PC Graphics with GKS

15 71 90.

IN.

☐ ☐ ■ PC GRAPHICS
■ WITH GKS

Introduction to Graphics Standards
(GKS, GKS-3D, PHIGS, CGI and CGM)
and to Graphics Programming

PETER R. BONO, JOSÉ L. ENCARNAÇÃO,
L. MIGUEL ENCARNAÇÃO and
WOLFGANG R. HERZNER

Original Translation from the German by
CYNTHIA SKRIPAK

Prentice Hall

First published 1990 by
Prentice Hall International Ltd
66 Wood Lane End, Hemel Hempstead
Hertfordshire HP2 4RG
A division of
Simon & Schuster International Group

This book was originally published in German under the title *Graphische Datenverarbeitung mit GKS* by J.L. Encarnação, L.M. Encarnação and W. Herzner. Revised, extended and updated for the English edition.
© 1987 Carl Hanser Verlag, Munich and Vienna

© 1990 P.R. Bono, J.L. Encarnação, L.M. Encarnação and W.R. Herzner

Typeset in 10/12 pt Palatino
by DMD Ltd, Oxford

Printed and bound in Great Britain at the
University Press, Cambridge

T
385
P3413
1990

Library of Congress Cataloging-in-Publication Data

Graphische Datenverarbeitung mit GKS. English.
    PC graphics with GKS: introduction to graphics standards (GKS, GKS-3D, PHIGS, CGI, and CGM) and to graphics programming/Peter R. Bono . . . [et al.].
        p.   cm.
    Translation of: Graphische Datenverarbeitung mit GKS.
    ISBN 0–13–654435–5: $44.95
    1. Computer graphics—Standards.   I. Bono, Peter R., 1945–
II. Title.
    T385.G73713 1989   89–39983
    006.6′0218—dc20   CIP

British Library Cataloguing in Publication Data

PC graphics with GKS: introduction to graphics standards (GKS, GKS-3D, PHIGS, CGI and CGM) and to graphics programming.
    1. Computer systems. Graphic displays. Software packages: Graphical Kernel system
    I. Bono, Peter R. (1945–)   II. Graphische Datenverarbeitung mit GKS. *English*
    006.6′8

ISBN 0–13–654435–5

1 2 3 4 5   94 93 92 91 90

□ □ ■ CONTENTS
■

v

 PREFACE

The Graphical Kernel System (GKS) achieved the status of a draft international standard in 1982 and was published as the first official international standard for computer graphics in the summer of 1985 (ISO, 1985). This event brought many years of cooperation by more than 100 American and European experts to a successful conclusion. The standard document is very large; the English version of the document contains approximately 250 pages and the German version over 200.

Everyone who was involved in the development of GKS knows that the standard is difficult to read because it contains no explanatory material. Almost every GKS programmer, who will undoubtedly need to refer to the standard, will occasionally wish for more exact clarification of one special case or another. However, it will not be necessary in most cases for an application programmer to read the entire document, especially if only a small portion of the total capabilities of GKS is needed for that application. This book is intended to guide the programmer's first foray into the use of GKS and, thus, cannot a priori deal with all GKS capabilities to the same degree; if it did, it would exceed the length of the original document!

Because GKS is specified independently of any programming language, function definitions are provided in two variations. One is the language-independent notation used by the GKS standard itself, and the other is FORTRAN77 (ISO, 1980), applying the FORTRAN language environment for GKS (ISO, 1988c), which is also internationally recognized as a standard. FORTRAN was chosen as the language environment for the examples, not only because it represents the first standardized GKS language environment, but also because it is utilized by an overwhelming majority of GKS implementations. More recently, the C programming language has become very popular. Consequently, in this edition we have provided both some sample programs written in C and an appendix showing the relationship between the abstract GKS functions and their realization as C procedure calls.

The contents of this book are structured to provide a brief introduction to computer graphics followed by an overview of the purpose of the GKS standard and its underlying concepts. Further chapters deal with these concepts as well as with the corresponding GKS functions. Discussions with several users convinced the authors to limit their examples to a few functions in the beginning in order to illustrate their principal applications with a detailed example. Finally, the concepts that were briefly covered in earlier chapters are discussed in detail, along with additional concepts such as GKS capabilities. The authors hope to achieve their goal of producing the fastest possible introduction to GKS. An appendix summarizes all GKS functions and indicates for each one whether it is discussed and, if so, in which chapter. In addition, another appendix contains some further examples and provides cross-references within the book.

The examples provided are programmed for the IBM PC/AT, and their code is available on floppy disk as a supplement to this book. Details can be obtained using the pre-printed order form in the back of this book. This gives the reader an opportunity to experiment with the functions described in the book's programming examples by receiving the examples as source code.

The GKS implementation used is the GSS*GKS product developed, marketed and sold by Graphic Software Systems (9590 SW Gemini Drive, Beaverton, OR 97005; telephone 503–641–2200). All the sample programs were developed and tested using this implementation. GSS offers a discount on its GSS*GKS product to all who use the discount coupon contained at the back of this book and purchase the product directly from them.

Chapters 10 and 11 provide an overview of further international developments in graphics standards. Because proposed standards can change significantly in a short period of time, it is possible that not every chapter will contain the most current information by the time this book appears. The intention is not to provide an exact representation but an outline of the scope of the areas being standardized.

Finally, one or two terms require elaboration:

GKS: GKS can be understood in this book as either the ISO document already mentioned or as a specific implementation of the standard. Clarification will be provided in cases where the meaning is not obvious from the context.

Functions: GKS functions are not, for the most part, functions in a mathematical sense. However, this terminology is retained because it is internationally recognized, on the one hand, and because it establishes an association with the so-called device functions or capabilities, on the other hand.

The authors would like to thank all those who contributed to the completion of this book. We thank Mrs Christ for inputting the text and for her careful editing and Mrs Skripak for her excellent translation of the original German text into English. We also thank Carl Hanser Verlag and Prentice Hall for their cooperation during the preparation and production of this book.

Peter R. Bono
José L. Encarnação
L. Miguel Encarnação
Wolfgang R. Herzner

November 1989

Chapter 1
INTRODUCTION

Computer graphics offers methods and techniques for producing and manipulating images, where the images are a special kind of output of internal computer representations (Encarnação and Strasser, 1988).

The main branches of computer graphics are:

- Generative computer graphics
- Image processing
- Image analysis

These areas are shown in Figure 1.1.

Output \ Input	Image	Description
Image	Image processing	Generative computer graphics
Description	Image analysis	'Everything else'

Figure 1.1   Areas of computer graphics

Computer graphics is used whenever visual representation of objects, activity, connections, values, results, positions, and concepts exists or is created. These representations can be realistic or abstract, they can correspond to actual objects, or they can render symbols (icons), concepts, or movement. The possibilities for applying computer graphics are limited only by the power of one's imagination. Here are some examples of areas in which computer graphics is successfully used:

- Data presentation
- Scientific visualization
- Cartography and surveying
- Simulation and animation
- Graphic arts and advertising
- Process control
- Office automation and documentation systems
- Electronic printing and publishing
- Computer-aided design and engineering (CAD/CAE)
- Computer-aided manufacturing (CAM)
- Computer-aided instruction (CAI)
- Medical diagnosis
- Robotics
- Video games

Plates 1–3 show examples of such applications.

Computer graphics is based on a simple reference model, which is shown in Figure 1.2. This configuration consists of three main components:

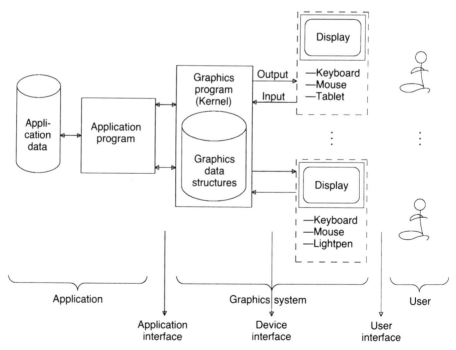

Figure 1.2   Reference configuration of a graphics system

- Application system
- Graphics system
- User (operator; client; system server)

The three essential system interfaces can also be inferred from Figure 1.2:

- Application interface
- Device interface
- User interface

For these interfaces there are standards or proposed standards (Bono, 1986; Enderle, 1986); the connection between these can be seen in Figure 1.3. These

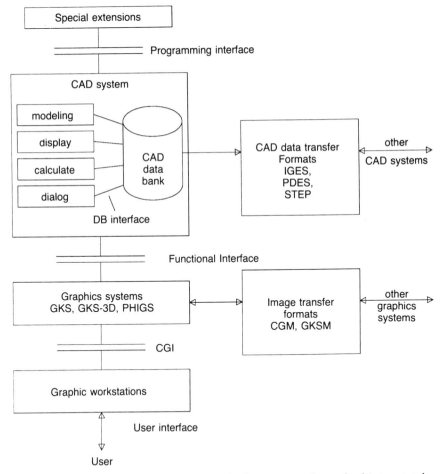

Figure 1.3   Integration of a graphics standard or proposed standard into a total system (using a CAD system as an example)

standards are as follows:

1. The standards for graphics programming (GKS, GKS-3D, PHIGS).
2. The interface to the device driver and to device-level graphics commands or command libraries (CGI).
3. Graphics-level archive and interchange (CGM, GKSM).
4. The data communication interface between different systems or between a system and the commercial database being used (IGES, STEP, PDES, EDIF, ODIF, etc.).

All of these standards or proposed standards serve a specific need and are enhanced by integration into a total system. Detailed discussion of these topics can be found in Encarnação and Schlechtendahl, 1983; and Encarnação, Schuster and Vöge, 1983. This book deals primarily with the theme of graphics programming at the application programmer interface and, in particular, with GKS.

1.1   The Graphics System and its Components

The composition and structure of a graphics system depends largely on the requirements of a given application. However, the most important parts for interactive processing of graphic information are as follows:

- A computer for storing generated pictures, for execution of calculations, and for generation of output data
- A display device with interactive potential
- Input tools to control the output, but also to input positions, text, etc.
- Hard copy devices like plotters, in order to create a permanent copy of the image

Devices for displaying images typically work in one of two modes:

- Vector display mode
- Raster display mode

In vector mode the device draws lines. A display file contains a series of line and positioning commands, which the display processor repeats, interprets, and executes on the screen with a refresh rate of 30–60 cycles per second. The processor also receives and processes input commands, which are entered by the user through the appropriate input peripherals. Raster systems, by contrast, generate pictures out of a matrix of points, which are stored in a so-called picture or frame buffer. The matrix is called a bitmap or, in the case of color displays, a pixel map. The display processor draws the image line by line (like a TV) and thereby activates all positions on the lines (pixels). The activated pixels in the bit-map are designated by a 1. On color devices, each pixel value (usually) represents an index into a so-called color table, which specifies the color assigned to the corresponding pixel. A vector drawing mode device is shown in Plate 4(a) and a raster drawing mode device in Plate 4(b).

Input devices allow the operator to input:

- Positions
- Object identification (by marking the object on an image display)
- Scalar values
- Text
- Commands

These input classes can be realized with a variety of hardware tools, including the following devices:

- Lightpen
- Tablet
- Mouse
- Keyboard
- Joystick
- Trackball
- Thumbwheels

Hard copy devices can also be used for output in addition to display devices. The most commonly used are:

- Pen plotter: flatbed or drum; pen up/down and x-/y-axis movement
- Electrostatic plotter: the paper moves in one direction, electrically-charged styli draw the image in rows
- Dot matrix printer: low-resolution raster device
- Ink jet plotter: nozzle instead of pen
- Xerographic plotter: laser rays produce the image; similar to Xerox method
- Photographing the image display by special exposure on special paper (for example, Tektronix or Polaroid units)
- Microfilm recorder
- Slide camera

Current systems utilize dedicated processors (chips) to support the capabilities of individual input and output devices (coding; decoding; generation of special primitives, like circles, ellipses and curve approximations; execution of local, device-specific functions, etc.). A few examples of these input and output devices are shown in Plates 5 and 6.

The graphics system components that have been briefly described (processor, image display, input and output devices, and peripherals) comprise a total system; such a system is called a workstation. The basic structure of a graphics workstation is illustrated schematically in Figure 1.4.

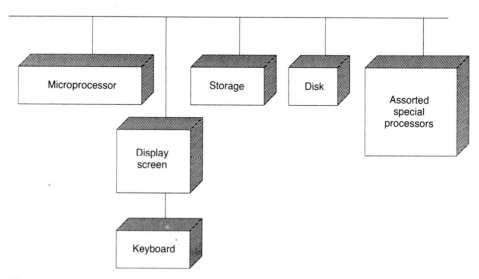

Figure 1.4   Basic structure of a graphics workstation system

1.2   Systems and Algorithms

Two fundamentally different classes of system can be differentiated, according to the capabilities of the graphics workstations used to realize them:

- Image-based, bitmapped systems
- Geometry-based, vector systems

Systems in the bitmapped class were first developed at the Xerox Corporation Palo Alto Research Center in 1974. These systems are based on a number of specialized micro programs that implement the image operations at the bit level (Guibas, Ingalls and Pike, 1984). These operations, called bitblt (bit block transfer; see Figure 1.5), allow a rapid change of the images that have been stored in the form of arrays of bits. Very efficient operations for the generation, manipulation, and storage of bit images are possible with this operation. Today's raster systems with page layout capabilities are based primarily on this

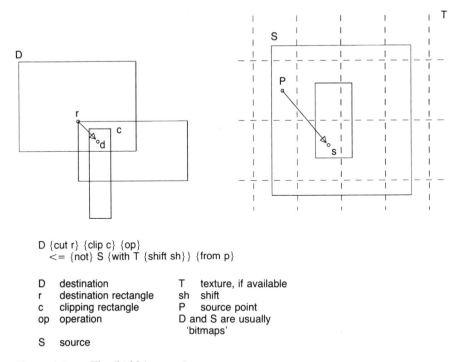

D {cut r} {clip c} {op}
   <= {not} S {with T {shift sh}} {from p}

D	destination	T	texture, if available
r	destination rectangle	sh	shift
c	clipping rectangle	P	source point
op	operation	D and S are usually	
			'bitmaps'
S	source		

Figure 1.5   The 'bitblt' operation

technology; a typical example is the Apple Macintosh. The extension of bitblt to color bitmaps is not a trivial problem; several approaches have been tried (Willis and Watters, 1988).

A great number of algorithms are used to create realistic-looking images; these algorithms have one or more of the following components:

- Coordinate (2D) and perspective (3D) transformations
- Visibility determination (hidden lines and surfaces)
- Intensity modulation
- Modeling of light sources
- Shadowing procedures
- Shading models (transparencies, reflections, etc.)
- Simulation and animation techniques

The majority of these algorithms are very computation-intensive; and, for this reason, efforts are currently under way to accelerate them through the use of special processing and/or VLSI building blocks or to realize them partially or completely in hardware. Further details on this theme are given by Encarnação and Strasser (1988); Fuchs (1985); and Strasser (1986). A few examples of the results which are possible with these algorithms can be seen in Plates 7 and 8. Geometry-based systems are tools for efficient and user-friendly execution of operations for the generation, manipulation, and display of geometric objects; that is, objects that are defined by their geometric parameters.

Many of today's workstations provide bitmapped and geometry-based systems in an integrated form. Increasing numbers of microprocessors and special building blocks (VLSI) will be utilized in such workstation environments in order to increase efficiency.

1.3   Goals and Purposes of GKS

A discussion of programming graphics systems is a natural sequel to this short introduction of the systems themselves. GKS was especially developed for programming (Enderle, Kansy and Pfaff, 1987; Hopgood *et al.*, 1988). The following goals were pursued during the development of GKS:

> *Provision of a uniform interface between the application and the graphics system.* The GKS standard specifies a uniform interface between the graphics support system and the application program. Consequently, application programs can be developed independently of the target graphics device, thereby increasing the portability of the application program.
>
> *Provision of an application-independent function set for computer graphics.* GKS makes available the following functions, which are independent of any specific application:

- Construction of graphic images
- Storage and manipulation of graphic information
- Dialog management and user input

> *Development of a methodology for computer graphics.* The concepts described in the ISO standards are not only the basis for the specifications of GKS functions but should also help the application programmer to understand and use graphics methods. In addition to that, standards act to systematize the technical terms of computer graphics.
>
> *Development of guidelines for manufacturers of computer devices.* The standard should suggest a number of useful combinations of graphics capabilities and functions to manufacturers of graphics devices.
>
> *Coverage of a variety of requests.* The goal of being able to implement as many applications as possible (the so-called '90% Rule', which was applied to the development of the GKS standard) means that GKS should reasonably

support at least 90% of all graphics applications. It also implies a considerable increase in GKS performance capacity. The cartographer places different demands (high image quality) on a graphics system than the CAD user (high interactivity) or process controller (rapid image updates) does.

Chapter 2
■ INTRODUCTION TO GKS

This chapter is concerned with the position of GKS in its computer-specific environment and provides an overview of its basic concepts.

2.1 What is GKS?

As already mentioned in the Preface, it is necessary to differentiate between two aspects of this concept. The *standard* describes a function set for computer graphics that is independent of applications and devices. It also describes the internal tables necessary for a description of the GKS state in a form independent of any particular programming language. A *GKS implementation* converts the specification of the standard into a collection of graphics services accessible from one or more specific programming languages and constitutes a basic computer graphics system.

2.2 Layer Model

In order to implement GKS, its abstract functions and parameters must be realized using a set of suitable constructs from the chosen implementation language; that is, GKS is embedded in a language-dependent layer. Because GKS does not represent a system aligned with a specific application area, separate environments will be developed for specific classes of applications (e.g., cartography or presentation graphics); these environments will support the most frequently used functions of these applications. The use of GKS is represented in Figure 2.1. Each layer above the dotted lines can act on others which lie directly beneath it or can utilize their functions. In this way, the application program has access to the functions of the application-oriented layer and also to the language-dependent GKS environment, as well as to other functions of the operating system. Graphics operations, however, should be addressed only by GKS.

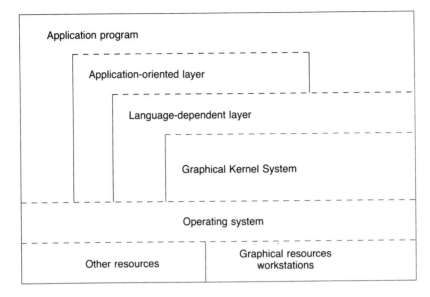

Figure 2.1 Layer model of GKS

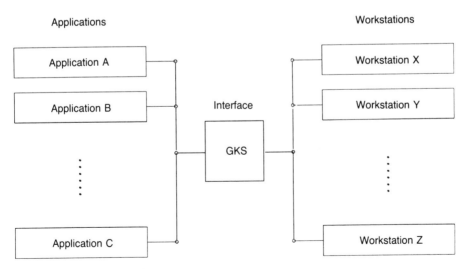

Figure 2.2 GKS interfaces

2.3 GKS Interfaces

Application programs do not act on the graphics devices themselves but through the application interface, which is clearly defined in the standard for GKS functions. GKS itself implements its tasks independently, for the most part, from the available graphics devices. The latter are combined, logically and technically, into the so-called graphics workstations, which communicate with GKS through a workstation interface. The adaptation of GKS functions to device-specific needs, as well as the control of the graphics devices, is implemented by so-called device drivers (see Figure 2.2). GKS therefore reflects the device's capabilities in the functions at the application interface.

2.4   Overview of Graphics Standards

Even a standard as extensive as GKS can have only limited objectives, and so there are also areas of computer graphics that are not subject to standardization by the ISO GKS document. GKS specifies or supports the following areas:

- Two-dimensional line graphics and limited raster graphics
- Graphics output and (graphics) input on a number of workstations
- Temporary storage of graphic information as well as image-structuring means (the so-called 'segments')
- Permanent storage of graphics information in metafiles
- Aids for tailoring the application program to use available device capabilities
- Several upwardly compatible implementation levels with appropriate functional capabilities

The concepts of 'segment' and 'metafile' will be further explained in Sections 2.6.6 and 2.6.7.

The following problem-specific areas are not, however, directly standardized by GKS:

- Representation of GKS functions in specific programming languages
- The internal structure of metafiles
- Interfaces between GKS and graphic workstations
- Three-dimensional line graphics and raster graphics

Standardization activities continue in all four areas:

- Standards for GKS FORTRAN, Pascal, and Ada have been published; for GKS C, there is a very advanced standard proposal, which is awaiting the approval of C as an ISO standard programming language (ISO, 1988c; 1988d; 1988e; 1988f; 1988h; 1989a; 1989b; 1989c; 1989d; 1989e; 1989f; 1989g; 1989i; 1989k).

■ The standardization of metafiles is available either as a GKS Metafile (specified in Annex E of the GKS standard) or as a CGM (Computer Graphics Metafile), specified in ISO (1987).

■ The interface to a single graphics device is called a CGI (Computer Graphics Interface); its definition is a proposed standard and should become an ISO standard in 1991 (Arnold and Bono, 1988).

■ Extensions to GKS for three-dimensional graphics are called GKS-3D (ISO, 1988g), which became available as a completed standard in the fall of 1988.

2.5 Operational Model

Figure 2.3 shows the communication links between GKS and the graphic devices it controls and between GKS and the application program. Segment storage handles workstation-independent management of image parts. Any number of segments and several metafiles can be in use simultaneously.

2.6 Concepts

There are approximately 200 GKS functions, which can be divided into a number of groups according to their underlying concepts. Because detailed discussion of one group or concept almost always requires some knowledge about the others, a brief overview of the individual concepts will be presented here. The individual groups will be discussed in detail in Chapters 3–9.

2.6.1 Primitives

Output primitives are the elementary components from which images are constructed. GKS uses six: polyline, polymarker, fill area, text, cell array, and the generalized drawing primitive (GDP). The GDP is used to access special workstation capabilities.

The appearance of an image is determined, on the one hand, by the geometric form of its elements and their positions, and, on the other hand, by the way it appears visually on the display surface. The former is achieved in GKS by the use of a cartesian coordinate system, in which control points are specified; the latter results from instructions specified by primitive attributes.

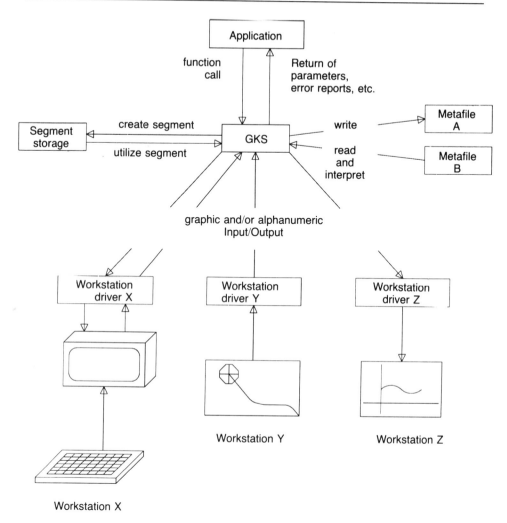

Figure 2.3 GKS operational model

2.6.2 Output Primitive Attributes

These describe the visual appearance of primitives. For line elements, such characteristics as line type (solid, dashed line), line width, and color can be specified; for text elements, such attributes as size, orientation, and color can be specified. For each primitive (except cell array and GDP) there is a set of attributes that can be specified either globally or in a workstation-specific manner.

2.6.3 Graphics Workstations

The abstract graphics workstation is a fundamental GKS concept. It is the combination of different graphics input and output devices and makes device-independent programming possible. More than one workstation can be used simultaneously by displaying a primitive on various workstations with different attributes and by taking into account the capabilities of the workstations. Various workstation categories can be distinguished, depending on whether input only, output only, or input and output can be executed on a single workstation.

Even workstations in one category can show widely differentiated capabilities. Many workstations capable of output will be able dynamically to change associations of attributes to primitives (like dynamic color changes by modification of internal color tables on raster devices). With others, this can lead to regeneration of the image (on storage tubes or plotters, for example).

2.6.4 Coordinate Systems and Transformations

Because the coordinate system in which the user defines the geometry of an image seldom agrees with that of the display surface, GKS separates the user's 'world coordinate system' in principle from the 'device coordinate system'. GKS, however, first represents the primitives defined in multiple, different world coordinate systems in a so-called 'normalized device coordinate system'. The mapping of world coordinates onto normalized device coordinates is called a 'normalization transformation' and is used for the composition of the image to be displayed. Only those coordinates transformed from normalized to real device coordinates via the so-called 'workstation transformation' are used for portraying the actual image seen on the display surface.

2.6.5 Input

GKS differentiates six classes of logical input device, which can be used in three different operating modes and which serve to pass on operator input to the application: *locator* (position), *stroke* (sequence of positions), *valuator* (floating point number, e.g., digitized position of a knob or thumbwheel), *choice* (natural number, e.g., function key), *string* (text), and *pick* (segment identification).

The operating modes are *request* (GKS waits until the appropriate input is entered), *sample* (the current value of the appropriate input device is obtained without operator action), and *event* (GKS manages an input queue, which can be generated asynchronously from the application). Coordinate inputs (locator and stroke) are transformed from device coordinates inversely through normalized device coordinates to world coordinates.

2.6.6   Segments

Segments are picture parts that can be created, transformed, deleted, transferred to workstations, and identified in interactive applications independently of each other. GKS can also manage segments in a separate workstation-independent segment storage (WISS) and on workstations that possess the capability for storing segments, that is, have a workstation-dependent segment storage (WDSS).

2.6.7   Metafiles

GKS allows the creation of sequential graphical metafiles, which contain picture drawing information in an abstract, device-independent form. The elements in metafiles can be read, examined, and then interpreted in a standardized way as a result of GKS calls. Metafiles can be used to transfer image descriptions between different locations or installations, but they can also be used to resume interrupted or suspended interactive sessions.

2.6.8   Inquiry Functions and GKS Lists

In addition to GKS functions, the standard also specifies the lists and tables that together describe the GKS operating state. All values of these tables and lists can be recovered from the application program by means of inquiry functions.

2.6.9 Error Handling

For every GKS function, the standard specifies a list of possible errors. If an error appears during the execution of a GKS function, GKS moves into an error state and activates an error handler. The reaction depends on the degree of the error and extends from 'reject function' to 'halt program'. It is possible for the application program to direct error handling itself because the program has GKS functions at its disposal (principally inquiry and control functions) that may be used even in error situations.

2.7   GKS State

GKS exists at any given time in just one of five, mutually exclusive operating states:

GKCL:	GKS closed
GKOP:	GKS open
WSOP:	At least one workstation open
WSAC:	At least one workstation active
SGOP:	Segment open

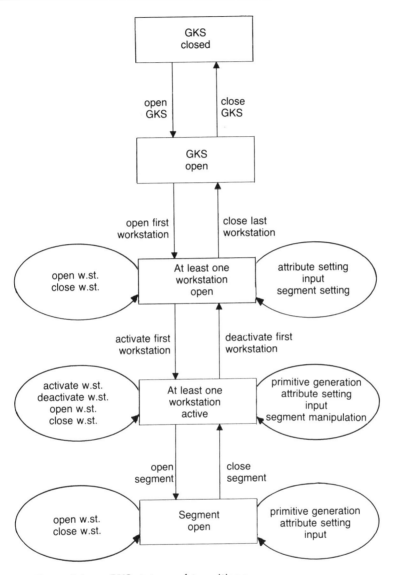

Figure 2.4   GKS states and transitions

State transitions result from invoking certain control functions. Only specific functions that belong to every group referred to in the loops on the right-hand side of Figure 2.4 are allowed in each state. All information necessary to the description of the GKS state while in use is combined into so-called state lists, which are created or destroyed according to the transition taken:

- **GKS state list:** One copy exists as long as GKS is open; it contains, among other things, information about open workstations and specific output primitive attributes.
- **Workstation state list:** One copy exists for each open workstation; it contains, e.g., workstation-specific output primitive attributes and the state of the input devices.
- **Segment state list:** One per segment exists; it contains segment attributes.
- **Error state list:** One copy, which exists like the GKS state list.
- **Input queue:** One copy, which exists like the GKS state list, but only if the GKS implementation is supporting an installation with event input.

In addition, there are description tables whose contents do not change during the running of a GKS application:

- **GKS description table:** One copy per installation. It contains information about the installation itself, e.g., levels (see Section 2.8) and a list of available workstation types.
- **Workstation description table:** One copy per workstation type. It contains details about the capabilities of the workstation type, like the maximum display surface size and the number of colors available on the workstation.

2.8 Levels

The entire spectrum of GKS capabilities, as outlined in Section 2.6, will be used by only a few applications; to implement GKS fully requires several person-years of effort. In addition, consider that the 'event' input operating mode and the corresponding management of the input queue on most host machines cannot be realized without intervention of the operating system or at least not without using special operating system capabilities; it will certainly not be utilized in all applications, however. It is desirable, therefore, to allow for GKS implementations that do not exhibit all the capabilities established in the standard. By matching application-specific requests with GKS functionalities, nine upwardly compatible levels were determined. These can be arranged into a 3×3 matrix (Figure 2.5), where the two axes are separated as follows:

- Input axis:
  - a.   no input
  - b.   request input only
  - c.   full input

Input

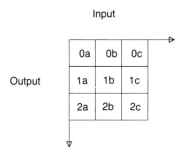

Figure 2.5   GKS levels

■ Output axis:

0.   minimal output; no segments; metafile not required but allowed; no pick input
1.   full output; WDSS only; metafile required
2.   like 1; but all segment facilities included

According to this scheme, level 0a is suitable for simple, passive applications without segment management, and with reduced management of output primitive attributes; level 2c embraces the full capability spectrum of GKS.

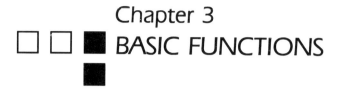

Chapter 3
BASIC FUNCTIONS

This chapter presents an introduction to programming with GKS. In order to do this, the chapter will be confined to a few important GKS functions, specifically those functions that activate a workstation and can draw lines. This is a small number of functions, as the concluding example in the chapter will illustrate. The example demonstrates how simple application programs that have previously used CalComp routines can be rearranged to use GKS.

3.1 Open, Close, Activate

In order to work with GKS it must first be opened. This is necessary because, prior to doing any graphical work, GKS must carry out a large number of actions which are not immediately evident, such as preparing the memory space, initializing its (internal) state, and so on. The function which does this is:

    OPEN GKS
        Input parameters: name   ERROR FILE
                            integer   NUMBER OF MEMORY UNITS

'name' and 'integer' are data types. The corresponding FORTRAN routine is expressed as:

            subroutine GOPKS   (ERRFIL,BUFA)
            integer   ERRFIL,BUFA

ERRFIL, in this case, is the logical unit number of the file to which GKS should write miscellaneous error reports. If the unit number of a dialog device were given, for example, error reports would appear directly on the screen during program execution. If the unit number corresponds to a disk file, a permanent record of any errors encountered can be created for later review. BUFA provides

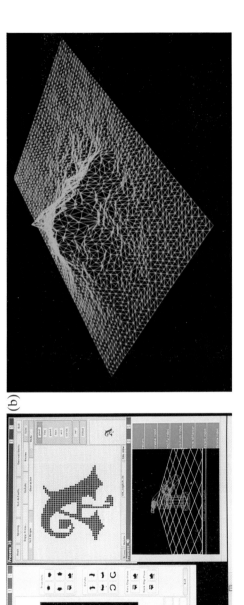

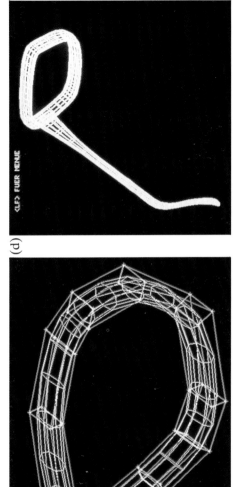

Plate 1 Examples of computer graphics applications

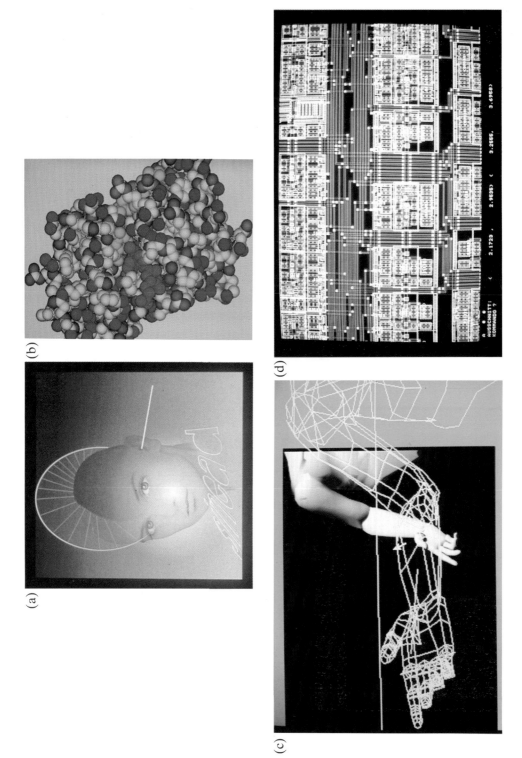

Plate 2 Examples of computer graphics applications

(a)

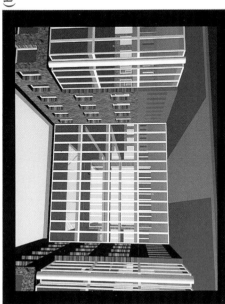

(c)

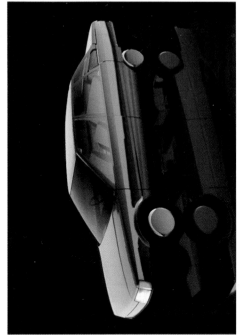

(b)

(d)

Plate 3   Examples of computer graphics applications

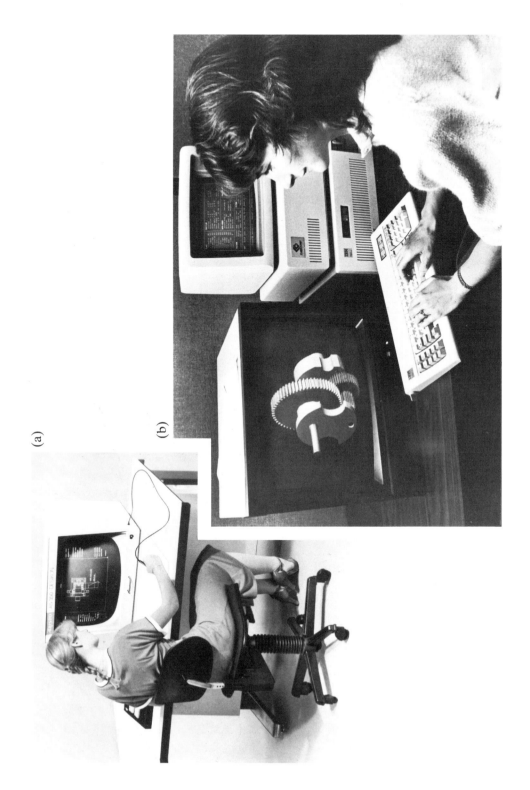

(a)

(b)

Plate 4 Examples of basic output methods (vector and raster). Photos: Aristo and Cubicomp

(a)

(b)

Plate 5 Input and output devices

(b)

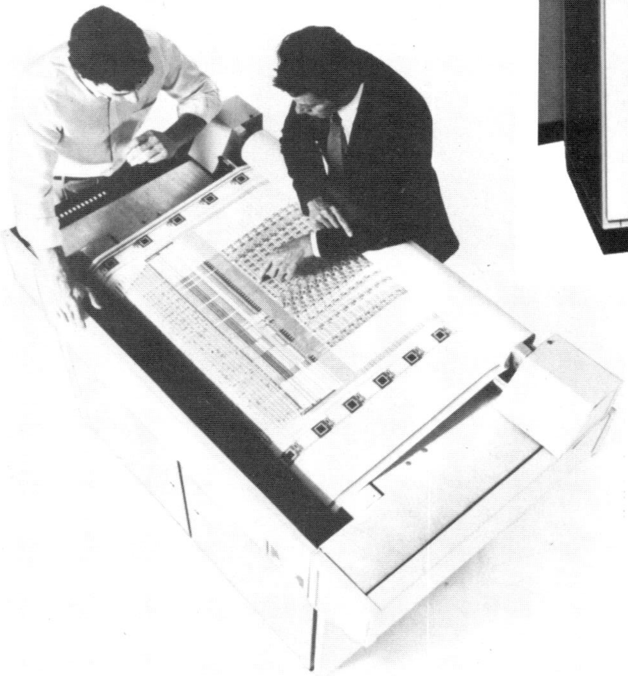

(a)

Plate 6 Input and output devices

(a)

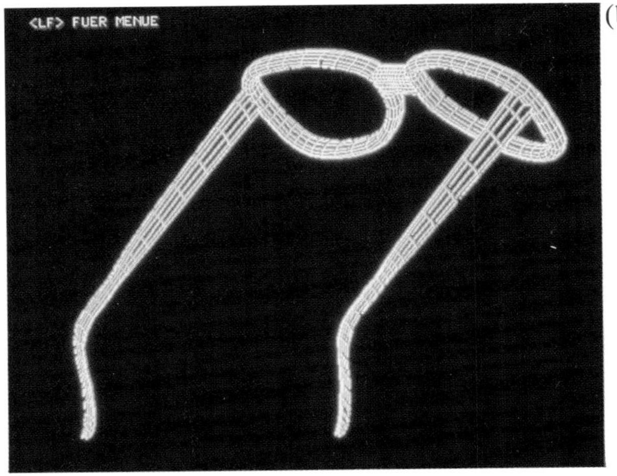

(b)

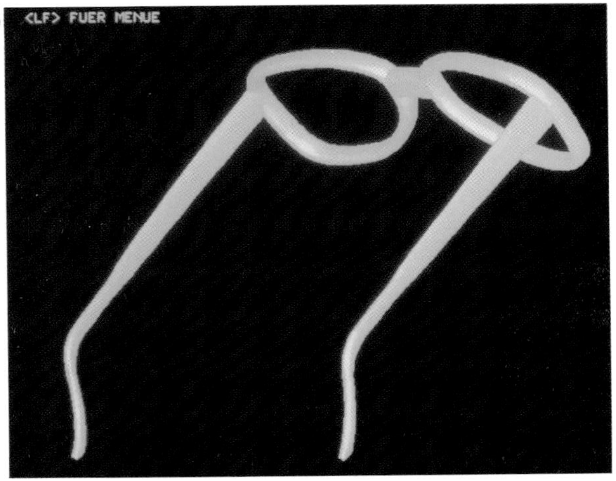

(c)

(d)

Plate 7 Examples of realism in computer graphics

(a)

(b)

(c)

(d)

Plate 8   Examples of realism in computer graphics

the size of the storage space available to GKS internally for its working storage, in implementation-dependent units.

Before discussing further functions, a few words are necessary about the description of GKS in FORTRAN. FORTRAN names for GKS functions were developed according to certain rules, to compensate for the fact that FORTRAN names can have a maximum length of only six characters (or, more precisely, in standard FORTRAN only the first six characters are significant), and GKS routines should be easily distinguishable from other subprograms. The rules are as follows:

1. The first letter is always 'G' (for GKS).
2. The remaining letters (up to five) are a clear abbreviation of the English function name, so that a given word is always represented by the same abbreviation in all function names, or is omitted everywhere. For example:

OPEN	by OP,
CLOSE	by CL,
GKS	by KS,
WORKSTATION	by WK.

Therefore, the FORTRAN designation for 'Open GKS' is G-OP-KS or GOPKS, and for 'Close Workstation', G-CL-WK or GCLWK. (This function will be dealt with later in this chapter.) So if a FORTRAN name contains the letter pair 'WK', it must be the abbreviation for 'workstation'. And the reverse follows; in most cases, the FORTRAN name can be derived from the given GKS name. With a little bit of practice, the most frequently used function names will become familiar.

Note that, because FORTRAN implementations of GKS almost always use a 'G' to begin the names of internal subroutines, common areas, etc., with which the user is generally not familiar, it is recommended that global names in the application program should *not* begin with the letter 'G'.

Now back to GKS itself. Because it is necessary to open GKS, it is also necessary to close it.

CLOSE GKS
        No parameters

or in FORTRAN
        subroutine GCLKS

Calling the parameter-less function GCLKS causes a release of the storage space occupied by GKS and shifts GKS into a state from which it can be reactivated exclusively by 'open GKS'.

Of course, to be able to open and close GKS is certainly necessary, but it is not enough for even a minimal application. The goal is to create visible images. In order to work on a specific workstation, the workstation must also be opened:

OPEN WORKSTATION

Input: name   WORKSTATION IDENTIFIER
           name   CONNECTION IDENTIFIER
           name   WORKSTATION TYPE

The corresponding FORTRAN routine is:

           subroutine GOPWK   (WKID,CONID,WKTYPE)
           integer   WKID, CONID, WKTYPE

The individual parameters have the following meanings:

WKID: Identification of the workstation; this parameter will be used from now on in all GKS calls which reference this workstation.

CONID: An implementation-dependent value. For example, unit numbers through which the workstation is addressed, that is, over which data must be output, if it is to be sent to this workstation.

WKTYPE: The type of workstation being opened. Each installation will have its own set of workstation types; different types indicate that different sets of capabilities are available to a GKS application.

This function, then, primarily establishes the connection to the workstation, and also positions and initializes the state list. A few internal updates will also occur. Unfortunately, this is still not sufficient for drawing on any workstation. Back to that a little bit later.

Of course, not only several workstations of different types, but also workstations of the same type can be available to a GKS installation. In this case, all similar workstations possess the same workstation type, but they are addressed via different connection identifiers and must be marked with different workstation identifiers in the application program.

The use of workstation identifiers and workstation types has another advantage, however. If a GKS program that uses a specific workstation is to be transferred to a workstation of a different type, then the third parameter is merely replaced by the new value in the corresponding GOPWK call. The same change occurs if the program is executed on another GKS installation using a similar type. The type descriptions are not standardized and, for this reason, different GKS installations can provide for different types on the same workstation. Check the documentation of your specific GKS installation for the valid workstation types.

Workstation types are also divided into categories (see Section 2.6.3):

OUTPUT: Workstations in this category can accept only graphic output.
INPUT: Workstations in this category can accept only graphic input.
OUTIN: Workstations in this category can accept graphic output or input.

There are three other special categories which will be introduced at an appropriate opportunity.

Workstations, like GKS, can also be closed.

CLOSE WORKSTATION

Input: name   WORKSTATION IDENTIFIER

The corresponding FORTRAN routine is:

        subroutine GCLWK   (WKID)
        integer   WKID

This function executes all delayed actions (see Section 4.2) and undoes all actions which 'Open Workstation' executes. The relevant workstation is, therefore, not available to the application program after this call, and it must be opened again if it is to be used again.

To the consternation of all those who are new to GKS, opening a workstation is still not enough to be able to draw with it. To do that, the workstation must first be activated.

ACTIVATE WORKSTATION

Input: name   WORKSTATION IDENTIFIER

or in FORTRAN:

        subroutine GACWK   (WKID)
        integer   WKID

A workstation can also be deactivated but left open. This is achieved by:

DEACTIVATE WORKSTATION

Input: name   WORKSTATION IDENTIFIER

or in FORTRAN:

```
subroutine GDAWK    (WKID)
integer             WKID
```

Why is this so complicated? Was it simpler with the older graphics systems? There are at least three answers to these questions. First, the GKS system allows one to control a workstation state more precisely; second, it allows multiple workstations to be used simultaneously (which the majority of older graphics systems could not); and third, it can offer greater operating reliability in cases of parallel use of several graphics devices by a number of application programs. Let us look at these arguments more closely.

As for workstation control, a workstation can exist in three states (see Section 2.7):

1. Workstation closed: the workstation is not available to the application program.
2. Workstation open: workstation attributes can be set (see Sections 3.3 and 5.4); segments can be manipulated (see Chapter 6); input can be accepted (see Chapter 8); and data about the state and capabilities of the workstation can be inquired.
3. Workstation activated: like (2), with the additional ability to accept output.

Operations can be performed on opened but deactivated workstations, but we will not discuss these functions until later in the book. The essential thing is that the stored information (the state of the display surface, its state list (see Section 2.7) and the available segments) is preserved if the workstation is deactivated, but not if the workstation is closed.

Finally, consider the simultaneous use of several operating modes by a number of programs. The classic case is the following. Two resources are being used in one multi-program facility. Program P uses Resource A, Program Q uses Resource B. After a while P also needs B and waits for B to be free. If Q now happens to need a second resource – namely A – a so-called 'deadlock' situation results, because both programs would wait forever for the release of the other resource if no possibility existed for reversal or a total avoidance of such deadlocks.

If resources are now replaced by graphics workstations, an analogous situation arises. By opening all workstations as early as possible, such dangerous moments are reduced because this should guarantee exclusive access to the open workstation according to the GKS concept. On the other hand, the 'author' of such application programs could be characterized by colleagues as antisocial for understandable reasons: for example, if the author starts the program and lets it run without interruption for hours.

A small example should illustrate these points. A drawing is constructed interactively and interim results are occasionally displayed on a plotter:

```
OPEN GKS (ERRFIL,BUFSIZE);
OPEN WORKSTATION (WK1, LNR1, SCREEN);
OPEN WORKSTATION (WK2, LNR2, PLOTTER);
ACTIVATE WORKSTATION (WK1);
```

repeat
  "Create and manipulate – with help from segments –
  the image on the screen; (nothing happens on plotter)"

  ACTIVATE WORKSTATION (WK2);

  "Draw actual image; (appears on both workstations)"

  DEACTIVATE WORKSTATION (WK2);

until finished;

```
DEACTIVATE WORKSTATION (WK1)
CLOSE WORKSTATION (WK1)
CLOSE WORKSTATION (WK2)
CLOSE GKS
```

The corresponding FORTRAN program could be expressed as follows:

```
C          6 is the unit number of the standard input,
C          11 and 21 are connection identifiers,
C          123 is the type identifier of the screen, and
C          456 is the identifier of the plotter.
           :
           :
C    Example 1
           :
           :
      call GOPKS (6,10000)
      call GOPWK (1,11,123)
      call GOPWK (2,21,456)
      call GACWK (1)
C
  100 continue
C          Create and manipulate (with the help of segments)
C          the image on the screen;
```

```
C            (nothing happens on plotter)
      call GACWK (2)
C            Draw current image; (appears on both workstations)
      call GDAWK (2)
   if(.not.FINISHED) goto 100
      call GDAWK (1)
      call GCLWK (1)
      call GCLWK (2)
      call GCLKS
          ⋮
          ⋮
```

This relatively long drawn-out treatment of the control of workstation states should offer some insight into the possibilities offered by GKS. The next section will concentrate mainly on the use of a single workstation.

☐ **Let us summarize the GKS functions introduced up to this point:**

OPEN GKS	GOPKS	(ERRFIL,BUFA)
CLOSE GKS	GCLKS	
OPEN WORKSTATION	GOPWK	(WKID,CONID,WKTYPE)
CLOSE WORKSTATION	GCLWK	(WKID)
ACTIVATE WORKSTATION	GACWK	(WKID)
DEACTIVATE WORKSTATION	GDAWK	(WKID)

3.2   Polyline and Polyline Index

The oldest primitive of computer graphics is the line, defined by two end points. Every graphics system allows the generation of this picture element. GKS, in fact, defines a connected series of lines of any length as a primitive rather than defining only single line segments. This is called a 'polyline' in the ISO document. The geometric form of a polyline is determined solely by the position of the control points, so the GKS function is:

POLYLINE

Input:	integer	NUMBER OF POINTS	(2,...,n)
	n*point	POINTS	(WC)

'Point' is a GKS type that represents the cartesian coordinates of a point (see Section 3.3); 'n*point' represents a series of points.

The following representation is established in GKS FORTRAN:

```
point     -> real X,Y
n*point   -> real X(N),Y(N)
```

The corresponding FORTRAN function is:

```
subroutine GPL   (N,X,Y)
integer          N
real             X(N),Y(N)
```

Now it's finally time to draw! Try it in a (FORTRAN) example:

```
C
C     Example 2: Drawing a polyline whose control points lie
C                              on a spiral
C
      real X(100),Y(100),S,T
         :
         :
C
C     Initialize points
C
      do 100 I=1,100
            T=0.2*(I−1)
            S=T/20.0
            X(I)=S*COS(T)
            Y(I)=S*SIN(T)
      100 continue
C
C     GKS and workstation already open
C
      call GACWK (1)
      call GPL          (100,X,Y)
```

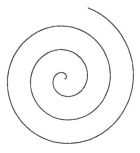

Figure 3.1   A spiral

The last function call causes the output of a 99-segment polyline on the activated workstation.

The 'polyline' primitive is considerably different – not only technically but also semantically – from drawing commands of older graphics systems, such as:

MOVE(X,Y):   'Move pen to point (X,Y) without drawing'
DRAW(X,Y):   'Draw visible line from current pen position to point (X,Y)'.

Drawing commands of this type have at least two disadvantages. One is that two calls are necessary to create a line and about a hundred calls would be needed for the series of lines described above; one call is enough in GKS. Of course, polyline calls require arrays with appropriate dimensions, while simple variables will suffice for MOVE/DRAW. Storage space, however, is playing an increasingly smaller role, while saving subroutine calls certainly has a positive effect on the execution time.

The other is that the concept of the so-called current position, which forms the basis for the older drawing commands, is ambiguous. According to this concept, the position of the drawing pen (on a plotter) or electron beam (on a display screen) is known after execution of each drawing command and the result of any subsequent DRAW call is dependent not only on this, but also on the last drawing command immediately preceding.

However, this concept is suitable only for graphic elements that have a 'natural' endpoint, so to speak. None of the surface-oriented primitives like polygons, disks, etc., or even the line-oriented primitives like circles possess a natural end. The end must be arbitrarily defined for them – not a very good solution, in general.

Finally, problems also arise in connection with workstations and segments because command sequences like:

MOVE (X0,Y0);
ACTIVATE WORKSTATION (PLOTTER);
DRAW (X1,Y1);

do not indicate where the line that ends at (X1,Y1) begins on the plotter. Of course, special treatment can be specified for these and similar cases, but the problems can be circumvented in an elegant and certainly more efficient way by using a self-contained graphics primitive. The general use of self-contained primitives that can be individually manipulated is an essential GKS concept.

Only the geometry of this type of graphic element is determined with the 'polyline' call, but its appearance on the display surface is not. The latter is determined by an array of properties like line width and color, which are called 'output primitive attributes' in GKS terminology. In order to differentiate between various groups of polylines in an image, they must be equipped with or display differing attributes.

The simplest way to distinguish between GKS primitives of the same type is to assign them varying values of a so-called 'display index'. Every primitive type has such an index; the one for polylines is simply called a 'polyline index'. If the index is set to a specific value by means of the following function:

SET POLYLINE INDEX

Input: integer   POLYLINE INDEX

or in FORTRAN:

                    subroutine GSPLI   (PLIND)
                    integer   PLIND

then all subsequent generated polylines will be associated with this index and will be displayed with each attribute that is chosen from the index. How this choice is made will not be discussed here. It should merely be stated at this point that the use of different indices also causes varied representations of the lines to be generated; the way these differences occur depends on the capabilities of the workstations utilized. Of course, one could ask which primitive attribute will be selected by a specific index on a given workstation or which primitive will determine this assignment for itself; this will be discussed later (Chapter 5). It is true, however, that all primitive indices like polyline index, polymarker index, and others must be natural numbers.

Now an example:

```
C
C     Example 3: Three different "spirals"
C
      real x(100),Y(100),S,T
C
C     Initialize points
C
      do 100 I=1,100
            T=0.2*(I−1)
            S=T/20.0
            X(I)=S*COS(T)
            Y(I)=S*SIN(T)
100 continue
C
C     workstation already activated
C
      do 200 I=1,3
            call GSPLI(I)
            call GPL(100,X,Y)
```

Figure 3.2   Three spirals

```
                if(I.ne.3) then
      C         shift "spirals" down
                    do 180 J=1,100
                        Y(J) = Y(J)−0.1
      180             continue
                endif
      200 continue
```

In this section the following GKS functions were introduced:

POLYLINE   GPL (N,X,Y)
SET POLYLINE INDEX   GSPLI (PLIND)

3.3   Coordinate Systems

The reader should now be in a position to map the basic CalComp routines onto GKS with the functions introduced thus far. (It is assumed that the reader is familiar with this graphics interface, once widely used. If this is not the case, refer to the commentary on the corresponding subroutines in Section 3.4.) There are, however, two CalComp routines that require additional GKS functions for their conversion. In fact, both functions (FACTOR and PLOT with special parameter values) change the coordinate system being used. In order to handle all CalComp basic routines in a similar manner, it seems sensible first to explain the coordinate systems used by GKS and their interrelationships.

Think back to the most important GKS goal: to make graphics application programs as device-independent as possible. In order to achieve this, it is necessary above all to give the application programmer the opportunity to specify images in a suitable coordinate system, without consideration for the devices being used.

The coordinate system in which the user describes an image is called the 'world coordinate' (WC) system. Although a wealth of different types of coordinate system (for example, cartesian or polar coordinates with linear or logarithmic scales) is possible, GKS restricts itself to the easiest and most widely used (90% rule!) in order to avoid unnecessary complexity in the transformation apparatus within GKS; GKS uses a linear-scaled cartesian coordinate system, with x increasing towards the right and y increasing towards the top.

In fact, all coordinate systems used in GKS are upright, two-dimensional cartesian systems with linear scaling on both axes so they can be mapped onto each other using translation and scaling operations (possibly different on both axes), but without requiring rotation.

GKS allows the use of several world coordinates during construction of an image, so it is possible to define different parts of the image in different parts of the world coordinate system. These individual image parts are shown on a so-called 'normalized device coordinate' (NDC) system with the help of a 'normalization transformation' (see Figure 3.3). In this way the whole image is composed in NDC (device- and application-independent)! This NDC is conceptually the unit square.

How does GKS determine which part of a world coordinate system is depicted in which portion of NDC? This is accomplished by obtaining 'window' and 'viewport' specifications from the application. These are used to specify which upright rectangle (i.e. window) of the definition area (here, WC) will be shown on which upright rectangle (i.e. viewport) of the image area (here, NDC). Each pair of windows and viewports is combined into a normalization transformation. These individual components of a normalization transformation can be

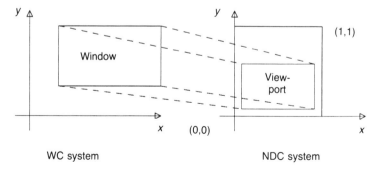

Figure 3.3   Normalization transformation

set by the following functions:

SET WINDOW

Input:	integer	TRANSFORMATION NUMBER	(1,...,n)
	4*real	WINDOW	
		LIMITS XMIN<XMAX,YMIN<YMAX	(WC)

and

SET VIEWPORT

Input:	integer	TRANSFORMATION NUMBER	(1,...,n)
	4*real	VIEWPORT	
		LIMITS XMIN<XMAX,YMIN<YMAX	(NDC)

or in FORTRAN:

```
subroutine GSWN    (TNR,XMIN,XMAX,YMIN,YMAX)
integer            TNR
real               XMIN,XMAX,YMIN,YMAX
```

and

```
subroutine GSVP    (TNR,XMIN,XMAX,YMIN,YMAX)
integer            TNR
real               XMIN,XMAX,YMIN,YMAX
```

The transformation number is the identification of a normalization transformation for which the appropriate call is valid (many normalization transformations can be defined simultaneously). The window limits specify the borders of those areas.

The simultaneous existence of several normalization transformations makes it possible to indicate which normalization transformation should be used for the display of primitives in NDC at the time of the primitives' creation. The function used for choosing a transformation is:

SELECT NORMALIZATION TRANSFORMATION

Input:	integer	TRANSFORMATION NUMBER	(0,...,n)

or in FORTRAN:

```
subroutine GSELNT    (TNR)
integer              TNR
```

The normalization transformation chosen by this function is used until another is chosen. But windows and viewports of all normalization transformations with index greater than zero can always be changed.

In general, when dealing with normalization transformations, it should be noted that:

- Viewports must always be completely contained in the NDC unit square.
- Viewports of different normalization transformations may overlap.
- The normalization transformation with the number 0 always represents the unity transformation and *cannot* be changed as an individual normalization transformation.
- The default normalization transformation is transformation number 0.
- Normalization transformations with TNR>0 always contain the unity transformation matrix at the beginning.
- Normalization transformations do *not* maintain the vertical-to-horizontal ratio if window and viewport show different aspect ratios.

Primitives (or parts of them) which lie outside a specific window are *not* automatically cut away or 'clipped' (see Section 9.1). In principle, all parts of an image in WC that lie inside the unit square after being transformed by the relevant normalization transformation can be displayed on the workstation (see Figure 3.4).

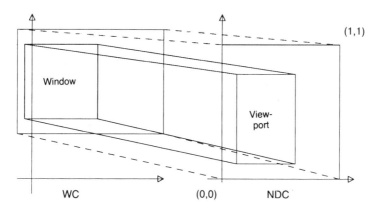

Figure 3.4   WC area bordered by dashed lines (inverse NT of the NDC unit square) can be displayed

Whether or not a window or viewport of the current normalization transformation should be clipped or not is determined by:

SET CLIPPING INDICATOR

Input: enum   CLIPPING INDICATOR (NO CLIP, CLIP)

'Enum' denotes an enumerative data type whose range will always be presented after the parameter name from now on. 'Clipping' here means trimming primitives at the viewport boundary. 'No clipping' conceptually leaves all primitives unchanged; because no primitive part lying outside of the unit square can ever be displayed, 'no clip' is synonymous with clipping at the unit square. (This rule will be clarified further with the use of segments in Chapter 6 and Section 9.1.)

Because no enumeration types exist in Fortran, these are generally shown as integer values 0 to n−1, where n represents the number of elements of the corresponding enumeration type.

The corresponding Fortran routine in this case is:

```
        subroutine  GSCLIP  (CLIPSW)
        integer     CLIPSW
C                                    0=NO CLIP, 1=CLIP
```

One small example (see Figure 3.5) demonstrates what is attainable through the use of several normalization transformations. Assume that the base and height of a three-dimensional object are to be drawn. The variables XMIN to ZMAX represent limits surrounding the object. The base will be maintained simply by parallel projection onto the x,y-plane and the height likewise onto the y,z-plane.

In order to maintain the impression of a folded-open base/height, the projection of the x-axis is given a negative sign. Because the window and viewport must always show coordinate values increasing towards the right and up, the positive x-axis of the base now points down. This corresponds to a 90-degree clockwise turn of world coordinates.

The two desired normalization transformations can now be easily defined:

```
        call GSWN (1,YMIN,YMAX,−XMAX,−XMIN)
        call GSVP (1,0.0,1.0,0.0,0.5)
        call GSWN (2,YMIN,YMAX,ZMIN,ZMAX)
        call GSVP (2,0.0,1.0,0.5,1.0)
```

Assume that $(XMAX−XMIN)/(YMAX−YMIN)=(ZMAX−ZMIN)/(YMAX−YMIN)=0.5$ is valid, because otherwise the angle between the base and height would be distorted. If X, Y, and Z are fields sufficiently large to receive point coordinates, and NP is an integer variable, the following loop generates base and height:

```
            ⋮
            ⋮
    100 continue
    C
    C    register the coordinates of the next series of edges
```

```
C    on X(N),Y(N),Z(N) and the number of its points in NP
C
C
     do 190 I=1,NP
          X(I)=−X(I)
 190 continue
C
C    output the base of the figure
C
     call GSELNT (1)
     call GPL (NP,Y,X)
C
C    height
     call GSELNT (2)
     call GPL (NP,Y,Z)
C
C    In case of additional figures:    GOTO 100
C
              :
              :
```

The normalization transformations, therefore, serve to assemble a device-independent image description in one unified coordinate system, the NDC.

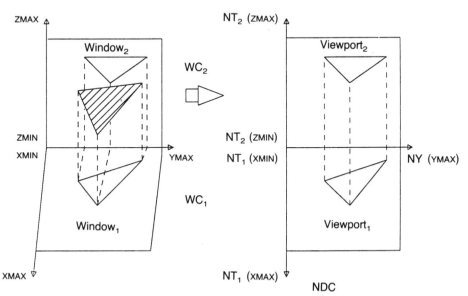

Figure 3.5   Base and height drawings using multiple normalization transformations

Now, in order to output the image on a specific workstation, the image must be shown on the so-called 'device coordinate' (DC) system of that workstation's display screen. This occurs with the help of the 'workstation transformation', which is specified analogously to normalization transformation by:

SET WORKSTATION WINDOW

Input: name   WORKSTATION IDENTIFIER
            4*real   LIMITS XMIN<XMAX,YMIN<YMAX   (NDC)

and

SET WORKSTATION VIEWPORT

Input: name   WORKSTATION IDENTIFIER
            4*real   LIMITS   XMIN<XMAX,YMIN<YMAX   (DC)

or in FORTRAN:

            subroutine GSWKWN   (WKID,XMIN,XMAX,YMIN,YMAX)
            integer   WKID
            real   XMIN,XMAX,YMIN,YMAX

            subroutine GSWVP   (WKID,XMIN,XMAX,YMIN,YMAX)
            integer   WKID
            real   XMIN,XMAX,YMIN,YMAX

The 'workstation window' here becomes part of the NDC unit square, which is shown in each area of the display surface specified by the 'workstation viewport'.

The following rules apply:

- The workstation transformation may not modify the aspect ratio of the selected portion of the image (in contrast to the normalization transformation). If the workstation viewport has an aspect ratio different from that of the workstation window, the image in the window will be shown in such a way that it touches the lower left-hand corner point of the workstation viewport and fills it to the maximum while maintaining its own aspect ratio (see Figure 3.6).
- There is only one workstation transformation per workstation. If the workstation transformation is changed, this results in a change of the image requested to be seen on the display device. The portion selected by 'set workstation window' may change, or the image's position on the display indicated by 'set workstation viewport' may change. If the image has already been displayed by the device, then a change of the workstation transformation on workstations that cannot immediately implement it (for

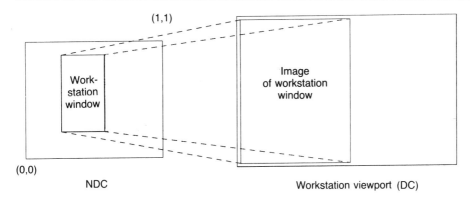

Figure 3.6 Workstation transformation

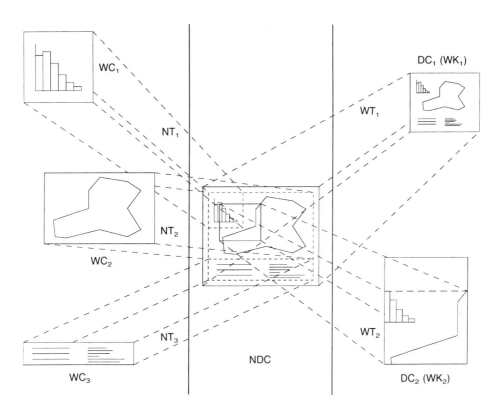

Figure 3.7 Image composition and viewport selection

example, by means of hardware capabilities) implies that the entire display must be redrawn (see Sections 4.2 and 6.1).

■ The default setting of each workstation's workstation transformation causes the largest possible display of the NDC unit square.

Device coordinates are dependent on the workstation, of course. Meters are used principally as DC units on plotters and related devices; for raster-oriented devices without exact correspondence to metric units, it is possible to specify the viewport in raster units.

In summary, the transformations described can be characterized as follows (see Figure 3.7). The normalization transformations serve for workstation-independent (and application-independent) image composition; the workstation transformation, in contrast, does the output and positioning of a portion of an image on the display surface of a specific workstation.

☐ **Let us summarize the GKS functions introduced in this section:**

SET WINDOW	GSWN	(TNR,XMIN,XMAX,YMIN,YMAX)
SET VIEWPORT	GSVP	(TNR,XMIN,XMAX,YMIN,YMAX)
SELECT NORM.TRANSFORMATION	GSELNT	(TNR)
SET CLIPPING INDICATOR	GSCLIP	(CLIPSW)
SET WORKSTATION WINDOW	GSWKSN	(WKID,XMIN,XMAX,YMIN, YMAX)
SET WORKSTATION VIEWPORT	GSWKVP	(WKID,XMIN,XMAX,YMIN, YMAX)

3.4 CalComp on GKS

The final example in this chapter will show the elementary subroutines of the CalComp interface written in terms of GKS functions, where the following (FORTRAN) subroutines are considered the core of the CalComp packet:

PLOTS	–	initialization
PLOT	–	move the pen, draw a line
FACTOR	–	change of scale of the drawing
WHERE	–	query of current pen position
NEWPEN	–	exchange drawing pen

All other basic subroutines like SYMBOL, NUMBER, SCALE, AXIS, and LINE call only PLOT; therefore, their implementation does not need to be modified, although to do so would make better use of GKS capabilities.

Before beginning this recoding, it is useful to compare the coordinate concepts of GKS and CalComp. First, CalComp has a single coordinate system, namely the drawing surface of the workstation being used. This is a cartesian coordinate system with linear scaling and length units in inches or centimeters. At the beginning of a drawing, it is assumed that the drawing pen is located at the origin of the coordinate system and that the drawing surface is not limited on any side.

Apart from the fact that this concept forces the user to work largely in device coordinates, the concept of an unrestricted drawing surface often created problems in practice. Specifically, if the plotter operator were not identical with the application programmer, he could not know how large a drawing was going to be and by how much it had to be separated from the earlier drawings that were already on the continuous roll of paper on a drum plotter. This is also the biggest problem encountered when developing an application on top of GKS as well, because GKS requires a (restricted) workstation viewport.

There are a number of possibilities for the specification of the drawing surfaces used, of course; but none of them gets around the fact that the coordinate area utilized is not known until *after* the construction of a drawing. Many solutions handle this by writing the drawing to a metafile first; the drawing is not generated on the actual drawing device until the end (by interpreting the previously created metafile). Here a simpler, albeit less elegant, solution is used – one that manages without metafiles.

For the run-time storage of important variables of the 'application-oriented shell' (as one could call this example), a FORTRAN common area /CALGKS/ defined in all subroutines is:

```
integer    ERRFIL, WKTYPE, CONID, PLIND, IND
real       XMIN,XMAX,YMIN,YMAX,FACT,X(100),Y(100)
logical    CLOSED
common     /CALGKS/ERRFIL, WKTYPE, CONID, PLIND, IND
common     /CALGKS/XMIN, XMAX, YMIN, YMAX, FACT, X, Y
common     /CALGKS/ CLOSED
```

ERRFIL, WKTYPE, CONID, and PLIND correspond to the parameters of GKS functions previously discussed. IND is the index of the point saved last in the fields X and Y; CLOSED acts as the control of the workstation state. In fact, an application program must call PLOTS before all other CalComp routines. One could enlist this routine, therefore, for opening and initializing GKS and the workstations used. After the end of a drawing, however, (by a specific PLOT call) the CalComp interface authorizes the creation of further drawings. If this call is not enlisted at the end by GKS (and this is important, because no other is available), then further calls of GKS must be activated again in all cases. For this reason PLOTS should initialize only a specific /CALGKS/-variable, and PLOT itself should open GKS, dependent on the value of the variable, CLOSED.

XMIN, XMAX, YMIN, and YMAX describe the current world coordinate window. We simply use one normalization transformation and modify its window by changing the scale factors or shifting the origin. With the help of a new function called CALSWN (CALcomp Set WiNdow) it is possible for the application program to explicitly set the window at run time, but only if GKS is closed (in order to simplify things). CALSWN can be called, therefore, only between PLOTS and the first PLOT call or after each PLOT call that ends a drawing. Using this new function necessitates a slight adjustment of the application, however.

FACT is the CalComp-specific scale factor, and X and Y are arrays to assemble the parameters passed in PLOT calls for a subsequent GKS polyline call.

Unfortunately, there are a few variables important for GKS that cannot be initialized with CalComp calls. Specifically, these are ERRFIL, WKTYPE, and the window limits. In this case, a FORTRAN block data subprogram is used to set these values exclusively. This makes it possible to tailor these values to the particular situation. (This is not a fail-safe method, but a simple one.)

```
block data    CALGKS
integer       ERRFIL, WKTYPE, IDUMMY(3)
real          XMIN, XMAX, YMIN, YMAX, RDUMMY(201)
logical       LDUMMY
common        /CALGKS/ ERRFIL, WKTYPE, IDUMMY
common        /CALGKS/ XMIN, XMAX, YMIN, YMAX
common        /CALGKS/ RDUMMY, LDUMMY
data          WKTYPE
              /"GKS type of the desired workstation"/
data          XMIN,XMAX,YMIN,YMAX
              /"window computed by the application"/
```

If the source code of the CalComp application is not available, block data offers the simplest approach in most operating systems to adapt the 'application-oriented environment' to the current needs. Another possibility would be to modify PLOTS. This is not convenient, however, because PLOTS also has other /CALGKS/ elements to set, which the application programmer does not need to handle. The listings for the modified CalComp subroutines are provided in Appendix D.

Chapter 4
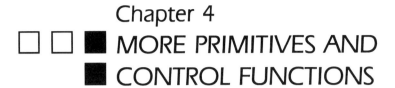
MORE PRIMITIVES AND
CONTROL FUNCTIONS

4.1 Primitives

GKS offers other primitives in addition to polylines. The following primitives have the same parameters as polylines:

POLYMARKER
Input:	integer	NUMBER OF POINTS	(1,...,n)
	n*point	POINTS	(WC)

or in FORTRAN:

subroutine GPM	(N,X,Y)	
integer	N	
real	X(N),Y(N)	

and

FILL AREA

Input:	integer	NUMBER OF POINTS	(3,...,n)
	n*point	POINTS	(WC)

or in FORTRAN:

subroutine GFA	(N,X,Y)	
integer	N	
real	X(N),Y(N)	

A 'polymarker' displays one or more instances of a centered symbol at the positions given by POINTS. A 'fill area' represents a closed surface that is bounded by a polygon determined by POINTS (the last point is automatically connected to the first by GKS); the surface can be filled in different ways (see Chapter 5).

As Figure 4.1 shows, the border of a fill area can intersect itself, so a clear definition is needed of what lies inside or outside a fill area. A point is inside a

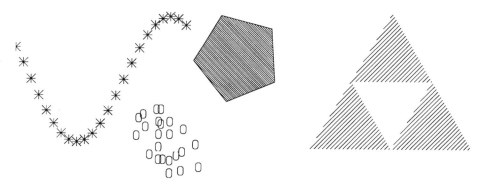

Figure 4.1   Examples of POLYMARKER and FILL AREA

fill area if a ray drawn from this point in any direction gives an odd number of
intersections with the borders of the fill area but without hitting any corner point
of the fill area (see Figure 4.2).

Another important primitive is

TEXT

Input: point   TEXT POSITION   (WC)
           string   CHARACTER STRING

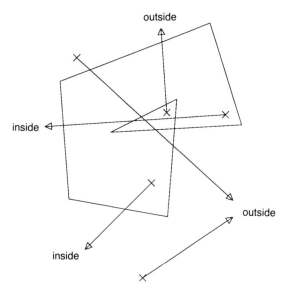

Figure 4.2   FILL AREA – outside/inside

In the FORTRAN language binding of GKS, there are two subroutines for this function, one for the full FORTRAN77 language environment and one for a subset in which the function LEN(text) – which delivers the number of characters in 'text' – is not available. The complete FORTRAN77 version is:

subroutine GTX	(PX,PY,CHARS)
real	PX,PY
character*(*)	CHARS

and the subset version is:

subroutine GTXS	(PX,PY,LSTR,CHARS)
real	PX,PY
integer	LSTR
character*(*)	CHARS

LSTR is the number of characters in CHARS. The subset version will be used in our examples because there are a fair number of FORTRAN compilers whose performance environment lies between subset and full FORTRAN77.

The text position (PX,PY) indicates where the character string should be placed and is, by default, the lower left-hand corner point of the rectangle in which the text is contained. Character height, font, character aspect ratio, text path, and alignment are specified by separate attributes. Section 5.1 discusses these attributes in greater detail. The GKS document specifies that, for font number 1, the character string be written in the code designated by ISO standard 646, which corresponds to the widely known and used ASCII code.

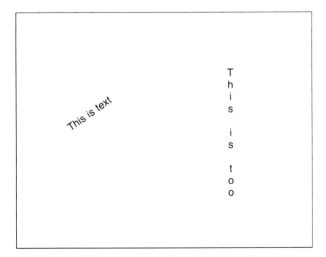

Figure 4.3   Examples of TEXT

Like polylines there are also indices for the new primitives, and thus we find the following functions:

SET POLYMARKER INDEX

Input: integer   POLYMARKER INDEX

or in FORTRAN:

subroutine GSPMI   (PMIND)
integer   PMIND

SET FILL AREA INDEX

Input: integer   FILL AREA INDEX

or in FORTRAN:

subroutine GSFAI   (FAIND)
integer   FAIND

SET TEXT INDEX

Input: integer   TEXT INDEX

or in FORTRAN:

subroutine GSTXI   (TXIND)
integer   TXIND

The use of varied indices here simply creates a visual difference between primitives of the same type. There is no indication yet of which attribute will actually be chosen by these indices on a workstation. A detailed discussion of these primitives occurs in the next chapter, so application examples will not be given here.

Another primitive conceived primarily for image processing applications is:

CELL ARRAY

Input: 2*point   CELL RECTANGLE (P,Q)   (WC)
           2*integer   DIMENSIONS OF THE COLOR INDEX
                            MATRIX DX,DY   (1,...,n)
           DX*DY*integer   COLOR INDEX MATRIX   (0,...,n)

The 'cell rectangle' drawn through the opposite corner points P and Q, parallel to the WC axis, consists of DY rows and DX columns. Thus, a total of DX*DY cells, each of the width |QX−PX|/DX and height |QY−PY|/DY (see Figure 4.4), are required. Each cell is filled with a single color. The element COLOR INDEX MATRIX(i,j) specifies the color with which the cell (i,j) will be filled. This color index should be handled exactly like the primitive indices previously discussed.

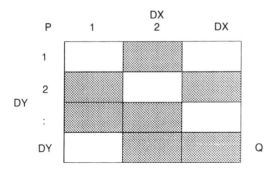

Figure 4.4   Cell array

COLOR INDEX MATRIX(1,1) is always at P, COLOR INDEX MATRIX(DX,DY) is always at Q, and (DX,1) is at (QX,PY) (see Figure 4.4).

If a workstation does not have the capability to display cell arrays in the form described, it is merely required to display the transformed border of the cell rectangle in a workstation-dependent color, line width, and line style.

This primitive makes it possible, therefore, to output images existing as an array of picture points and obtained by some kind of (image processing) method with a single GKS call. Of course, cell arrays as large as 500*500 cannot be displayed with complete assurance that all GKS implementations will actually be able to transfer the 250,000 color indices necessary in a single call.

The FORTRAN language environment allows for the transfer of partial arrays:

subroutine GCA	(PX,PY,QX,QY,DIMX,DIMY,ISC,ISR,DX,DY, COLIA)
real	PX,PY,QX,QY
integer	DIMX,DIMY,ISC,ISR,DX,DY,COLIA(DIMX,DIMY)

(PX,PY) and (QX,QY) are the coordinates of the cell rectangle points P and Q, respectively. DIMX and DIMY are the dimensions of the color index matrix COLIA. ISC is the index of the first *column*, and ISR is the index of the first *row* of a submatrix with DX columns and DY rows, which are to be extracted by GKS and used for the cell array.

If, for example, only the upper right 5*5 submatrix of a 20*15 matrix is to be transferred (see Figure 4.5), this can be done by the following call:

call GCA (PX,PY,QX,QY,20,15,16,1,5,5,COLIA)

Of course, ISC=ISR=1 and DX=DIMX or DY=DIMY must be set if the entire color matrix is to be transferred to GKS at one time. In addition, cell arrays are subject to the same transformations as all other primitives.

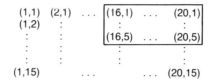

Figure 4.5   The partial matrix within
the frame is to be transferred

Nothing further will be said about cell array except in Section 5.1, where the color model will be discussed.

The final GKS primitive will now be introduced to address special workstation capabilities like circle or rectangle generators. This primitive is called:

GENERALIZED DRAWING PRIMITIVE (GDP)

Input: integer   NUMBER OF POINTS
             n*point   POINTS   (WC)
             integer   GDP IDENTIFIER
             data   GDP DATA RECORD

or in FORTRAN:

subroutine GGDP   (N,X,Y,GDPID,LDR,DATREC)
integer   N
real   X,Y
integer   GDPID
integer   LDR
character*80   DATREC(LDR)

The GDP IDENTIFIER chooses the desired primitive (e.g., 'arc') to be generated using the (transformed) POINTS. If the transformation causes a distortion, this must be accounted for by the rendering process; circular arcs, for example, can become elliptical arcs. If the GDP does not require transformed data (like the weights for a smooth spline /Boor 78/), then the data will be transferred in the GDP DATA RECORD, rather than the POINTS array.

Because the GKS standard does not specify any specific GDPs, further discussion of this primitive will be avoided, except to say that no GKS implementation is forced to support GDP. (If an implementation supports a specific GDP, however, it is imperative that it is interpreted in the same way on every workstation available for this implementation.) If the GKS installation at your disposal offers GDP, you will surely be able to find information about the corresponding parameter arguments in the implementation documentation.

Of course, the use of GDP reduces the portability of application programs. In order to improve this situation, the ISO subcommittee responsible for GKS created a working group to collect, register, and publish approved proposals for GDP (as well as other graphics 'entities' like 'escape' – see Section 4.2 – and new line and marker types).

☐ **Here is a summary of the GKS functions introduced in this section:**

POLYMARKER	GPM	(N,X,Y)
FILL AREA	GFA	(N,X,Y)
TEXT	GTX	(PX,PY,CHARS)
	GTXS	(PX,PY,LSTR,CHARS)
SET POLYMARKER INDEX	GSPMI	(PMIND)
SET TEXT INDEX	GSTXI	(TXIND)
CELL ARRAY	GCA	(PX,PY,QX,QY,DIMX,DIMY, ISC,ISR,DX,DY,COLIA)
GENERALIZED DRAWING PRIMITIVE	GGDP	(N,X,Y,GDPID,LDR,DATREC)

4.2 Additional Control Functions (Updating Images)

There are other control functions in addition to those for setting workstation states, which were presented in Section 3.1. It needs to be possible, for example, to clear an already 'used' display surface:

CLEAR WORKSTATION

Input: name   WORKSTATION IDENTIFIER
         enum   CONTROL FLAG   (CONDITIONALLY,ALWAYS)

This function clears the display surface of a given workstation according to the second parameter. If the second parameter is set to CONDITIONALLY, it merely ensures that the display surface is empty; at all other times, the display surface is cleared regardless of whether it is currently empty.

On a workstation that utilizes a permanent storage medium like paper or film as a display surface, it is guaranteed in a workstation-specific way that a new drawing surface is available (by inserting a new sheet of paper, for example). The corresponding FORTRAN routine is:

```
        subroutine GCLRWK  (WKID,CONDFL)
        integer            WKID,CONDFL
C                          0=CONDITIONALLY,1=ALWAYS
```

After opening a workstation, its drawing surface is as empty as it is immediately following 'Clear workstation'; therefore, this function need not be called at the beginning of a program.

Two other functions are concerned with one of the most complicated mechanisms of the Graphical Kernel System, controlling the update of image changes. This concept is of more significance for highly interactive applications, however, so the aspects essential for simpler applications will be dealt with while avoiding a more complete description.

There are two main types of image changes. There are those that are caused by adding new picture parts to an already existing image, and there are those that arise from manipulating an existing image.

Consider the first type. This type is caused by a group of GKS functions that includes all operations – in addition to the generation of primitives – that send predefined segments to the workstation (see also Section 6.2): essentially, all output functions. In specific cases, it can be useful to delay the visualization of these functions on a single workstation – in other words, to buffer them in order to optimize data transfer to the device.

The so-called 'update mode' controls the point in time which is the latest possible time the effect of such functions must be visible; to do this, the update mode can take the following values:

ASAP: Each function has an immediate, visible effect on the
        workstation; that is, 'As Soon As Possible'.
BNIG: Each function has a visible effect on the workstation
        'Before the Next Interaction Globally' on any workstation.
BNIL: Each function has a visible effect on the workstation
        'Before the Next Interaction Locally' on this workstation.
ASTI: Each function has a visible effect on the workstation
        'At Some Time'.

All delayed functions are executed by the time a workstation is closed, if not carried out sooner.

None of the cited values requires a workstation to delay the visible effects of functions that generate primitives. If this is explicitly called for by the application, it can be accomplished with the help of segments. It is assumed, however, that most implementations will make use of the buffering control option. The most useful practice is to drive the plotter and related devices in ASTI mode, interactive screens in BNIG or BNIL mode, and to use ASAP only in special cases (for example, real-time process control).

The second type of image changes are caused by use of GKS functions that result in image manipulation. These uses include:

■ Changes of the workstation transformation

- Changes in the association between primitive indices and primitive attributes
- Changes of segment attributes (see Section 6.3)
- Deleting segments
- Under certain circumstances, functions of the first group (which will not be discussed here)

Imagine the following situation. A map is being created. First, the whole map is drawn on a plotter. (The prerequisite for further action is having stored the map in segments.) If the workstation window of this workstation is set afterwards to select a small detail of this map, then this part may be enlarged and displayed on the plotter. Plotters normally cannot execute these changes immediately like most interactive displays can, so the first consequence is that the drawing already created must be advanced and a new drawing surface made available to the plotter. Finally, the desired detail is drawn using the new workstation transformation.

Image changes in this second category can therefore cause so-called 'implicit regeneration' (IRG). Whether the operation will cause an implicit regeneration on a workstation or whether it can be carried out immediately without an implicit regeneration can be determined from the respective workstation description tables (see Section 2.7).

The following important points need to be noted:

- Before every implicit regeneration, all delayed actions on the corresponding workstation are implicitly carried out.
- In the case of an implicit regeneration, only the primitives that are stored in segments will be redrawn; all other primitives are lost.

Occasionally it makes sense not to allow an implicit regeneration to occur immediately (within the GKS function that affects this implicit regeneration), but to delay the regeneration. Let us return to the map example, but now we also want to change the position of the image on the display surface. To accomplish this, we change the workstation viewport. It is certainly not desirable for the call 'set workstation window' to cause an implicit regeneration at this point; it should follow the call of both 'set workstation window' and 'set workstation viewport'. With the help of the so-called 'regeneration mode', each workstation can be individually designated to SUPPRESS or ALLOW an implicit regeneration.

GKS provides a single function to set both modes:

SET DEFERRAL STATE

Input:	name	WORKSTATION IDENTIFIER	
	enum	DEFERRAL MODE	(ASAP, BNIG, BNIL, ASTI)
	enum	REGENERATION MODE	(SUPPRESS, ALLOW)

or in FORTRAN:

```
            subroutine GSDS      (WKID,DEFMOD,REGMOD)
            integer              WKID
            integer              DEFMOD
C                                        0=ASAP,1=BNIG,2=BNIL,3=ASTI
            integer              REGMOD
C                                        0=SUPPRESS,1=ALLOW
```

Another function allows a workstation to update regardless of the current values of both modes:

UPDATE WORKSTATION

Input: name   WORKSTATION IDENTIFIER
          enum   REGENERATION FLAG   (SUPPRESS,PERFORM)

or in FORTRAN:

```
            subroutine GUWK      (WKID,REGFL)
            integer              WKID,REGFL
C                                        0=SUPPRESS,1=PERFORM
```

This function first causes all delayed actions to be carried out. If an implicit regeneration is also necessary but is currently suppressed, it is implemented only if the regeneration flag is set to PERFORM. Otherwise, only the transfer of buffered data is initiated.

Now with these functions, the problem of the map detail enlargement is easily solved (assuming that the map is stored in segments):

```
            :
            : (Draw entire map)
            :
C           suppress IRG
      call GSDS (WKID,3,0)
C           set new WT
      call GSWKWN (WKID,...)
      call GSWKVP (WKID,...)
C           update WK
      call GUWK (WKID,1)
```

The use of

```
      call GSDS (WKID,3,1)
```

instead of the GUWK call would have had the same effect.

After this example of image changes, two final GKS control functions, MESSAGE and ESCAPE, will be discussed.

MESSAGE

Input:	name	WORKSTATION IDENTIFIER
	string	MESSAGE

or in FORTRAN77:

```
subroutine GMSG    (WKID,MESS)
integer            WKID
character*(*)      MESS
```

and in the subset version:

```
subroutine GMSGS   (WKID,LSTR,MESS)
integer            WKID,LSTR
character*(*)      MESS
```

LSTR is the number of characters in MESS. The effect of this function is that the 'message' will be readable at an implementation-dependent location in the workstation viewport or on a separate device that is assigned to the workstation, and it will be displayed in an implementation-dependent way.

Finally, the 'escape function' is used to address certain capabilities of one workstation, a group of workstations, or a GKS installation-dependent capability that is not covered by GDP. Like GDP, this function has its own parameter, which identifies the escape function desired. At the time of writing, there are no standardized uses for the escape function. One can imagine, however, that with this function the capabilities of raster hardware could be used to manipulate images already stored and displayed on the device or the drawing speed of vector plotters could be controlled. The essential thing is that this function produces no graphical output and leaves the GKS state unchanged.

ESCAPE

Input:	name	ESCAPE FUNCTION IDENTIFICATION
	data	ESCAPE INPUT DATA RECORD
Output:	data	ESCAPE OUTPUT DATA RECORD

or in FORTRAN:

```
subroutine GESC    (FID,LDIN,DATIN,MLDOUT,LDOUT,DATOUT)
integer            FID,LDIN
```

character*80	DATIN(LDIN)
integer	MLDOUT,LDOUT
character*80	DATOUT(MLDOUT)

The actual length of the output data in LDOUT is returned in DATOUT. If the GKS installation available to you supports the escape function, you will be able to find out about the corresponding arguments in the implementation documentation.

Here is a summary of the GKS functions introduced in this section:

CLEAR WORKSTATION	GCLRWK	(WKID,CONDFL)
SET DEFERRAL STATE	GSDS	(WKID,DEFMOD,REGMOD)
UPDATE WORKSTATION	GUWK	(WKID,REGFL)
MESSAGE	GMSG	(WKID,MESS)
	GMSGS	(WKID,LSTR,MESS)
ESCAPE FUNCTION	GESC	(FID,LDIN,DATIN,
		MLDOUT,LDOUT,DATOUT)

Chapter 5

ATTRIBUTES

As emphasized earlier, the construction of an image from primitives essentially describes only its geometric characteristics. Additional characteristics such as color or text font are assigned to the primitive by so-called 'attributes'. In order to do this, methods are needed to specify the appearance of a polyline. For example, should it be displayed as a thin, green line or a thick, dark blue stroke? One must also consider the capabilities of the workstation used, of course, because it is unrealistic to expect varied color representations on a monochrome vector display. On the other hand, it is reasonable to demand that a specific polyline be represented by a dashed line on each workstation, because all graphic output devices known to the authors can draw at least a dashed line in software, if not in hardware.

Separating geometric from visual (non-geometric) attributes is an essential step forward from older graphics concepts and graphics packages because, through this, the geometric characteristics of an image can be defined independently of the device and the visual attributes can be matched to the capabilities of the workstation being used.

How are specific attributes assigned to the primitives? We have already learned a group of so-called 'device-independent primitive attributes', or 'primitive attributes' for short, for which it was said that different indices cause different representations. Recall that polyline, polymarker, fill area, and text have such indices; the cell array does not; and GDP uses the indices of whatever other primitives appear to be most useful in each case.

These indices are primitive attributes in the sense that they are bound to the primitive at its creation and this connection remains unchanged during the entire lifetime of the primitive; they are workstation-independent because this relationship is the same for all workstations.

The calls

        call GSPLI (11)
        call GPL (N,X,Y)

create a connection between polyline index 11 and the polyline (with N points) created afterward; index 11 is attached to the polyline as long as the polyline exists.

Before describing how such an index selects attributes on a specific workstation, it is useful to examine the primitive attributes used in GKS.

5.1   Visual Attributes of Primitives

5.1.1   Color

One attribute that all primitives possess, to the extent that they can be said to possess attributes in general, is color. The color of an object is a function of the portion of the electromagnetic spectrum which meets the eye of the observer. If the whole visible area of a spectrum were brought into play to describe the color of an object, a high expenditure of effort would be necessary to process the information. Fortunately, it has been shown that the human eye is satisfied with a reduction to three spectral regions if the intensity shading within these regions is sufficiently large. The concept of overlapping three monochrome images to create a complete colored image has pervaded all technical disciplines that deal with the reproduction of color-printing, film, photography, video, and computer graphics. (In printing, another color layer, black, is usually added.)

There are two principal variations on this method. In a 'subtractive' color model, the basic colors are cyan (light blue), yellow, and magenta (purple-pink); and overlapping them creates black. In the 'additive' color model, the basic colors are red, green, and (dark) blue; and overlapping them produces white. The first variation is called subtractive because the individual spectrum fields are removed from white light; this makes it especially suitable for printing. In the second variation, in contrast, the individual spectrum fields are added; and this is useful primarily for self-lighting media. Both models are complementary in the sense that the corresponding overlap of two basic colors of one model yields a basic color of the other model.

The additive color model is used by GKS because of the great number of color display screens currently in use. This means that a color is described by a number triplet R/G/B, which describes the intensities of red/green/blue. The numbers range between 0 and 1; 0 means no intensity and 1 means full intensity. Table 5.1 contains a few examples of the assignment of these numbers to colors.

The color actually displayed is dependent on the capabilities of the workstation. In many cases it may not be necessary for an application to utilize specific colors; sometimes it is sufficient that the colors simply be different from one another. Therefore, the choice of colors is analogous to the choice of other visual attributes. Disregarding cell array and GDP, all primitives have a so-called color index as a visual attribute instead of having a specific color triplet. This

Table 5.1 Examples of R/G/B color compositions

Intensity			Resulting color in additive color model
red	green	blue	
0.0	0.0	0.0	black
1.0	0.0	0.0	red
0.0	1.0	0.0	green
0.0	0.0	1.0	blue
1.0	1.0	0.0	yellow
1.0	0.0	1.0	magenta
0.0	1.0	1.0	cyan
1.0	1.0	1.0	white
0.5	0.0	0.0	dark red
0.7	0.2	0.1	brown
1.0	0.5	0.0	orange
0.5	0.5	0.5	gray

index selects a specific R/G/B combination on each workstation. The selection mechanism will be discussed in detail in Section 5.2. (On monochrome workstations, color triplets are mapped to workstation-specific intensity values.)

In addition to the additive and subtractive color models, there are also a number of other color models in use. These will not be discussed in this book.

5.1.2 Polyline Attributes

Polylines have the visual (non-geometric) attributes 'linetype', 'linewidth', and 'polyline color index'. The linetypes 1 to 4 mean *solid, dashed, dotted,* and *dashed-dotted*; every workstation must be able to depict these. Linetypes of greater values are reserved for future standardization. Negative values may be used, but they are implementation-dependent. It is required that every linetype be similarly represented on all workstations of one installation. Whether the period of an interrupted line begins anew with each polyline, at every node of a polyline, or whether it continues across nodes of a polyline (that is, begins with the remainder of the previous interrupted line) is implementation-dependent.

The linewidth is calculated from a workstation-specific 'nominal linewidth' multiplied by the value of the line width scale factor attribute. The result is represented on the workstation by the nearest available linewidth.

Table 5.2 shows a few examples of polylines (in black, of course).

Table 5.2   Polyline attributes

Linewidth scale factor	Linetype			
	1	2	3	4
1.0	————	·············	··············	— · — · —
2.0	————	··············	••••••••••••	— • — • —

5.1.3   Polymarker Attributes

Polymarkers have the attributes 'marker type', 'marker size', and 'polymarker color index'. The marker types 1–5 correspond to the symbols *dot* (.), *plus* (+), *asterisk* (*), *circle* (O), and *cross* (×). The marker size is calculated analogously to linewidth from a nominal marker size and a marker size scale factor.

5.1.4   Fill Area Attributes

Disregarding color index, fill area attributes are different from those already introduced. First, it is possible to specify how a fill area is filled. The corresponding attribute is called 'fill area interior style'; it is an enumeration type parameter and can take on one of the following four values:

HOLLOW: The boundary of the polygon is drawn in the current fill area color index.

SOLID: The fill area is filled completely with the color selected by the fill area color index.

PAT-TERN: The fill area is filled with a pattern. A pattern is a kind of cell array, which conceptually replicates in the x- and y-directions as often as necessary to cover the whole primitive (see also Section 5.3). An additional attribute, 'fill area interior style index', points to a workstation-specific pattern table to specify which pattern will be used.

HATCH: The fill area is hatched with the color determined by the fill area color index. The fill area interior style index again specifies which hatch style will be used; this time it acts as a pointer to a (workstation-specific) hatch list.

This is summarized in Table 5.3.

Table 5.3   Usage of fill area attributes depending on 'fill
area interior style'

FA interior style	FA interior style index	FA color index
HOLLOW	—	Edge color
SOLID	—	Interior color
PATTERN	Index in pattern table	—
HATCH	Index in hatch list	Hatch color

If a fill area is supplied with a pattern, two other attributes are used: 'pattern size' and 'pattern reference point'. The pattern size specifies the size of the cell array, and the reference point determines the position of the pattern. These attributes are specified in world coordinates and, like primitives, are subject to all transformations. Workstations that display patterns but cannot transform them do not have to use either attribute.

5.1.5   Text Attributes

Text is actually more than a primitive. Aside from the fact that there are different fonts (other character sets like Arabic and Greek also have different forms), text can also be represented in different sizes, widths, directions, etc. Due to the fact that almost every output device can realize text in some form and because almost every application requires text, GKS contains a graphic text primitive that possesses a wealth of attributes. These include 'character height', 'character expansion factor', 'character spacing', 'text path', 'character up vector', 'text alignment', 'text font index', 'text precision', and 'text color index'.

These attributes are more easily understood using a character body model. For each text font – in a coordinate system specific to this font – the lines shown in Figure 5.1 are defined. If proportional text is being described, as in Figure 5.1, the width of the individual character and its respective relationship of width to height are different; otherwise, all characters are of equal width. The height and width indicated here are called 'normal'.

CHARACTER HEIGHT specifies the desired character height in WC. The character body is enlarged so it nominally agrees with the desired character height.

CHARACTER EXPANSION FACTOR changes the width/height ratio from the nominal setting to the specified value according to:

$$\frac{desired\ width}{desired\ height} = \text{CHAR. EXPANSION FACTOR} \times \frac{nominal\ width}{nominal\ height}$$

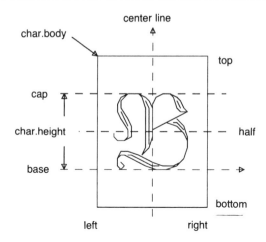

Figure 5.1   Character body

CHARACTER SPACING controls the spacing between consecutive characters as a portion of their height. Positive values insert space between character bodies; negative values cause character bodies to move closer together, overlapping in extreme cases.

TEXT PATH specifies the direction in which consecutive text characters should be arranged. GKS recognizes the text paths RIGHT, LEFT, DOWN, and UP. RIGHT and LEFT arrange the characters so that their bottom lines form a line. DOWN and UP cause the center lines of the characters to form a line.

These four attributes describe the size and form of a text string and define a 'text extent rectangle' (see Figure 5.2). The text extent rectangle is the minimal rectangle that contains all of the character bodies of the text. The following attributes determine the orientation and position of this rectangle in the WC system.

CHARACTER UP VECTOR specifies the upright direction of the character body.

TEXT ALIGNMENT controls the positioning of the text extent rectangle in relation to text position (see Section 4.1). The horizontal components of this attribute can accept the values LEFT, CENTER, RIGHT, or NORMAL depending on whether the left line, center line, or right line should go through the text position or whether the text alignment follows in accordance with the text path (see Table 5.4). The vertical components can accept the values TOP, CAP, HALF, BASE, BOTTOM, or NORMAL. They specify (together with text paths LEFT and RIGHT) each line of the character body that should go through the text position. In the case of the other two text paths (UP and DOWN), vertical alignments TOP, HALF, and BASE are interpreted the same as for LEFT and RIGHT. CAP refers to the uppermost character and BOTTOM refers to the lowest character of the text extent rectangle. NORMAL realigns the text in reference to the text path (see Table 5.4). Text fonts

Ch. Height = 1.0
Ch. Exp. = 1.0
Ch. Spacing = 0.0
T. path = right
Ch. Up Vector = (0.0,1.0)
T. Alignment = <normal,normal>

T. Alignment = <normal,bottom>
Ch. Up Vector = (1.0,4.0)
T. path = up
Ch. Height = 0.75
Ch. Exp. = 0.8
Ch. Spacing = 0.0

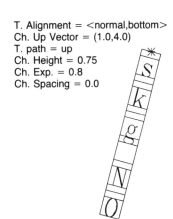

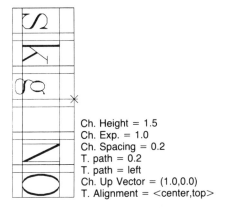

Ch. Height = 1.5
Ch. Exp. = 1.0
Ch. Spacing = 0.2
T. path = 0.2
T. path = left
Ch. Up Vector = (1.0,0.0)
T. Alignment = <center,top>

T. Alignment = <normal,base>
T. path = right
Ch. Up Vector = (−1.0,2.0)
Ch. Height = 1.0
Ch. Exp. = 2.0
Ch. Spacing = −0.5

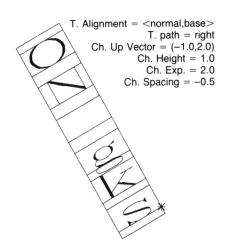

Figure 5.2   More examples of TEXT

Table 5.4   Text alignment for NORMAL

Text path	(horizontal,vertical) alignment for NORMAL
RIGHT	(LEFT,BASE)
LEFT	(RIGHT,BASE)
TOP	(CENTER,BASE)
BOTTOM	(CENTER,TOP)

are allowed in which upper and cap lines or base and bottom lines coincide. Now consider another text attribute; namely:

TEXT FONT AND PRECISION is an attribute consisting of two components. As already mentioned, there are a number of different fonts. These are selected by an index, which is specified by the first component of the attribute, and which takes the form of an integer. Not all workstations of a GKS installation must be able to display all of the fonts supported by the installation. The following rules apply:

- Font 1 contains the character set defined in ISO 646 (ASCII in the US) and must be available on every workstation.
- A font number must represent the same font on all workstations.
- If a font is selected on a workstation that cannot supply it, it must be replaced by Font 1.

The second component of the TEXT FONT AND PRECISION attribute, which takes an enumerated value, specifies the text precision. This attribute makes it possible for the programmer to specify how precisely a workstation must take into account the text attributes and the clipping specifications. Text precision can have the following values:

STRING: Text font and text position must be taken into consideration. Character height and character expansion factor must be accounted for as well as possible, and the other text attributes do not have to be considered at all. Clipping occurs in a device-dependent fashion.

CHARACTER: This precision is similar to STRING precision, but the individual characters of a text string must be precisely positioned, and clipping occurs at least character by character. The character up vector must be evaluated as closely as possible.

STROKE: All attributes are fully applied, and precise clipping occurs. This is also true, of course, for fonts whose characters are created as polylines or from other elements (like fill area or raster text).

This attribute exploits device capabilities because texts with 'string' quality can often be generated quickly. For stroke quality, a software text generator is often necessary, greatly slowing down the speed of character generation. Figure 5.3 illustrates the different pictures that result from different settings of text precision – all other text attributes remaining the same. The existence of a higher-quality text font on a specific workstation implies the existence of all lower-quality fonts as well. It should also be mentioned that normalization transformations and segment transformations can distort the text-extent rectangles into parallelograms.

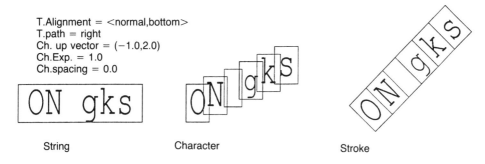

Figure 5.3   Text precisions

The final text attribute, TEXT COLOR INDEX, has a meaning analogous to the color indices previously discussed. Table 5.5 contains the initial values of text attributes.

5.1.6 Cell Array and GDP Attributes

These two primitives do not have any of their own attributes. All parameters necessary for describing the cell array are specified in its call. Individual GDPs use the attributes of the primitives to which they correspond most closely, according to their nature. In this way, a GDP that represents a circular arc uses the polyline attributes, and a GDP representing a disk (a filled circle) uses the fill area attributes.

We have finished describing the attributes of GKS primitives. The following section will discuss how these attributes are assigned to primitives.

Table 5.5 Defaults for text attributes

Text attribute	Defaults
Character height	0.01 (1% of the window height)
Character expansion factor	1.0
Character spacing	0.0
Text path	RIGHT
Character up vector	(0.0,1.0)
Text alignment	<NORMAL,NORMAL>
Text font and precision	<1,STRING>
Text color index	1

5.2 Choosing Visual Attributes

5.2.1 Workstation-specific Attributes

As discussed earlier, the primitive indices select specific visual attributes on each workstation. To do this, each workstation manages a so-called 'bundle table' in its state list (see Section 2.7) for each primitive element type that possesses such an index. The bundle table is composed of fixed columns and a variable number of rows. Each entry in the table describes a valid combination of visual attributes of the corresponding primitive and is called a 'bundle'. Each entry is referenced by an index for identification. The polyline table of a workstation can be represented as shown in Table 5.6.

Table 5.6 Example of a polyline bundle table

Polyline index	Linetype	Width factor	Color index
1	1	1.0	1
2	2	1.0	1
3	1	2.0	1
4	2	2.0	1
5	1	1.0	2
:	:	:	:

The polyline index is, therefore, a pointer into the polyline bundle table of each open workstation. For example, in Table 5.6 polyline index 3 selects line type 1 (solid), linewidth scale factor 2.0 (double the nominal linewidth), and color index 1. Again, the latter is itself a pointer into a color table, contained on each workstation and built similarly to the bundle table (with four columns, of course). Figure 5.4 illustrates how a specific polyline index completely determines the visual aspects of a polyline on different workstations. On workstation A (in Figure 5.4), therefore, white, solid lines of 'double' thickness will be produced, while on workstation B, green, dotted nominal width lines will appear.

Section 5.4 deals with additional bundle tables and their manipulation.

5.2.2 Workstation-independent Attributes

At times it is desirable to be able to set certain attribute values globally, that is, identically for all workstations being used. This principle is, in fact, possible in the former model as well; the corresponding bundle entries could be set to fit,

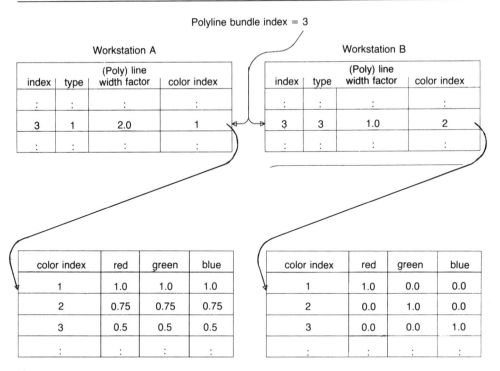

Figure 5.4   Attribute selection using primitive bundle index

but not very conveniently. Here, it would be better to use application sequences of the following kind:

> set LINETYPE to SOLID;
>
> generate POLYLINE; (*will be displayed as solid line on all active workstations*)
>
> set LINETYPE to DASHED;
>
> generate POLYLINE; (*will be displayed as dashed line everywhere*)

GKS does enable this method of attribute selection. To do this, it manages its own table in its state list, which contains an entry for each visual attribute described in Section 5.1. (The functions with which these tables can be changed are handled in Section 5.3.) When a primitive is produced, the values relevant to that attribute are selected from each table and remain connected to the element throughout its lifetime.

5.2.3   Aspect Source Flags

Global attribute values are passed along with the index of a primitive when it is output to a workstation; the index itself selects attribute values (from the corresponding bundle table of the workstation). For each visual attribute, which can be set globally and in a workstation-specific manner, it is necessary to be able to decide which value is to be used. This is possible with the help of so-called 'aspect source flags' (ASFs). Each attribute to be defined either globally or in a workstation-specific manner (i.e. via a bundle table) has an ASF. Each ASF can accept the values BUNDLED or INDIVIDUAL, depending on whether the workstation-specific or global (that is, individual) value is to be used. The collection of ASFs can be compared to switches, which control the choice of attribute values. When creating a primitive, therefore, the values of all relevant ASFs as well as the values of each global attribute, which has the value INDIVIDUAL from the ASF associated with it, are connected to the corresponding primitive.

   When GKS is opened, the implementation sets all ASFs uniformly and in an implementation-specific manner to either BUNDLED or INDIVIDUAL. To change the values of the ASF, you must use the following function:

SET ASPECT SOURCE FLAGS

Input:	ASF linetype	(BUNDLED, INDIVIDUAL)
	ASF linewidth scale factor	(BUNDLED, INDIVIDUAL)
	ASF polyline color index	(BUNDLED, INDIVIDUAL)
	ASF marker type	(BUNDLED, INDIVIDUAL)
	ASF marker size scale factor	(BUNDLED, INDIVIDUAL)
	ASF polymarker color index	(BUNDLED, INDIVIDUAL)
	ASF text font and precision	(BUNDLED, INDIVIDUAL)
	ASF character expansion factor	(BUNDLED, INDIVIDUAL)
	ASF character spacing	(BUNDLED, INDIVIDUAL)
	ASF text color index	(BUNDLED, INDIVIDUAL)
	ASF fill area interior style	(BUNDLED, INDIVIDUAL)
	ASF fill area interior style index	(BUNDLED, INDIVIDUAL)
	ASF fill area color index	(BUNDLED, INDIVIDUAL)

The corresponding FORTRAN routine uses a 13-element integer field, whose elements can accept the values 0 (=BUNDLED) or 1 (=INDIVIDUAL) and which represents the ASF in the previous sequence by:

```
subroutine GSASF    (LASF)
integer             LASF(13)
```

   There are no ASFs for the attributes character height, character up vector, pattern size, pattern reference point, text path, and text alignment. The reason for this is that the first four attributes are specified in WC and the last two decidedly influence the position and form of a text string (and therefore its geometric properties). In both cases, it would violate GKS concepts to permit workstation-specific differences when these attributes can be set only globally.

5.3 (Workstation-independent) Primitive Attributes

A GKS implementation maintains a table that contains the current values of each visual attribute introduced in Section 5.1, where the following rules apply to the use of these attributes:

- The current values of each attribute from that table are bound to any primitive whose ASF is set to INDIVIDUAL at the time of its creation; this connection remains during the whole lifetime of the primitive.
- The bound values of visual attributes of each primitive override the values from the corresponding bundle table chosen by the index, at the time of outputting a primitive on a workstation in the category OUTPUT or OUTIN.
- The entries in this table can be changed.
- The entries in this table can be inquired.

Default values for workstation-independent primitive attributes are given in Table 5.7. Now it is time to introduce the separate GKS functions with which individual attributes are set.

Table 5.7   Defaults for workstation-independent primitive attributes

linetype	1	
linewidth scale factor	1.0	
polyline color index	1	
marker type	3	
marker size scale factor	1.0	
polymarker color index	1	
fill area interior style	HOLLOW	
fill area style index	1	
pattern size	<1.0,1.0>	(WC)
pattern reference point	(0.0,0.0)	(WC)
character height	0.01	
character expansion factor	1.0	
character spacing	0.0	
text path	RIGHT	
character up vector	(0.0,1.0)	(WC)
text alignment	<NORMAL,NORMAL>	
text font and precision	<1,STRING>	
text color index	1	

5.3.1 Polyline Attribute Functions

SET LINETYPE

Input: integer LINETYPE $(-n,...,-1,1,...,n)$

or in FORTRAN:

subroutine GSLN (LINTYP)
integer LINTYP

SET LINEWIDTH SCALE FACTOR

Input: real L!NEWIDTH (>0.0)

or in FORTRAN:

subroutine GSLWSC (LINWDT)
integer LINWDT

SET POLYLINE COLOR INDEX

Input: integer POLYLINE COLOR INDEX $(0,...,n)$

or in FORTRAN:

subroutine GSPLCI (PLCOLI)
integer PLCOLI

5.3.2 Polymarker Attribute Functions

SET MARKER TYPE
Input: integer MARKERTYPE $(-n,...,-1,1,...,n)$

or in FORTRAN:

subroutine GSMK (MRKTYP)
integer MRKTYP

SET MARKER SIZE SCALE FACTOR

Input: real MARKER SIZE SCALE FACTOR (>0.0)

or in FORTRAN:

>   subroutine GSMKSC   (MRKSCF)
>   integer   MRKSCF

SET POLYMARKER COLOR INDEX

Input: integer   POLYMARKER COLOR INDEX   (0,...,n)

or in FORTRAN:

>   subroutine GSPMCI   (PMCOLI)
>   integer   PMCOLI

5.3.3 Fill Area Attribute Functions

SET FILL AREA INTERIOR STYLE

Input: enum   FILL AREA INTERIOR STYLE
                        (HOLLOW,SOLID,PATTERN,HATCH)

or in FORTRAN:

>   subroutine GSFAIS   (FAINST)
>   integer   FAINST
> C   0=HOLLOW,1=SOLID,2=PATTERN,3=HATCH

SET FILL AREA STYLE INDEX

Input: integer   FILL AREA STYLE INDEX   (-n,...,-1,1,...,n)

or in FORTRAN:

>   subroutine GSFASI   (FASTIN)
>   integer   FASTIN

SET FILL AREA COLOR INDEX

Input: integer   FILL AREA COLOR INDEX   (0,...,n)

or in FORTRAN:

>   subroutine GSFACI   (FACOLI)
>   integer   FACOLI

SET PATTERN SIZE

Input: real   SIZE IN X, SIZE IN Y   (2*wc)   (>0.0)

or in FORTRAN:

        subroutine GSPA   (SZX,SZY)
        real   SZX,SZY

SET PATTERN REFERENCE POINT

Input: point   PATTERN REFERENCE POINT   (2*WC)

or in FORTRAN:

        subroutine GSPARF   (RFX,RFY)
        real   RFX,RFY

5.3.4 Text Attribute Functions

SET CHARACTER HEIGHT

Input: real   CHARACTER HEIGHT   (WC)   (>0.0)

or in FORTRAN:

        subroutine GSCHH   (CHHGT)
        real   CHHGT

SET CHARACTER EXPANSION FACTOR

Input: real   CHARACTER EXPANSION FACTOR   (>0.0)

or in FORTRAN:

        subroutine GSCHXP   (EXPFAC)
        real   EXPFAC

SET CHARACTER SPACING

Input: real   CHARACTER SPACING

or in FORTRAN:

        subroutine GSCHSP   (CHSPAC)
        real   CHSPAC

SET TEXT PATH

Input: enum   TEXT PATH   (RIGHT,LEFT,UP,DOWN)

or in FORTRAN:

       subroutine GSTXP   (TXPATH)
       integer   TXPATH
C   0=RIGHT,1=LEFT,2=UP,3=DOWN

SET CHARACTER UP VECTOR

Input: 2*real   CHARACTER UP VECTOR   (2*WC)

or in FORTRAN:

       subroutine GSCHUP   (CHUX,CHUY)
       real   CHUX,CHUY

SET TEXT ALIGNMENT

Input: 2*enum   TEXT ALIGNMENT
                          <(NORMAL,LEFT,CENTER,RIGHT),
                     (NORMAL,TOP,CAP,HALF,BASE,BOTTOM)>

or in FORTRAN:

       subroutine GSTXAL   (TXALH,TXALV)
       integer   TXALH
C   0=NORMAL,1=LEFT,2=CENTER,3=RIGHT
       integer   TXALV
C   0=NORMAL,1=TOP,2=CAP,3=HALF,4=BASE,5=BOTTOM

SET TEXT FONT AND PRECISION

Input: <integer,enum>   TEXT FONT/PRECISION
                                <(-n,...,-1,1,...,n),
                     (STRING,CHARACTER,STROKE)>

or in FORTRAN:

       subroutine GSTXFP   (FONT,PREC)
       integer   FONT,PREC
C   PREC: 0=STRING,1=CHARACTER,2=STROKE

SET TEXT COLOR INDEX

Input: integer   TEXT COLOR INDEX   (0,...,n)

or in FORTRAN:

       subroutine GSTXCI   (TXCOLI)
       integer   TXCOLI

There are no corresponding 'set' functions for cell array and GDP because they do not possess any visual attributes of their own. GDP functions may be defined so as to use some combination of the other attributes when the result of calling the GDP is realized on a workstation.

5.4 Workstation Attributes

Each workstation capable of output maintains six attribute tables, one for each of the four primitive classes, the color table, and a table of patterns for the corresponding fill area. However, the GKS standard does not mandate that pattern tables be implemented on all workstations. These tables have the following entries:

> Polyline bundle table:
> > Polyline index
> > Linetype
> > Linewidth factor
> > Polyline color index
>
> Polymarker bundle table:
> > Polymarker index
> > Marker type
> > Marker size scale factor
> > Polymarker color index
>
> Text bundle table:
> > Text index
> > Text font and precision
> > Character expansion factor
> > Character spacing
> > Text color index
>
> Fill area bundle table:
> > Fill area index
> > Fill area interior style
> > Fill area style index
> > Fill area color index
>
> Color table:
> > Color index
> > Intensity red
> > Intensity green
> > Intensity blue

Pattern table:
    Pattern index
    Dimensions of the matrix
    Pattern matrix

Each workstation must provide control over the display of at least two colors (via color indices 0 and 1); 0 is always the background color and cannot be changed on some workstations. The use of the tables above is subject to the following rules:

- Each workstation possesses its own set of these tables.
- Every entry of a table describes a 'bundle' of attribute values, which are identified by a unique index.
- If a primitive is output on a workstation, a bundle is chosen in the corresponding table by the index bound to this primitive. The attribute values contained in this bundle are, however, enlisted for visualization of the primitive only if the corresponding (and therefore bound) ASF is set to BUNDLED.
- If there is no bundle for an index in a table, index 1 is used. If there is no entry for index 1 either, the result is workstation-dependent. An exception is the color tables, because the use of a non-defined color index is principally workstation-dependent.
- The contents of bundle tables can be modified under application program control.
- The entries in bundle tables can be inquired.
- The values of the tables are valid for *all* primitives of a displayed image on a given workstation. If a bundle is changed and its index is used for an already displayed primitive, the corresponding attributes of all these primitives are changed. If this change is really necessary (the primitive is neither clipped away nor in invisible segments – see Section 6.3) and if the workstation cannot implement this change dynamically, then a regeneration of the image is implied (see Section 4.2). In simpler applications using non-dynamic workstations, therefore, it is often advantageous to set all the bundle tables before beginning output and then to use them as much as is desired during output. This will minimize the number of implicit regenerations.
- The default value of all indices is 1.

Adapting these tables to the application program's needs takes place through setting the individual bundle entries, for which GKS provides the following functions:

SET POLYLINE REPRESENTATION
Input: name   WORKSTATION IDENTIFIER
           integer POLYLINE INDEX   (>0)
           integer LINETYPE   (−n,...,−1,1,...,n)
           real   LINEWIDTH FACTOR   (>0.0)
           integer POLYLINE COLOR INDEX   (>=0)

or in FORTRAN:

subroutine GSPLR   (WKID,PLIND,LTYPE,LWIDTH,PLCOLI)
integer   WKID,PLIND,LTYPE
real   LWIDTH
integer   PLCOLI

SET POLYMARKER REPRESENTATION

Input: name   WORKSTATION IDENTIFIER
           integer POLYMARKER INDEX   (>0)
           integer MARKER TYPE   (−n,...,−1,1,...,n)
           real   MARKER SIZE SCALE FACTOR   (>0.0)
           integer POLYMARKER COLOR INDEX   (>=0)

or in FORTRAN:

subroutine GSPMR   (WKID,PMIND,MTYPE,MSZSF,PMCOLI)
integer   WKID,PMIND,MTYPE
real   MSZSF
integer   PMCOLI

SET FILL AREA REPRESENTATION

Input: name   WORKSTATION IDENTIFIER
           integer FILL AREA INDEX   (>0)
           enum   FILL AREA INTERIOR STYLE
                                  (HOLLOW,SOLID,PATTERN,HATCH)
           integer FILL AREA STYLE INDEX   (−n,...,−1,1,...,n)
           integer FILL AREA COLOR INDEX   (>=0)

or in FORTRAN:

subroutine GSFAR   (WKIND,FAIND,FAINST,FASTIN,FACOLI)
integer   WKIND,FAIND,FAINST

C   FAINST: 0=HOLLOW,...,3=HATCH
            integer   FASTIN,FACOLI

SET TEXT REPRESENTATION

Input: name   WORKSTATION IDENTIFIER
            integer   TEXT INDEX
            <integer,enum>   TEXT FONT AND
                               PRECISION $<(-n,...,-1,1,...,n)$
                                       (STRING,CHARACTER,STROKE)>
            real   CHARACTER EXPANSION FACTOR (>0.0)
            real   CHARACTER SPACING
            integer   TEXT COLOR INDEX $(0,...,n)$

or in FORTRAN:

            subroutine GSTXR   (WKID,TXIND,TXFONT,TXPREC,CHEXP,
                               CHSPAC,TXCOLI)
            integer   WKID,TXIND,TXFONT,TXPREC
C   TXPREC:0=STRING,1=CHARACTER,2=STROKE
            real   CHEXP,CHSPAC
            integer   TXCOLI

SET COLOR REPRESENTATION

Input: name   WORKSTATION IDENTIFIER
            integer   COLOR INDEX $(0,...,n)$
            3*real   COLOR(RED/GREEN/BLUE) $[0.0,1.0]$

or in FORTRAN:

            subroutine GSCR   (WKID,CIND,RED,GREEN,BLUE)
            integer   WKID,CIND
            real   RED,GREEN,BLUE

SET PATTERN REPRESENTATION

Input: name   WORKSTATION IDENTIFIER
            integer   PATTERN INDEX
            2*integer   PATTERN DIMENSION (>0)
            n*m*
            integer   PATTERN ARRAY $(0,...,n)$

or in FORTRAN:

        subroutine GSPAR   (WKID,PAIND,DIMX,DIMY,NCS,NRS,DX,DY,
                                        COLIA)
        integer   WKID,PSINF,DIMX,DIMY,
                                        NCS,NRS,DX,DY,COLIA(DIMX,DIMY)

C   The parameters DIMX,...,DY are handled exactly
C   like the cell array parameters.

5.5 Inquiry Functions

As mentioned earlier, a description of all inquiry functions would be beyond the scope of this book. Because attribute inquiry functions contain some new concepts, however, one set of functions that is representative of all those used – namely, the functions to inquire about the color capabilities of the implementation – will be described.

First, one can inquire about the general color facilities of a workstation:

INQUIRE COLOR FACILITIES

Input:	name	WORKSTATION TYPE	
Output:	integer	ERROR INDICATOR	
	integer	NUMBER OF AVAILABLE COLORS	
		OR INTENSITIES	$(0,2,3,...,n)$
	enum	AVAILABLE COLOR	(MONOCHROME,COLOR)
	integer	NUMBER OF PREDEFINED	
		COLOR INDICES	$(2,...,n)$

The corresponding FORTRAN routine is:

        subroutine GQCF   (WKTYPE,ERRIND,NCOLI,COLA,NPCI)
        integer   WKTYPE
        integer   ERRIND,NCOLI,COLA

C   0=MONOCHROME,1=COLOR

        integer   NPCI

Because all workstations of the same type exhibit identical facilities, the inquiry here refers to the facilities of a workstation type, not to a specific individual workstation.

ERRIND is given the value 0 if the call was made correctly; in other cases, it receives the number of the error encountered (see also Section 9.2 on this subject). If ERRIND is equal to 0, the other parameters contain the inquired values; otherwise, their values are implementation-dependent, but unusable as a rule.

If NCOLI has the value 0 (with ERRIND equal to 0), then a continuous color or intensity range is available on the workstation type. If NCOLI is greater than 0, NCOLI different colors or intensities are available. COLA equal to 0 means that only one color (different intensities in NCOLI) is supported on workstations of this type. COLA equal to 1, on the other hand, means that several colors can be supported simultaneously. Finally, NPCI provides the number of predefined color indices.

In order to know which colors are actually predefined, it helps to know that the series of predefined (color) indices should not contain any 'holes'. Therefore, if a call to 'inquire color facilities' delivers the value N for NPCI, the color indices 0 to N−1 are predefined. Predefined color representations can be determined directly with the help of the function:

INQUIRE PREDEFINED COLOR REPRESENTATION

Input:	name	WORKSTATION TYPE
	integer	PREDEFINED COLOR INDEX
Output:	integer	ERROR INDICATOR
	3*real	COLOR (RED/GREEN/BLUE INTENSITY)

or in FORTRAN:

```
subroutine GQPCR    (WKTYPE,PRCOLI,ERRIND,RED,GREEN,BLUE)
integer             WKTYPE,PRCOLI
integer             ERRIND
real                RED,GREEN,BLUE
```

The predefined colors of a workstation type can be inquired with the following FORTRAN program segment (with the assumption that the fields R,G,B are of appropriate dimensions).

```
        call GQCF (WKTYPE,ERRIND,NCOLI,COLA,NPCI)
        if (ERRIND.eq.0) then
            do 100 I=1,NPCI
            call GQPCR (WKTYPE,I−1,ERRIND,R(I),G(I),B(I))
100         continue
        endif
C           we do not show the code to check ERRIND
C           within the loop.
```

Color representations of a specific workstation can, of course, be inquired. In fact, these values are identical in the beginning (after opening) to the predefined values of the corresponding workstation type, but the values can be changed by using the 'Set Color Representation' function. The corresponding inquiry function is:

INQUIRE COLOR REPRESENTATION

Input: name   WORKSTATION IDENTIFIER
          integer COLOR INDEX
          enum   KIND OF RETURNED VALUE (SET, REALIZED)
Output: integer ERROR INDICATOR
          3*real   COLOR (R/G/B INTENSITY)

or in FORTRAN:

```
        subroutine GQCR    (WKID,COLI,TYPE,ERRIND,RED,GREEN,BLUE)
        integer            WKID,COLI,TYPE
C                                        TYPE: 0=SET,1=REALIZED
        integer            ERRIND
        real               RED,GREEN,BLUE
```

Here is the explanation for the third parameter 'kind of returned value'. If a workstation cannot precisely realize an R/G/B triplet defined by means of 'set color representation', the workstation maps it to a triplet, which is displayable and which represents the desired color as well as possible. With this TYPE parameter, it is possible to determine whether the returned R/G/B values are those originally set or are those actually being used in the rendering of the image.

An analogous situation holds true for all attributes saved in workstation tables for which the workstation is not required to be able to achieve precisely the specified effect.

This is the end of our treatment of GKS inquiry functions, at least in the context of attributes.

☐ **Here is a summary of the inquiry functions introduced in this section:**

INQUIRE COLOR FACILITIES	GQCF	(WKTYPE,ERRIND,NCOLI,COLA,NPCI)
INQUIRE PREDEFINED COLOR REPRESENTATION	GQPCR	(WKTYPE,PRCOLI,ERRIND,R,G,B)
INQUIRE COLOR REPRESENTATION	GQCR	(WKID,COLI,TYPE,ERRIND,R,G,B)

5.6 Minimal Workstation Display Capabilities

Table 5.8 summarizes the minimal capabilities required for supporting primitive attributes on all workstations capable of output.

Table 5.8 Minimal requirements for output-capable workstations

Colors	2	(0=background, 1=foreground)
Linetypes	4	(1=solid,2=dashed, 3=dotted,4=dashed-dotted)
Linewidths	1	
Predefined polyline bundles	5	
Settable polyline bundles	20^1	
Marker types	5	$(1,...,5=.,+,*,\bigcirc,\times)$
Marker sizes	1	
Predefined polymarker bundles	5	
Settable polymarker bundles	20^1	
Fill area interior styles	1	(HOLLOW)
Predefined fill area bundles	5	
Settable fill area bundles	10^1	
Predefined patterns	1^2	
Settable patterns	$10^{2,3}$	
Hatches	3^2	
Character heights	1^4	
Character expansion factors	1^4	
Text fonts STRING	1	
Text fonts CHARACTER	1	
Text fonts STROKE	0^5	
	2	
Predefined text bundles	2^5	
	6	
Settable text bundles	20^1	

1 Relevant only for performance levels 1a, 1b, 1c, 2a, 2b, 2c (see Section 2.8).
2 Relevant only for workstations that support the corresponding fill area interior style.
3 Can be reduced by implementation techniques to save space.
4 Relevant only for character and stroke quality.
5 Distributed according to performance level: 0a–c/1a–2c '(see Section 2.8).

Chapter 6

SEGMENTS

A segment is a collection of primitives together with their attributes and clipping rectangles (see Section 9.1). Segments are used to store information created during program execution.

The essential difference between primitives inside and outside of segments is that application programs do not have further access to primitives located outside of segments once the primitives have been created. Primitives within segments can be manipulated to a certain degree and can be identified with interactive operations. In addition, only primitives stored in segments can be redrawn at the time of image regeneration on a workstation.

The use of segments rests on the following principles:

- Each segment available at any given time in GKS has a unique name.
- A segment is created by collecting all primitives (and their attributes) generated between the segment's opening and closing.
- The contents of a closed segment cannot be further altered, and existing segments cannot be reopened.
- Only one segment can be open at a time.
- Entire segments can be:
  □ renamed;
  □ deleted; or
  □ inserted into an open segment as well as into the stream of primitives outside of segments (see Section 6.2).
- Primitives within a segment can be provided with a so-called 'pick identifier', which allows detailed identification of image parts (see Section 8.11).
- Segments can be associated with individual workstations, and these associations can also be canceled (see Section 8.2). Initially, a segment is associated only with those workstations that are active at the time the segment is opened.

■ A segment is available only on its associated workstations. Only these segments can be displayed and 'picked' during dialog sessions on these workstations.

These principles will be discussed in detail in the following sections.

6.1 Creating and Deleting Segments

A segment is created or opened by the following function:

CREATE SEGMENT

Input: name   SEGMENT NAME

or in FORTRAN:

subroutine GCRSG   (SGNAME)
integer   SGNAME

All subsequently generated primitives will be collected in this segment, until the following function is used:

CLOSE SEGMENT

no parameters

or in FORTRAN:

subroutine GCLSG

Once the segment is closed, the primitives contained in the segment can no longer be individually changed, but the whole segment can be manipulated. For example, segments can be renamed with:

RENAME SEGMENT

Input: name   OLD SEGMENT NAME
          name   NEW SEGMENT NAME

or in FORTRAN:

subroutine GRENSG   (OLDNAM,NEWNAM)
integer   OLDNAM,NEWNAM

Segments can also be deleted.

DELETE SEGMENT

Input: name   SEGMENT NAME

or in FORTRAN:

subroutine GDSG   (SGNAME)
integer   SGNAME

A deleted segment is no longer available to any workstation. Its state list is released (see Section 2.7), and its name can now be used for a new segment.

A segment can be removed from one specific workstation without being deleted everywhere using the following function:

DELETE SEGMENT FROM WORKSTATION

Input: name   WORKSTATION IDENTIFIER
           name   SEGMENT NAME

or in FORTRAN:

subroutine GDSGWK   (WKID,SGNAME)
integer   WKID,SGNAME

To delete *all* segments from a workstation, use the function previously introduced in Section 4.2, namely, 'clear workstation'. Note that if a segment is deleted from one workstation, it remains available to all other workstations with which it is associated. If a segment is deleted from the last workstation with which it is associated, however, this is equivalent to deleting the segment from the whole system. The usefulness of this rule is explained in Section 6.2.

Deleting a segment from a specific workstation will principally cause a change in the image displayed there. As with many other segment manipulations, this can lead to implicit regeneration, which can be suppressed (see Section 4.2). In the case of a suppressed implicit regeneration, image regeneration can be done by using the 'update workstation' function described earlier, among other methods. It is sometimes desirable, however, to redraw the image despite the update workstation state. If this image is constructed of segments, GKS provides a separate function:

REDRAW ALL SEGMENTS ON WORKSTATION

Input: name   WORKSTATION IDENTIFIER

or in FORTRAN:

        subroutine GRSGWK   (WKID)
        integer   WKID

This function causes:

- Execution of all delayed actions
- Clearing of the display surface
- Drawing of all visible segments assigned to the workstation (see Section 6.3)

   The difference between this function and the otherwise identical function 'update workstation' is that 'redraw' always causes image regeneration.

   Because only primitives stored in segments are drawn at the time of image regeneration, this function can be usefully employed if, for example, an image of an unnecessary primitive, created during an interactive dialog with the operator and not stored in segments, must be cleared away.

☐ **Let us summarize the functions introduced in this section:**

CREATE SEGMENT	GCRSG	(SGNAME)
CLOSE SEGMENT	GCLSG	
RENAME SEGMENT	GRENSG	(OLDNAM,NEWNAM)
DELETE SEGMENT	GDSG	(SGNAME)
DELETE SEGMENT FROM WORKSTATION	GDSGWK	(WKID,SGNAME)
REDRAW ALL SEGMENTS ON WORKSTATION	GRSGWK	(WKID)

6.2 Duplicating Segments

Each available segment exists just once at any given point in time during the implementation of an application program in GKS. Recall that a segment is associated with all workstations active when the segment is opened. If, at a later time, you want to display the segment on a newly active workstation, you can explicitly achieve this effect with the following function:

ASSOCIATE SEGMENT WITH WORKSTATION

Input:	name	WORKSTATION IDENTIFIER
	name	SEGMENT NAME

or in FORTRAN:

           subroutine GASGWK   (WKID,SGNAME)
           integer   WKID,SGNAME

If the segment is not yet available on the given workstation, it is assigned there. The 'associate segment' function is, therefore, the inverse of 'delete segment from workstation' in some respects.

We have seen that it is possible to store GKS segments in some form. In order to better understand the behavior of the above, as well as related functions, it is appropriate to examine this storage a bit more closely.

In principle, any logical or physical unit that the storage of segments utilizes is called 'segment storage'. Keeping in mind the trend to provide graphic workstations with local memory, GKS offers workstation-dependent segment storage (WDSS). Conceptually, this is the part of a workstation in which segments can be stored locally. Using WDSS relieves some of the strain on the main memory, and image generation time can be considerably reduced. However, in order to be able to maintain GKS applications independent of the workstation, GKS implementations beginning at output level 1 (see Section 2.8) must support WDSS on all workstations.

A segment stored in WDSS is conceptually available only to the corresponding workstation and cannot be transferred to other workstations. WDSS is insufficient, therefore, for implementing 'associate segment with workstation'. The prerequisites to do that (that is, 'associate segment with workstation') are much better met by a centrally administered workstation-*in*dependent segment storage (WISS). This is regarded as a separate workstation of the special category WISS (and of the type WISS) and is exclusively for device-independent segment storage. This means that WISS must be opened and activated by the application program if a segment is to be stored in it (for later duplication). If no duplication is planned, WISS can simply be deactivated before opening the segment. Closing WISS causes the same result as clearing (that is, using 'clear workstation'); all segments stored in WISS are lost. The function 'delete segment from workstation' is also applicable here, of course. For that reason it is also sensible to equate the deletion of a segment from the last workstation to which it is associated with the segment's removal from the system. Most of the remaining GKS functions relating to workstations, however, cannot in general be applied usefully to the WISS workstation.

The function 'associate segment with workstation' causes the segment to be copied out of WISS into the WDSS of the corresponding workstation. Whether this transfer is actually implemented or is merely simulated by WISS for lack of physically available WDSS is irrelevant from the application program's point of view.

Before describing further segment duplication possibilities, here is a summary of the valid rules for segment storage:

- At most one WISS exists per GKS installation.
- At most one WDSS exists per graphic workstation.
- All segments existing in WDSS are available only on the workstation to which the WDSS belongs.
- All segments existing in WISS can be duplicated.
- All copies of a segment (in WISS and the different WDSSs) are identical, and each segment storage can contain at most one copy of each segment.

Figure 6.1 illustrates these facts. The segment transformations portrayed in Figure 6.1 are segment attributes and will be discussed in the next section. This

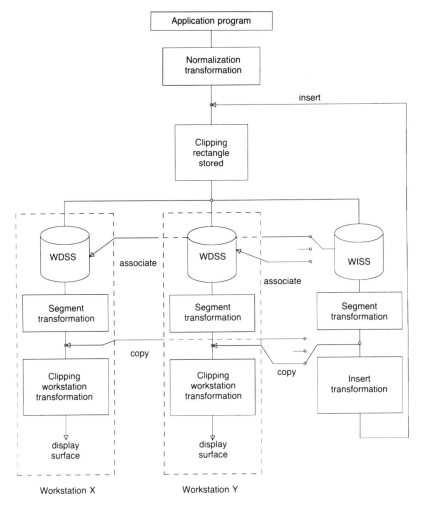

Figure 6.1   Segment flow in GKS

figure also exhibits all possibilities for duplicating GKS segments:

- *Association* with a specific workstation:
  the segment is stored on the given workstation (as previously mentioned).
- *Copying* onto the display surface of a specific workstation:
  the segment is transferred to the given workstation without being stored there.
- *Inserting* into the stream of primitives:
  the segment's contents are copied into the stream of calls coming from the application program. If a segment is open, it will be saved here.

The segment must be closed for all of these operations. In the last two operations, the copied segment loses its identity as a segment. In this fashion, a segment can be duplicated any number of times.

The two newly-introduced copy operations are implemented with the following GKS functions:

COPY SEGMENT TO WORKSTATION

Input: name   WORKSTATION IDENTIFIER
           name   SEGMENT NAME

or in FORTRAN:

        subroutine GCSGWK   (WKID,SGNAME)
        integer   WKID,SGNAME

This sends the contents of the segment from the WISS to the appropriate workstation after they have been transformed by the current segment transformation. The workstation outputs the segment contents immediately *without* saving them in its own WDSS.

INSERT SEGMENT

Input: name   SEGMENT NAME
           2*3*real TRANSFORMATION MATRIX

or in FORTRAN:

        subroutine GINSG   (SGNAME,TM)
        integer   SGNAME
        real   TM(2,3)

This applies, first, the specified transformation and, then, the corresponding segment transformation (see Section 6.3) to the primitives stored in the segment in WISS. Finally, the transformed primitives are sent to all active workstations. If a segment is open, the transformed primitives are stored in it. If WISS is active, the transformed primitives are reinserted into WISS (in the open segment), where they can be associated, copied, or inserted again.

The GKS functions introduced in this section were as follows:

ASSOCIATE SEGMENT WITH WORKSTATION	GASGWK	(WKID,SGNAME)
COPY SEGMENT TO WORKSTATION	GCSGWK	(WKID,SGNAME)
INSERT SEGMENT	GINSG	(SGNAME,TM)

6.3   Displaying Segments/Segment Attributes

Segments have attributes, which are used both to affect the display of the segment contents on the workstation and to control their use in interaction. These attributes are comparable to workstation attributes in so far as they can be changed and – because these changes cause image modifications – changing attributes can cause implicit regenerations on workstations that cannot dynamically implement the changes. In all other respects, the segment attributes are identical for all copies of a segment.

Segment transformations are set by the following function:

SET SEGMENT TRANSFORMATION

Input:	name	SEGMENT NAME
	2*3*real	TRANSFORMATION MATRIX

or in FORTRAN:

subroutine GSSGT	(SGNAME,TM)
integer	SGNAME
real	TM(2,3)

If a segment is displayed on a workstation of the category OUTPUT or OUTIN, all of the segment's primitives are transformed prior to display. All point coordinates (already mapped in NDC) and vectors are transformed as follows:

$$\begin{bmatrix} x' \\ y' \end{bmatrix} = \begin{bmatrix} T(1,1) & T(1,2) & T(1,3) \\ T(2,1) & T(2,2) & T(2,3) \end{bmatrix} \times \begin{bmatrix} x \\ y \\ 1 \end{bmatrix}$$

where T is the transformation matrix; (x,y) is the point vector to be transformed; and (x',y') is the transformed point.

Following the segment transformation, the workstation transformation will be executed and the resulting primitives displayed. (In most implementations, these transformations are combined into a single matrix multiplication operation for reasons of efficiency.)

It is possible not only to rotate segments with this matrix and to translate or variably scale them in the x- and y-directions, but also to shear them (by cropping the coordinate axes, for instance). However, it is not always easy to find the right matrix to achieve the desired effects. Consequently, GKS provides two utility functions which allow the matrix to be derived from the transformation parameters without causing the cropping effect. Using the following function:

EVALUATE TRANSFORMATION MATRIX

Input:	point	FIXED POINT	(WC,NDC)
	2*real	SHIFT VECTOR	(WC,NDC)
	real	ROTATION ANGLE	radians
	2*real	SCALE FACTORS IN X AND Y	
	enum	COORDINATE SWITCH	(WC,NDC)
Output:	2*3*real	TRANSFORMATION MATRIX	

or in FORTRAN:

```
        subroutine GEVTM    (XO,YO,DX,DY,PHI,FX,FY,SW,TMOUT)
        real                XO,YO,DX,DY,PHI,FX,FY,SW
C                                          SW:0=WC,1=NDC
        real                TMOUT(2,3)
```

the matrix is derived from the parameters FIXED POINT, SHIFT VECTOR, ROTATION ANGLE, and SCALE FACTORS, so that the use of the function is equivalent to applying the following operations in the specified order:

- First, scale relative to the fixed point (XO,YO)
- Then, rotate around the fixed point (PHI>0→ counterclockwise)
- Finally, translate

If the coordinate switch is set to WC, fixed point and shift vector are accepted in world coordinates and are first transformed by the current normalization transformation. If the following function is used:

ACCUMULATE TRANSFORMATION MATRIX

Input:	2*3*real	SEGMENT TRANSFORMATION MATRIX	
	point	FIXED POINT	(WC,NDC)
	2*real	SHIFT VECTOR	(WC,NDC)

	real	ROTATION ANGLE IN RADIANS	
	2*real	SCALE FACTORS IN X AND Y	
	enum	COORDINATE SWITCH	(WC,NDC)
Output:	2*3*real	TRANSFORMATION MATRIX	

or in FORTRAN:

```
        subroutine GACTM      (TMIN,XO,YO,DX,DY,PHI,FX,FY,SW,TMOUT)
        real                  TMIN(2,3),XO,YO,DX,DY,PHI,FX,FY,SW
C                                       SW:0=WC,1=NDC
        real                  TMOUT(2,3)
```

the input transformation matrix is composed and a matrix derived as before from the other input parameters to produce the output matrix.

For example, if a segment is to be repeatedly rotated through a constant angle and shrunk, this can be accomplished with the following small FORTRAN program:

```
C
C     at the beginning TMIN is the matrix              [1 0 0]
C                                                      [0 1 0]
C     N is the desired number of loops
      do 100 I=1,N
            call GACTM (TMIN,XO,YO,0.0,0.0,0.1,0.9,0.9,0,TMOUT)
            call GSSGT (SGNAME,TMOUT)
            do 100 J=1,2
                  do 100 K=1,3
                  TMIN(J,K) = TMOUT(J,K)
100         continue
```

The execution of this program causes a visible spiraling of the segment around the point (XO,YO) on all workstations that can dynamically transform segments and that allow implicit regeneration.

Other segment attributes also can be changed:

SET VISIBILITY

Input:	name	SEGMENT NAME	
	enum	VISIBILITY	(VISIBLE,INVISIBLE)

or in FORTRAN:

```
        subroutine GSVIS      (SGNAME,VIS)
        integer               SGNAME,VIS
C                                   VIS: 0=INVISIBLE,1 = VISIBLE
```

Here, the specified segment becomes visible or invisible depending on the value of the second parameter. Invisible segments are not displayed on any workstations, nor can they be picked.

SET HIGHLIGHTING

Input: name   SEGMENT NAME
          enum   HIGHLIGHT   (NORMAL,HIGHLIGHT)

or in FORTRAN:

          subroutine GSHLIT   (SGNAME,HLIT)
          integer   SGNAME,HLIT
    C   HLIT:0=NORMAL,1=HIGHLIGHT

Using this function, if the given segment is visible, the primitives contained in it will either be highlighted (by blinking, for example) or not, in a workstation-dependent way, according to the value of the second parameter.

SET SEGMENT PRIORITY

Input: name   SEGMENT NAME
          real   SEGMENT PRIORITY   [0.0,...,1.0]

or in FORTRAN:

          subroutine GSSGP   (SGNAME,PRIOR)
          integer   SGNAME
          real   PRIOR

Now, when segments are displayed on a workstation, the segment priority determines the order in which they are displayed; they are displayed in order of increasing priority. (Segments with highest priority are displayed last.) With this feature, certain visibility algorithms can be supported on raster workstations; but, on workstations that do not support this concept in hardware, implementations are not required to check for segment overlap in software.

Segment priority is also important for pick input (see Section 8.11).

SET DETECTABILITY

Input: name   SEGMENT NAME
          enum   DETECTABILITY   (NOT DETECTABLE,DETECTABLE)

or in FORTRAN:

          subroutine GSDTEC   (SGNAME,DTEC)
          integer   SGNAME,DTEC
    C   DTEC:0=NOT DETECTABLE,1=DETECTABLE

Pick input allows segments to be identified by an interactive dialog between the operator and the graphics system (see Section 8.11). A segment can be picked on a specific workstation, however, only if it is both visible *and* detectable. This function is used to turn the detectability of a specified segment on and off.

When a segment is first opened, the following default values for the segment attributes are in effect:

Transformation matrix : $\begin{bmatrix} 1 & 0 & 0 \\ 0 & 1 & 0 \end{bmatrix}$

Visibility	:	VISIBLE
Highlighting	:	NORMAL
Priority	:	0.0
Detectability	:	NOT DETECTABLE

Finally, let us summarize the functions introduced in this section:

SET SEGMENT TRANSFORMATION	GSSGT	(SGNAME,TM)
EVALUATE TRANSFORMATION MATRIX		GEVTM(XO,YO,DX,DY, PHI,FX,FY,SW,TMOUT)
ACCUMULATE TRANSFORMATION MATRIX	GACTM	(TMIN,XO,YO,DX,DY, PHI,FX,FY,SW,TMOUT)
SET VISIBILITY	GSVIS	(SGNAME,VIS)
SET HIGHLIGHTING	GSHLIT	(SGNAME,HLIT)
SET SEGMENT PRIORITY	GSSGP	(SGNAME,PRIOR)
SET DETECTABILITY	GSDTEC	(SGNAME,DTEC)

Chapter 7
◻ ◻ ■ METAFILES
■

7.1 Basic Concepts

GKS metafiles, abbreviated GKSM, are sequential data files that can be generated, stored, transmitted, reread, and interpreted with the help of GKS. Metafiles are used principally for:

- Exchanging image representations between different applications, systems, or installations.
- Saving the transactions of an interactive session in order to be able to continue at a later time after an interruption ('audit trail').

The use of GKSMs is based on the following concepts:

- GKSMs behave like graphic workstations; in particular, GKSMs are created by workstations of the category MO (= Metafile Output) and they are read by workstations of the category MI (= Metafile Input).
- Any number of MO and MI workstations can be in use simultaneously.
- If a metafile is to be created, an MO workstation must be activated (because output can be produced only on active workstations).
- If an existing metafile is to be read, an MI workstation must be opened.
- If an MO workstation is activated, then every GKS call that is of importance for the image representation causes the output of a corresponding record on the metafile; this is essentially true for all functions except:
  ◻ inquiry functions;
  ◻ functions concerned with graphic input; and
  ◻ functions that explicitly affect other workstations.
- Attributes of MO workstations can be set (like other output workstations).
- There is a separate function with which application-specific data can be written to the metafile.
- The records of a GKSM are processed in the order in which they were created.
- Processing a GKSM occurs in a maximum of three steps:

☐ Reading the item type; this uniquely identifies the function stored in the item. Item type is an integer; the numbers 1 to 100 are reserved for GKS items. User records have type > 100. (However, it seems a good idea to use the numbers over 1000 for private item types and to reserve the numbers between 100 and 999 for future standards like GKS-3D – see Chapter 10).
☐ Reading the record, if desired.
☐ Interpreting the record, if desired.
■ The interpretation of a GKSM record has conceptually the same effect as each GKS function that generates this record. Functions concerning individual workstations can be interpreted on all active workstations, if no workstation is explicitly indicated.

Figure 7.1 illustrates the dataflow when using metafiles.

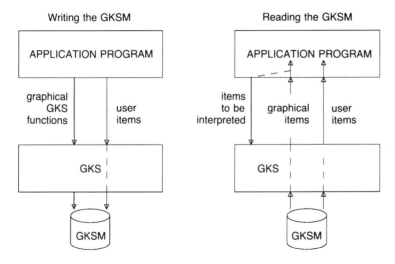

Figure 7.1   GKSM dataflows

7.2   Use

The functions with which workstations controlling GKS metafiles are opened and activated are identical to those already introduced in Chapter 3. In addition, with

WRITE ITEM TO GKSM

Input: name   WORKSTATION IDENTIFIER
           integer   DATA RECORD TYPE   (>100)
           integer   DATA RECORD LENGTH   (>1)
           data   DATA RECORD

an application record can be written on a GKSM. GKS does not examine the contents of the record. The corresponding function in FORTRAN is:

```
subroutine GWITM        (WKID,TYPE,IDRL,LDR,DATREC)
integer                 WKID,TYPE,IDRL,LDR
character*80            DATREC(LDR)
```

The record length, LDR, is given in units of 80 characters. IDRL specifies the number of characters to put into DATREC.

The following functions are used for reading and interpreting GKSM data records.

GET ITEM TYPE FROM GKSM

Input: name   WORKSTATION IDENTIFIER
Output: integer ITEM TYPE
          integer ITEM LENGTH

or in FORTRAN:

```
subroutine GGTITM       (WKID,TYPE,LDR)
integer                 WKID
integer                 TYPE, LDR
```

This returns the item type and item length of the current GKSM item.

READ ITEM FROM GKSM

Input: name   WORKSTATION IDENTIFIER
          integer MAXIMUM ITEM LENGTH in chars   (>0)
Output: data   ITEM STORAGE

or in FORTRAN:

```
subroutine GRDITM       (WKID,AKTLDR,MAXLDR,DATREC)
integer                 WKID,AKTLDR,MAXLDR
character*80            DATREC(MAXLDR)
```

This copies the current item to DATREC. If the item is longer than the 'maximum item length', part of the data record is lost. AKTLDR shows how many characters should be read in to DATREC. AKTLDR = 0 causes the record to be skipped. Usually, AKTLDR is the value LDR returned by GGTITM.

INTERPRET ITEM

Input: integer ITEM TYPE
          integer LENGTH OF DATA RECORD
          data   DATA RECORD

or in FORTRAN:

```
subroutine GIITM      (TYPE,IDRL,LDR,DATREC)
integer               TYPE,IDRL,LDR
character*80          DATREC(LDR)
```

This causes the data record contained in DATREC to be interpreted by the GKS implementation. The meaning of IDRL here is analogous to its meaning in GWITM; it is usually set to the LDR value of the previous GGTITM call. It is useful to call 'interpret item' only with data which has been retrieved previously by 'get item from GKSM' and 'read item from GKSM'. It is not a good idea, however, to do this with user records or to manipulate GKS records before subjecting them to 'interpret item'. In general, one needs implementation-specific knowledge to do this correctly. Doing so reduces the portability of the resulting program.

A FORTRAN program for interpreting a GKSM on a plotter follows:

```
        program INTPRT
integer               ERRFIL,EOFTYP,BUFSIZ
integer               GKSM,CON1,TYP1
integer               PLOT,CON2,TYP2
integer               TYPE,MLDR,IDRL,LDR
character*80          DR(100)
     C
           data ERRFIL /1/
     C           ERRFIL is arbitrarily set here
           data BUFSIZ /1000/
     C           BUFSIZ also arbitrarily set
           data EOFTYP /0/
     C           see Section 7.3
     C
     C The workstation-dependent parameters, shown as ? below, must be
     C filled in to follow implementation-dependent conventions.
           data GKSM, CON1, TYP1
     *      / 1 ,     ? ,     ? /
           data PLOT, CON2, TYP2
     *      / 2 ,     ? ,     ? /
     C
           data MDLR/100/
     C
     C Opening
           call GOPKS (ERRFIL,BUFSIZ)
           call GOPWK (GKSM,CON1,TYP1)
           call GOPWK (PLOT,CON2,TYP2)
           call GACWK (PLOT)
```

```
C
C Interpret, but read over application record
C (The DR length is assumed to be sufficient)
C
  100      call GGTITM (GKSM,TYPE,LDR)
           if (TYPE .eq. EOFTYP) goto 200
           call GRDITM (GKSM,LDR,MLDR,DR)
           if (TYPE .gt. 100) goto 100
           call GIITM (TYPE,LDR,MLDR,DR)
           goto 100
C
C Finish
  200      call GDAWK(PLOT)
           call GCLWK(PLOT)
           call GCLWK(GKSM)
           call GCLKS
           stop
           end
```

This section introduces the following metafile functions:

WRITE ITEM TO GKSM	GWITM	(WKID,TYPE,IDRL,LDR,DATREC)
GET ITEM TYPE FROM GKSM	GGTITM	(WKID,TYPE,LDR)
READ ITEM FROM GKSM	GRDITM	(WKID,AKTLDR,MAXLDR,DATREC)
INTERPRET JTEM	GIITM	(TYPE,IDRL,LDR,DATREC)

7.3 Formats

7.3.1 Annex E

The GKS standard defines only the functional capabilities of GKS metafiles; it does not define the format in which these metafiles or their data records are constructed. Consequently, there are no standards at this moment that stipulate a specific format. However, a proposal has been drawn up by DIN that is adequate for the GKS requirements. It is included as a non-mandatory appendix (called Annex E) to the ISO GKS standard. It is used by virtually all current GKS implementations. This proposal is binding as an appendix to national standards in West Germany and in Austria and will also become binding in the majority of the other European countries. The standardized CGM-encodings are described in Section 7.3.2.

According to the DIN proposal, the first item of each metafile has a fixed format and contains, among other things, instructions for the coding of integer and real numbers. Characters are always coded in ASCII code (ISO standard

Table 7.1 Assignment of GKSM item types to GKS functions

Item type   GKS function

  0   END OF GKSM
  1   DELETE WORKSTATION
  2   REDRAW ALL SEGMENTS ON WORKSTATION
  3   UPDATE WORKSTATION
  4   SET DEFERRAL STATE
  5   MESSAGE
  6   ESCAPE

11   POLYLINE
12   POLYMARKER
13   TEXT
14   FILL AREA
15   CELL ARRAY
16   GDP

21   SET POLYLINE INDEX
22   SET LINETYPE
23   SET LINEWIDTH SCALE FACTOR
24   SET POLYLINE COLOR INDEX
25   SET POLYMARKER INDEX
26   SET MARKER TYPE
27   SET MARKER SIZE SCALE FACTOR
28   SET POLYMARKER COLOR INDEX
29   SET TEXT INDEX
30   SET TEXT FONT AND PRECISION

31   SET CHARACTER EXPANSION FACTOR
32   SET CHARACTER SPACING
33   SET TEXT COLOR INDEX
34   SET CHARACTER VECTORS[1]
35   SET TEXT PATH
36   SET TEXT ALIGNMENT
37   SET FILL AREA INDEX
38   SET FILL AREA INTERIOR STYLE
39   SET FILL AREA STYLE INDEX
40   SET FILL AREA COLOR INDEX
41   SET PATTERN SIZE[2]
42   SET PATTERN REFERENCE POINT
43   SET ASPECT SOURCE FLAGS
44   SET PICK IDENTIFIER[3]

Table 7.1   contd.

Item type	GKS function
51	SET POLYLINE REPRESENTATION[4]
52	SET POLYMARKER REPRESENTATION[4]
53	SET TEXT REPRESENTATION[4]
54	SET FILL AREA REPRESENTATION[4]
55	SET PATTERN REPRESENTATION[4]
56	SET COLOR REPRESENTATION[4]
61	SET CLIPPING INDICATOR[5]
71	SET WORKSTATION WINDOW[4]
72	SET WORKSTATION VIEWPORT[4]
81	CREATE SEGMENT
82	CLOSE SEGMENT
83	RENAME SEGMENT
84	DELETE SEGMENT[6]
91	SET SEGMENT TRANSFORMATION
92	SET VISIBILITY
93	SET HIGHLIGHTING
94	SET SEGMENT PRIORITY
95	SET DETECTABILITY
>100	USER ITEMS

1   With changes in character height, character up vector, or the current normalization transformation, the border vectors of the character body transformed to NDC will be written to the metafile.
2   Like (1), but with the use of the pattern table border vectors.
3   This function will be discussed in Section 8.11.
4   Will be written to the metafile in case it is called with the corresponding workstation identifier.
5   With each change of the current normalization transformation or by selecting another normalization transformation, the resulting clipping rectangle will be written to the metafile.
6   Will be produced by 'delete segment from workstation' as well as by 'delete segment'.

For 1 and 2, the vectors will be transformed back from 'read item from GKSM' by the (inverse) current normalization transformation and will be returned in world coordinates.

646). All other items are of variable lengths and contain data in the format specified by the first item. It is possible, however, that the physical structure of a GKSM does not match its logical structure. Metafiles can be subdivided into physical items of fixed lengths in order to simplify the exchange between different GKS installations.

This makes it possible, therefore, to create metafiles by using different encodings of numbers. The two most frequently used are binary and the so-called external, which is similar to a character display of FORTRAN I or F formats. Typically, the binary encoding is used within a single installation because it is quick to process, but it often is very difficult to interchange binary-encoded GKSMs between different installations. The external format requires more computation for creating and interpreting, but this format is machine-independent to a great extent.

Through GKS, the program cannot specify which format should be used to create a GKSM. (Reading presents no problem here, because GKS always obtains the necessary information from the first item of the metafile being interpreted.) Consequently, the implementation should provide a different workstation type for each different format. The best thing to do is to ask the person in charge of your GKS installation how the choice of specific metafile formats is carried out. In most cases, it simply depends on choosing the right parameter when opening the corresponding workstation.

For those users who would like to examine GKSM in detail, Table 7.1 shows the assignment of item type to GKS function as these assignments are defined in the DIN proposal mentioned earlier. Some GKS functions produce more than one GKSM item (e.g. 'copy segment to workstation'). Table 7.1 contains only those assignments that are important for interpretation.

7.3.2 CGM Encodings

In Chapter 11, we introduce the Computer Graphics Metafile, an ISO standard (ISO 8632; see ISO, 1987) designed for static picture capture, storage, and interchange. The CGM can be used in place of the GKSM for some of the purposes of a GKS metafile. In particular, Annex E of the CGM standard contains guidelines for implementers who would use the CGM as a GKSM.

A given CGM may be represented in any one of three different standardized formats: character, binary, and clear text. These formats are described further in Chapter 11.

As we noted above, the CGM standard does not provide sufficient functional support for it to serve as a complete replacement for the GKSM. This is because the CGM does not contain elements that allow it to satisfy the workstation audit trail capabilities of the GKSM. Consequently, work is now under way within ISO to specify an addendum to GKS – containing extensions to CGM – that would allow the CGM to serve as a fully functional GKSM. This addendum to GKS should be approved and published in late 1990.

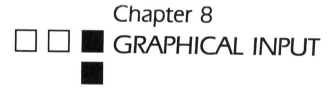

Chapter 8
GRAPHICAL INPUT

Graphical input occurs as a result of operator action on a physical input device. The types of operation and the input values available to the program are extremely varied and are subject to rapid technological change. Many physical input devices are not of a graphical nature at all (like keyboards), but they have a direct connection to graphics environments because the values obtained from them must be included in the output on the display surface. In the standard, therefore, because of the variety of input hardware, uncoupling the physical behavior of these devices must occur in order to be able to operate an application program with different input devices. Thus, the concept of *logical input devices* was created for GKS.

8.1 Logical Input Devices

An application program draws input from one or more logical input devices, which the operator controls by the use of physical input devices. A logical input device is characterized by its *input class* and can exist in one of three *operating modes*. A logical input device is identified (in a programming environment) by three characteristics: a workstation identifier, its input class, and its device number.

The workstation identifier indicates an open workstation of category INPUT or OUTIN, to which the logical input device belongs. It is realized by one or more physical input devices available on that workstation.

The input class determines the type of the logical input device. GKS specifies six classes: LOCATOR, STROKE, VALUATOR, CHOICE, PICK, STRING. Each logical input device can return *logical* input values to the application program.

The device number differentiates between various logical input devices of the same class on the same workstation.

8.2 Input Classes

Because GKS recognizes only six input classes (see Figure 8.1), the majority of possible physical input devices must be assigned to these classes. This happens through the GKS implementation (in the workstation drivers), which can provide several logical input devices of one class on the same workstation; it can also use the same physical input device (e.g., keyboard) to provide the values delivered by several logical input devices.

Figure 8.1   Input classes in GKS

The values returned by the six input classes are:

LOCATOR: a position in world coordinates and
              a transformation number;
STROKE: a sequence of points in world coordinates and
              a transformation number;
VALUATOR: a real number;
CHOICE: a non-negative whole number that represents
              a choice from a number of possible alternatives;
PICK: a segment name and a pick identifier;
STRING: a character string.

The *locator* and *stroke* devices are required to deliver their input values in world coordinates. However, we have already seen that the ranges of normalization transformations can overlap in NDC space. Consequently, in order to map an NDC location indicated by the operator into a unique WC value, it is necessary to provide a function that allows for the choice or selection of the intended normalization transformation.

Figure 8.2 shows three normalization transformations that overlap in NDC space. The user has the option of controlling the transformation of the device

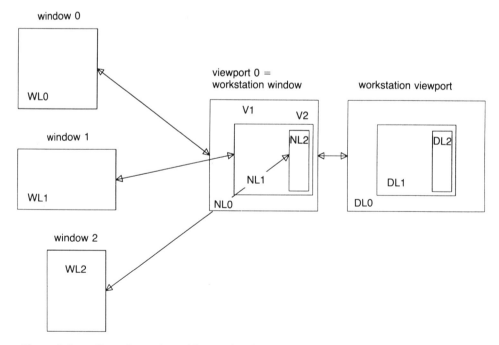

Figure 8.2   Transformation of locator/stroke input (Enderle *et al.*, 1987)

coordinates back into world coordinates by allocating priorities for normalization transformations. The function SET VIEWPORT INPUT PRIORITY performs this. For LOCATOR, the function will select the normalization transformation that has the highest priority and in whose viewport the NDC position of the input point lies. For STROKE, all points must lie within the viewport, that is, all points of an input are from the same world coordinate system and, in combination with it, provide the basis for the same normalization transformation. In order to guarantee that the NDC position lies in at least one viewport, there is the default transformation, '0', which cannot be changed and has a fixed window and viewport of 0 to 1 in X and 0 to 1 in Y; it therefore specifies the identity transformation. This transformation also has the highest default priority, so positions are returned in normalized coordinates by default, or whenever no other normalization transformation fits.

8.3   Operating Modes of Logical Input Devices

Each logical input device always operates in one of three *operating modes*: REQUEST, SAMPLE, or EVENT. Sample and event are available only in GKS performance level 'c'. The operating mode is determined individually for each input device, with the function SET <input class> MODE; the default mode is REQUEST.

> REQUEST: GKS waits until the operator has provided the input (like a FORTRAN READ) or has interrupted the request.
>
> SAMPLE: GKS returns the current logical input value of the logical input device without waiting for any operator action.
>
> EVENT: GKS manages an input queue, which contains the event reports in chronological order. Events are created asynchronously and only by operator action on each input device, which has been placed in EVENT MODE.

8.4   The Logical Input Device Model

A logical input device has a *measure*, a *trigger*, an *initial value*, a *prompt and echo*, an *echo area*, and a *data record*. The measure and trigger of a logical input device are parts of the graphic workstation implementation that contains the logical input device.

The *measure* of a logical input device is a value which is determined by one or more physical input devices. A single physical device can simultaneously determine more than one measure; however, logically, a separate measure process is used for each measure.

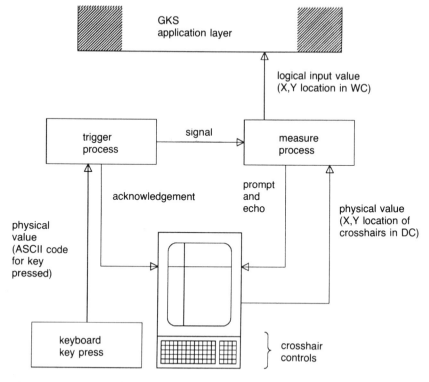

Figure 8.3   Logical input model in GKS as illustrated by LOCATOR input
(ISO, 1985)

The *trigger* of a logical input device is an action performed on a physical input device. The operator can use a trigger in order to indicate essential points in time. A single operator action (e.g., pressing a key or a switch on a lightpen) causes the firing of no more than one trigger. Several logical input devices can use the same trigger, however. This model (see Figure 8.3 and Figure 8.4) describes the behavior of all logical input devices in all operating modes.

The trigger is necessary for input in Request mode and Event mode. If a REQUEST has been set for a logical output device when the trigger is activated, then the measure will use this device to fulfill the REQUEST.

The state of a logical input device can be changed by the function SET <input class> MODE. After calling this function with the parameter REQUEST, no measure process exists for the given device, and the device identifier is not on the receiver list of its trigger. After a call with the parameter EVENT, a newly initialized measure process arises for the given device, and the device identifier is placed on the receiving list of its trigger. After a call with the parameter

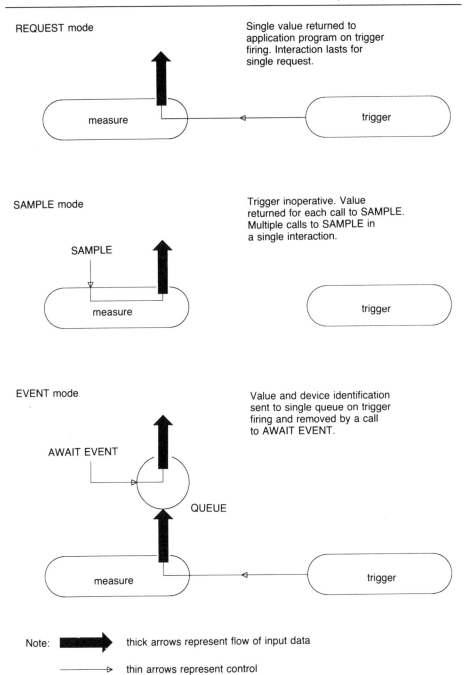

REQUEST mode

Single value returned to
application program on trigger
firing. Interaction lasts for
single request.

measure   trigger

SAMPLE mode

Trigger inoperative. Value
returned for each call to SAMPLE.
Multiple calls to SAMPLE in
a single interaction.

SAMPLE

measure   trigger

EVENT mode

Value and device identification
sent to single queue on trigger
firing and removed by a call
to AWAIT EVENT.

AWAIT EVENT

QUEUE

measure   trigger

Note: thick arrows represent flow of input data

thin arrows represent control

Figure 8.4   Interaction between measure and trigger (ISO, 1985)

SAMPLE, a new measure process arises; the device identifier is not placed on the list of recipients of its trigger, however.

If a device is in REQUEST mode, logical input can be done by calling a request function (REQUEST <input class>). The consequences are that a measure process for the given device is created and its value is set to the initial value; GKS pauses until the trigger of the given device fires or the operator interrupts the input; the logical value is set to the current value of the measure process; the measure process is terminated and the logical input value is returned.

If a logical input device is in SAMPLE mode, a logical input value can be obtained by calling the appropriate function (SAMPLE <input class>). This causes the current state of the measure process to be accepted as the input value without waiting for designation by the trigger and, therefore, without (direct) user action.

If a logical input device is in EVENT mode, the logical input values are placed in the input queue as event reports. This occurs with the activation of the trigger, asynchronously with the sequencing of the GKS application program.

The GKS function 'AWAIT_EVENT' causes the oldest (first) entry of the queue to be placed in the *current event report* of the GKS state list. This function delivers only the workstation, the input class, and the input device number as return values. With the function 'GET <device class>' the application program finally obtains the logical input value of the current event report. Figure 8.5 illustrates EVENT input.

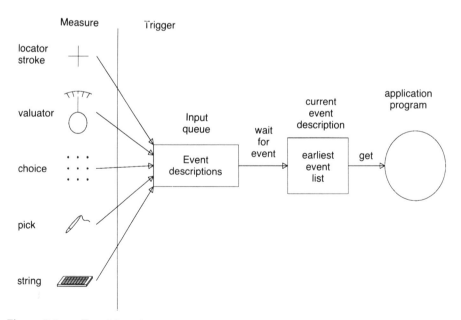

Figure 8.5   Event input

8.5 Input Class Measures

The details of logical input device measures in different classes are presented in the following.

The measure of a *locator* device consists of a position, P, in world coordinates and the number, N, of a normalization transformation. P lies inside the device window transformed into normalized coordinates by the inverse workstation transformation. P also lies inside the viewport determined by N; and, additionally, P must lie outside all viewports with higher priority than N (after transformation into normalized device coordinates). Figure 8.6 illustrates some possible different ways of echoing the locator value.

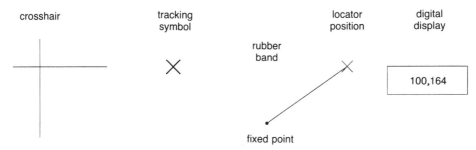

Figure 8.6   Locator echoes to indicate measure

The measure of a *stroke* device consists of a sequence of points, $P_1,\ldots,P_m$ in world coordinates and the number, N, of a normalization transformation. Then, the P_i ($1 \leq i \leq m$) lie inside the device window after transformation by the inverse workstation transformation into normalized device coordinates. Furthermore, the P_i ($1 \leq i \leq m$) lie inside the viewport determined by N; and, in addition, there is no viewport with higher priority than N that contains all the points. It is clear that N can change as new points are added to the sequence.

The measure of a *valuator* device provides a logical input value, which is a real number (see Figure 8.7). Each value lies between minimum and maximum values which are specified in the data record of the workstation state list.

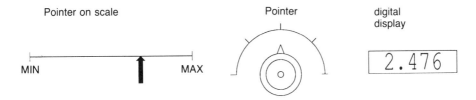

Figure 8.7   Valuator echoes to indicate measure

The measure of a *choice* device delivers a logical input value, which is a whole number and lies in the value range between 0 and a device-dependent maximum; this maximum is specified in the workstation description table. The value 0 is normally interpreted as 'no choice was made by the operator'.

The measure of a *pick* device delivers a logical input value, which identifies a segment name and a pick identifier.

The measure of a *string* device delivers a sequence of characters.

For each input class, there is an INITIALIZE function. This function can be called only if the logical device that specifies the function is in REQUEST mode. The initial value, the prompt and echo, the echo area, and a data record that can comprise the internal implementation can all be initialized.

In the following sections, the GKS functions for input in request mode will be specified in detail.

8.6   Locator

The locator provides the coordinates of a point. Because the application program works in world coordinates, it is desirable to deliver point coordinates in world coordinates instead of in the device coordinates with which they were actually registered. In order to manage this, the specified point is transformed to a normalized coordinate system by means of the inverse workstation transformation of the specified workstation. The value is accepted only if the input point lies in that area of the workstation viewport on which the device window is projected, so that the point remains in the unit square (see Figure 3.6).

Then, the point must be transformed into world coordinates. If, however, the point lies in several normalization transformations in the viewports, into which associated world coordinates system should the point be transformed? In order to be able to determine clearly the inverse normalization transformation to be used, a so-called 'input priority' can be assigned to each normalization transformation, as already mentioned in Section 8.2:

SET VIEWPORT INPUT PRIORITY

Input: integer   NT NUMBER
           integer   REFERENCE NT NUMBER
           enum   RELATIVE PRIORITY   (HIGHER,LOWER)

or in FORTRAN:

           subroutine GSVPIP   (NTNR,RNTNR,RELPRI)
           integer   NTNR,RNTNR,RELPRI
     C   RELPRI: 0=HIGHER, 1=LOWER

A corresponding priority will be given to the specified normalization transformation relative to the reference normalization transformation. This is used by successive locator and stroke input to determine each inverse normalization transformation with which the input coordinates are transformed out of NDC to world coordinates. If the application is not using too many NDC systems simultaneously, these calculations can be carried out quickly by the implementation.

A locator value is requested with the following GKS function:

REQUEST LOCATOR

Input:	name	WORKSTATION IDENTIFIER	
	integer	LOCATOR DEVICE NUMBER	(1,...,n)
Output:	enum	STATUS	(NONE,OK)
	integer	NT NUMBER	
	point	LOCATOR POSITION	(WC)

or in FORTRAN:

```
          subroutine GRQLC    (WKID,LCDNR,STAT,NTNR,PX,PY)
          integer             WKID,LCDNR
          integer             STAT
C                                                   0="NONE", 1="OK"
          integer             NTNR
          real                PX,PY
```

This installs an input process as described in Section 8.4 for the specified locator input device. If the operator 'breaks' (i.e. terminates input without providing a location), it provides the status 'NONE' and invalid values for the other output parameters. Otherwise, status is set to 'OK' and the other output parameters are set to the appropriate values provided by the operator.

8.7   Stroke

Stroke provides a series of points. In principle, the same processing applies here as to locator, but here *all* points must lie within the projection of the device window into the device viewport and the viewport of the normalization transformation to be chosen.

REQUEST STROKE

Input:	name	WORKSTATION IDENTIFIER	
	integer	STROKE DEVICE NUMBER	(1,...,n)

Output:	enum	STATUS	(NONE,OK)
	integer	NT NUMBER	
	integer	NUMBER OF POINTS	$(0,\dots,n)$
	n*point	POINTS	(WC)

or in FORTRAN:

```
subroutine GRQSK   (WKID,SKDNR,NMAX,STAT,NTNR,NP,PX,PY)
integer            WKID,SKDNR,NMAX
integer            STAT,NTNR,NP
real               PX(NMAX),PY(NMAX)
```

8.8 Valuator

The valuator provides a real number from an available range. This range is set to the initial values [0,1] but can be changed with the function 'initialize valuator', which will not be described further here.

REQUEST VALUATOR

Input:	name	WORKSTATION IDENTIFIER	
	integer	VALUATOR DEVICE NUMBER	$(1,\dots,n)$
Output:	enum	STATUS	(NONE,OK)
	real	VALUE	

or in FORTRAN:

```
subroutine GRQVL   (WKID,VLDNR,STAT,VAL)
integer            WKID,VLDNR
integer            STAT
real               VAL
```

8.9 Choice

Choice provides a non-negative whole number that represents the choice of one of several possibilities, where the value zero means 'no choice'. Many realization options are possible; e.g., function keys or other special keys, input of a specific choice text, specifying a graphic primitive by selecting it with a lightpen, etc. It is obviously important to be able to communicate to the operator the alternatives available; the initialization function is introduced here as one example of all input classes. The function used to set the initial state of a given choice is:

INITIALIZE CHOICE

Input:	name	WORKSTATION IDENTIFIER	
	integer	CHOICE DEVICE NUMBER	$(1,...,n)$
	enum	INITIAL STATUS	(OK, NOCHOICE)
	integer	INITIAL CHOICE NUMBER	$(1,...,n)$
	integer	PROMPT/ECHO TYPE	$(-n,...,-1,1,...,n)$
	4*real	ECHO AREA	
		XMIN<XMAX, YMIN<YMAX	(DC)
	data	CHOICE DATA RECORD	

or in FORTRAN:

```
          subroutine GINCH      (WKID,CHDNR,INCHNR,INSTAT,PET,
                                     XMIN,XMAX, YMIN,YMAX,LDR,DATREC)
          integer               WKID,CHDNR,INCHNR,INSTAT,PET
 C                                       PET=Prompt/Echo Type
          real                  XMIN,XMAX,YMIN,YMAX
          integer               LDR
          character*80          DATREC(LDR)
```

The individual parameters mean:

'INITIAL CHOICE NUMBER': Default choice suggested to the user.

'PROMPT/ECHO TYPE': Can be chosen from among several options described in the user guide. '1' means workstation-dependent form for all input classes. Each input device must be able to realize at least one form of prompting and echoing.

'ECHO AREA': This is an upright rectangle in the workstation's display area, in which specific prompt/echo types are displayed.

'DATA RECORD': Some prompt/echo types require additional information. For example, prompt/echo type '3' means that text strings will be presented in the echo area, one string corresponding to each individual choice (see Figure 8.8). The text strings to be used for labeling the choice buttons are passed in the data record. Describing the exact handling of this transfer would go beyond the limits of our discussion here, however.

The initialization functions of the other input classes have the same or analogous parameters.

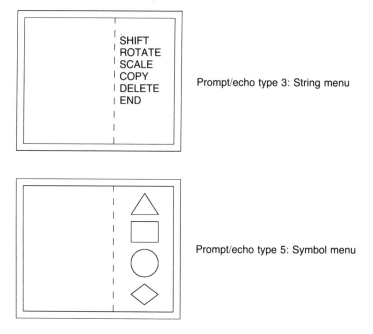

Prompt/echo type 3: String menu

Prompt/echo type 5: Symbol menu

Figure 8.8   Choice echoes to indicate measure

Choice input in request mode is done with the following function:

REQUEST CHOICE

Input:	name	WORKSTATION IDENTIFIER	
	integer	CHOICE DEVICE NUMBER	(1,...,n)
Output:	enum	STATUS	(NONE,OK,NOCHOICE)
	integer	CHOICE VALUE	(0,...,n)

or in FORTRAN:

```
          subroutine GRQCH     (WKID,CHDNR,STAT,CHNR)
          integer              WKID,CHDNR
          integer              STAT,CHNR
    C                          CHNR: 0= NONE,1=OK,2=NOCHOICE
```

8.10 String

String delivers a sequence of characters (usually keystrokes).

REQUEST STRING

Input:	name	WORKSTATION IDENTIFIER	
	integer	STRING DEVICE NUMBER	(1,...,n)
Output:	enum	STATUS	(NONE,OK)
	string	CHARACTER STRING	

In FORTRAN, there are two corresponding functions – one for complete FORTRAN77, another for the FORTRAN77 subset. The FORTRAN77 version is:

```
          subroutine GRQST     (WKID,STDNR,STAT,LOSTR,STR)
          integer              WKID,STDNR
          integer              STAT,LOSTR
C                                     LOSTR=number of characters in STR
          character*(*)        STR
```

And the subset version is:

```
          subroutine GRQST     (WKID,STDNR,STAT,LOSTR,STR)
          integer              WKID,STDNR
          integer              STAT,LOSTR
          character*80         STR
```

Note that the names of both FORTRAN routines are the same. This is true for all functions that are concerned with text input.

8.11 Pick

The final input class handles segment identification. It allows the operator to 'pick' a segment displayed on one workstation and return the name of this segment to the application program. The following conditions apply, however:

■ A segment can be picked on an OUTIN workstation only if the segment is visible, detectable, and associated with the workstation.
■ If several segments in a pick area overlap one another, the one with the highest segment priority will be selected.

In order to be able to pick not only whole segments, but also smaller units, a so-called 'pick identifier' was introduced, whereby each primitive within a segment can be associated with its own identifier. This identifier is a primitive attribute and is subject to the same rules as other primitive attributes. It is communicated to the application program during pick input. This attribute is set with the function:

SET PICK IDENTIFIER

Input: name   PICK IDENTIFIER

or in FORTRAN:

subroutine GSPKID   (PKID)
integer   PKID

and the following rules govern its use:

■ The current pick identifier is assigned to all subsequent primitives that are stored in segments, until a new pick identifier is set.
■ Pick identifiers do not have to be unique.

A program part like this is perfectly legal.

SET PICK IDENTIFIER (P1);

CREATE SEGMENT (S1);

    . . .
    Primitive definition   (S1,P1)
    . . .
    SET PICK IDENTIFIER (P2);
    . . .
    Primitive definition   (S1,P2)
    . . .
CLOSE SEGMENT;

CREATE SEGMENT (S2);

    . . .
    Primitive definition   (S2,P2)
    . . .
    SET PICK IDENTIFIER (P1);
    . . .
    Primitive definition   (S2,P1)
    . . .
CLOSE SEGMENT;

The input function is:

REQUEST PICK

Input:	name	WORKSTATION IDENTIFIER	
	integer	PICK DEVICE NUMBER	
Output:	enum	STATUS	(NONE,OK,ŅOPICK)
	name	SEGMENT NAME	
	name	PICK IDENTIFIER	

or in FORTRAN:

subroutine GRQPK	(WKID,PKDNR,STAT,SGNAME,PKID)	
integer	WKID,PKDNR	
integer	STAT	
C		0=NONE,1=OK,2=NOPICK
integer	SGNAME,PKID	

The status NOPICK is returned if no segment can be identified; NONE registers an interruption of input from the user, as with the other REQUEST mode input functions. In both of these special cases, the values of the associated parameters are meaningless.

Let us summarize the input functions introduced in this chapter:

SET VIEWPORT INPUT PRIORITY	GSVPIP	(NTNR,RNTNR,RELPRI)
REQUEST LOCATOR	GRQLC	(WKID,LCDNR,STAT,NTNR,PX,PY)
REQUEST STROKE	GRQSK	(WKID,SKDNR,NMAX,STAT,NTNR, NP,PX,PY)
REQUEST VALUATOR	GRQVL	(WKID,VLDNR,STAT,VAL)
INITIALIZE CHOICE	GINCH	(WKID,CHDNR,INCHNR, INSTAT,PET,XMIN,XMAX, YMIN,YMAX,LDR,DATREC)
REQUEST CHOICE	GRQCH	(WKID,CHDNR,STAT,CHNR)
REQUEST STRING	GRQST	(WKID,STDNR,STAT,LOSTR,STR)
SET PICK IDENTIFIER	GSPKID	(PKID)
REQUEST PICK	GRQPK	(WKID,PKDNR,STAT,SGNAME,PKID)

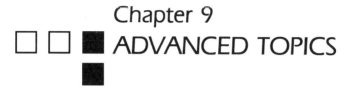

Chapter 9
ADVANCED TOPICS

9.1 Clipping

Clipping is generally understood in computer graphics as the cutting away of any part of a graphics primitive that lies outside certain borders. In GKS, there are only upright clipping rectangles; namely, the normalization transformation viewport, the window, and the NDC unit square. Because clipping is conceptually applied to very diversified circumstances within GKS, the essential rules are summarized here.

- A clipping rectangle is assigned to each primitive when it is generated. If the clipping indicator is switched on (see Section 3.3), this rectangle will be the viewport of the current normalization transformation; otherwise, it is the NDC unit square. The clipping rectangle remains bound to the primitive like an attribute during the lifespan of the primitive and, therefore, exists in segments and metafiles as well.
- When a primitive is displayed on a workstation, it is clipped to the intersection of its clipping rectangle and the workstation window.
- Note that clipping rectangles in segments are *not* affected by segment transformations. This means not only that the clipping rectangle always remains upright, but also that the contents of segments during segment transformations can shift with respect to clipping rectangles just as they do with respect to the window.
- The function 'insert segment' replaces the clipping rectangle of every inserted segment's primitive with the current clipping rectangle, which is determined according to the first rule listed above.

9.2 Error Handling and Logging

A small number of error possibilities are specified for each GKS function; each of them causes the ERROR HANDLING procedure to be called. Every GKS implementation enables this error checking. The ERROR HANDLING procedure provides an interface between GKS and the application program. The default ERROR HANDLING procedure can be replaced by one supplied by the application program.

If the ERROR HANDLING procedure is provided by the application program, error information can be interpreted and corresponding data can be saved in a data record. After the end of the GKS function that caused the error, the application program can read and interpret this data record.

The EMERGENCY CLOSE GKS procedure is an implementation-dependent capability. Its goal is to save as much graphical information as possible. The effects of this procedure on graphics workstations are not specified in the GKS document. The procedure can be called directly from the application program.

    EMERGENCY CLOSE GKS

       No parameters

or in FORTRAN:

      subroutine GECLKS

It attempts to perform the following steps:

CLOSE SEGMENT	(if it is open)
UPDATE	(all open workstations)
DEACTIVATE	(all active workstations)
CLOSE	(all open workstations)
CLOSE GKS	

Typically, the default ERROR HANDLING procedure available in an implementation of GKS simply calls the ERROR LOGGING procedure with the same set of parameters. The default ERROR LOGGING procedure can also be replaced by one supplied by the application program.

GKS distinguishes among errors according to where they are detected:

(A)   in GKS procedures,
(B)   in procedures activated by GKS (workstation driver, operating system),
(C)   in other parts of the application program,

and also according to their consequences:

(1)   simple error with a clearly specified error reaction,
(2)   serious error with unforeseeable and consequently unknown effects.

GKS handles the individual error situation according to the following scheme:

(A1) Concerned mainly with incorrect calls (e.g., wrong parameters or incorrect GKS state).

(A2) Situations like storage overflow or transfer error. An error report is generated, and GKS tries to save as much graphics data as possible and may try to rectify the error.

(B1) Similar to A1; however, in this case, the implementation cannot guarantee that the GKS procedures might not have already effected some irreversible operations.

(B2) Result is totally unknown.

(C1) Not appropriate to be covered by the GKS standard.

(C2) GKS provides the function EMERGENCY CLOSE GKS (see above).

An error report minimally consists of the identification of the GKS function where the error arose and an error number. The meaning of the error numbers are summarized in Annex B of the GKS standard; they should be listed in your GKS installation documentation. The function identifiers are part of the respective language environments and are also available for each language (e.g., FORTRAN or C) in your documentation.

9.3 Minimal Capabilities ·

The minimal capabilities of workstations have already been listed in Section 5.6; Table 9.1 is a summary of the capabilities that every GKS installation of a given performance level must possess.

9.4 Initial Values

When GKS, a workstation, or a segment is opened, specific initial values apply to the corresponding attributes or state variables. Table 9.2 summarizes all initial values that are neither workstation-specific nor implementation-dependent.

Table 9.1 Minimal GKS capabilities

Capabilities	Levels								
	0a	0b	0c	1a	1b	1c	2a	2b	2c
No. of settable NTs	1	1	1	10	10	10	10	10	10
No. of seg. priorities[1]	–	–	–	2	2	2	2	2	2
Input classes[2]	–	5	5	–	6	6	–	6	6
Prompt/echo types per device	–	1	1	–	1	1	–	1	1
Max. length of STROKE-buffer	–	64	64	–	64	64	–	64	64
Max. length of STRING–Buffer	–	72	72	–	72	72	–	72	72
W.St. of category OUTPUT or OUTIN	1	1	1	1	1	1	1	1	1
W.St. of category INPUT or OUTIN	–	1	1	–	1	1	–	1	1
W.St. of category MO	0	0	0	1	1	1	1	1	1
W.St. of category MI	0	0	0	1	1	1	1	1	1
W.St. of category WISS[3]	–	–	–	–	–	–	1	1	1

1 Relevant only for workstations that support segment priority
2 Pick is useful only in performance levels that support segmentation
3 '1' here means 'exactly 1'

Key
0 = Not required for this performance level
– = Not defined in this level

Table 9.2 Workstation and implementation defaults

GKS state list

polyline index	1
linetype	1
linewidth scale factor	1.0
polyline color index	1
polymarker index	1
marker type	3
marker size scale factor	1.0
polymarker color index	1
text index	1
text font and precision	<1,STRING>
character expansion factor	1.0
character spacing	0.0
text color index	1
character height	0.01
character up vector	(0.0,1.0)
text path	RIGHT
text alignment	<NORMAL,NORMAL>
fill area index	1
fill area interior style	HOLLOW
fill area style index	1
fill area color index	1
pattern size	<1.0,1.0>
pattern reference point	<0.0,0.0>
current NT	0
clipping indicator	CLIP

list of normalization transformations ordered by viewport input priority (initially in numerical order with 0 highest)

window	<0.0,1.0,0.0,1.0>
viewport	<0.0,1.0,0.0,1.0>

Workstation state list
for every logical input device

operating mode	REQUEST
prompt/echo type	1

Segment state list

transmation matrix	$\begin{bmatrix} 1 & 0 & 0 \\ 0 & 1 & 0 \end{bmatrix}$
visibility	VISIBLE
highlighting	NORMAL
priority	0.0
detectability	NOT DETECTABLE

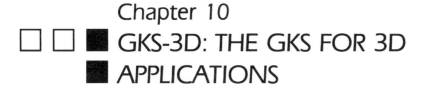

Chapter 10
□ □ ■ GKS-3D: THE GKS FOR 3D
■ APPLICATIONS

10.1 Why GKS-3D?

GKS was developed to work exclusively in two dimensions; that is, images are defined on such planes as image or drawing surfaces. This is useful in many application areas, and at first glance it appears totally natural: after all, the final result of your work will end up on a flat surface, a piece of paper, for example, or a slide, even if a three-dimensional object is being represented.

Two considerations argue against a complete generalization of this 2D graphics model. First of all, there are areas of application for computer graphics where considerable handling of spatial objects occurs; and their representation – in 3D, if possible – is very important not only for aesthetic appeal, but also from the standpoint of communicating information to the viewer. Examples that come to mind are flight simulation, CAD, physical models (e.g., spatial representation of internal body organs), and molecular biology (e.g., spatial representation of organic molecules frequently allows direct conclusions to be made about their interaction with the environment). It could be argued that the projection of such anatomical organs or flight scenes is, in fact, 2D on the user's screen and is therefore supported by 'classical' GKS. This is true for the most part. However, there are tasks such as projections from three dimensions onto two or calculating hidden object parts that must be handled by 3D applications. Why not just hand this task over to a central graphics system?

The second argument arises from the increasing number of graphics devices in existence that are able to process three spatial coordinates directly. These displays show 3D data on their display surface in accordance with settable transformation matrices. They actually do nothing more than the corresponding applications; but they do it in their hardware and, thus, much faster than would be possible with software.

There are two main groups of graphics output devices: those whose output area is a surface, like conventional devices, and those that can actually project objects three-dimensionally into space. Even if examples of the second type are still rare, devices equipped with this technology (holography, vibrating mirror, plastic model-making machines, to name three) will become increasingly available in the future.

There is actually a third argument for introducing GKS-3D into the field: three-dimensional digitizing. This allows spatial coordinates like surface points of objects to register exactly like surface coordinates with conventional digitizing.

10.2 Relationship with GKS

With these facts in mind, a subcommittee of the ISO working group on GKS standardization was formed in 1982 to work out a proposal for extending GKS to 3D (GKS-3D), which became a standard (ISO 8805) in late 1988. The following guidelines were applied:

- Application programs used by GKS should be able to work with GKS-3D without modification and should deliver the same results as often as possible.
- All GKS functions should remain unchanged and must be fully supported by GKS-3D.
- Any new functions should serve 3D exclusively. This means that no functions should be added that are not directly necessary to support 3D graphics. Any inclusion of new primitives or attributes was consciously avoided.

This last guideline often drew the critics' fire and is likely to continue to do so. To critics it seems absolutely necessary that a 3D graphics system also contain solid graphics primitives (Requicha, 1980) such as cubes, spheres, tetrahedrons, and cylinders.

There are good rebuttals to these very reasonable arguments, however. First, until very recently, developments in the area of solid modeling have not been sufficiently advanced that there have been commonly accepted graphics primitives. Premature standardization could, therefore, bring with it the danger of undesirable influence on this field's development. Furthermore, in addition to solid modeling, there is a series of other 3D models like fractals (Magnenat-Thalmann and Thalmann, 1985), finite-element surfaces and particle systems (Reeves, 1983) which would have to be taken into consideration. Indeed, in 1988 work on standardizing an extension of PHIGS (see Section 11.3) was started (PHIGS PLUS) (Van Dam *et al.*, 1988), which will cover this area. And finally, an old development principle of GKS remains valid: GKS should support only the visual representation of objects, but not the application-oriented geometric description.

There may still be some confusion as to how GKS-3D relates to GKS. From a functional standpoint and, thus, from the view of the application program,

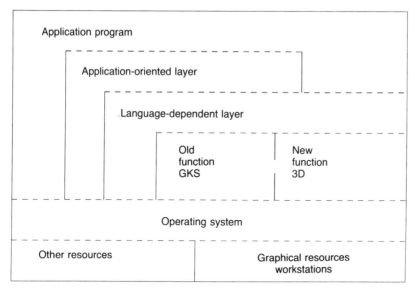

Figure 10.1   GKS-3D layer model

GKS-3D (ISO, 1988g) should be considered as an extension of GKS. Figure 10.1 illustrates the relationship; contrast this figure with Figure 2.1.

Figure 2.4 and especially Figure 2.5 (GKS levels) remain valid. For example, GKS-3D in performance level 2b must support not only all corresponding GKS functions, but also 3D segments (see Section 10.3.6) and 3D input (see Section 10.3.5).

For the GKS-3D implementer, this functional expansion does not mean that it is sufficient to add a few functions to the GKS implementation. Actually, much more of a general adjustment of a large part of GKS will be required, if a totally new implementation does not appear economical. One should also note that ISO 8805 (ISO, 1988g), which describes GKS-3D, is not a simple addendum to ISO 7942 (ISO, 1985) but is a complete document; however, neither does it contradict ISO 7942, because ISO 7942 conceptually is contained in ISO 8805.

10.3   GKS-3D Concepts

The rest of this chapter will elaborate on modifications of GKS features described earlier in the book, as well as new GKS-3D concepts.

10.3.1   Primitives

GKS-3D has the same primitives as GKS, of course. In addition to these primitives, GKS-3D offers a 3D counterpart for each GKS primitive. In other words, alongside POLYLINE there is POLYLINE 3 and alongside TEXT is TEXT 3, where point parameters are given with three coordinates. To summarize, for each GKS output function PRIMITIVE there is also a function PRIMITIVE 3 in GKS-3D.

In addition, GKS-3D provides new primitives – FILL AREA SET and FILL AREA SET 3 – both of which will be explained in greater detail in Section 10.4.6.

The 'expansion' of GKS primitives into 3-space (that is, into a 3D cartesian coordinate system) creates a distinction between actual spatial primitives (POLYLINE 3, POLYMARKER 3) and planar ones (TEXT 3, FILL AREA 3, FILL AREA SET 3, CELL ARRAY 3). This subject will also be discussed in Section 10.4.

10.3.2 Primitive Attributes

The complete attribute model remains unchanged, and a few attributes have been added (see Sections 10.4 – 10.6).

10.3.3 Graphics Workstations

The essential difference between GKS workstations and those for GKS-3D is that the latter are generally considered to be 3D workstations. Therefore, workstation windows and display surfaces are parallelepipeds instead of rectangles; and whether or not the third coordinate is ignored or interpreted is determined in a workstation-specific manner.

10.3.4 Coordinate Systems and Transformations

Herein lies the greatest difference between GKS and GKS-3D. First, all coordinate systems already existing in GKS (WC, NDC, and DC) are expanded to right-handed systems (WC3, NDC3, and DC3) with a third dimension (the z-coordinate). Now, the WC3 area is a three-dimensional, real cartesian system, NDC3 is the unit cube, and individual DC3s are cuboids (see Figure 10.2).

In order to set the window of a specific normalization transformation, call:

```
SET WINDOW 3

    Input:     integer   TRANSFORMATION NUMBER
               6*real    WINDOW LIMITS                            (WC3)
```

or in FORTRAN:

```
              subroutine GSW3    (TNR,WNLIM)
              integer            TNR
              real               WNLIM(6)
```

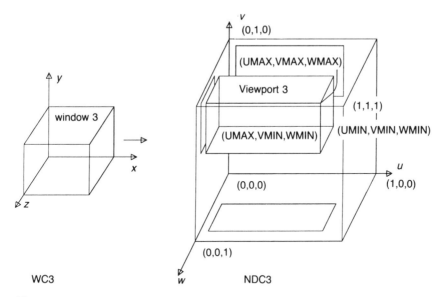

Figure 10.2 3D normalization transformation

to specify the 3D area of WC3 that is to be displayed on VIEWPORT 3 (in NDC3). SET VIEWPORT 3 is derived from SET VIEWPORT in a similar way to SET WINDOW 3.

The examples of new functions just discussed can be generalized in this way; every GKS-3D function that is derived from a GKS function FUNCTION by expansion into three dimensions is named FUNCTION 3.

How are the original GKS functions like SET WINDOW adapted to the new model? Here is the fundamental rule:

Rule for embedding 2D functions in GKS-3D
Each GKS function FUNCTION is handled as a special case of FUNCTION3. It is immediately extended to the third dimension when called, according to the following guidelines:

- Primitives lie in the z=0 plane.
- Bounding rectangles in WC or NDC contain the Z-area [0,1].
- Workstation viewports contain a workstation-specific Z-area.
- Transformation matrices are 3×4 instead of 2×3 (see Section 10.3.6).

In addition to the coordinate systems WC3, NDC3, and DC3, GKS-3D uses two others:

VRC – View Reference Coordinates
NPC – Normalized Projection Coordinates

VRC and NPC are used for the workstation-specific determination of projections. Section 10.5 discusses 'viewing' in detail.

10.3.5   Input

GKS-3D differs from GKS only in the area of coordinates, so GKS-3D offers two additional input classes; namely, LOCATOR 3 and STROKE 3. Because both classes can be implemented exactly like their 2D counterparts, there is a corresponding GKS-3D function for each GKS function to control LOCATOR and STROKE. For example:

INITIALIZE LOCATOR 3	INITIALIZE STROKE3
SET LOCATOR 3 MODE	SET STROKE 3 MODE
REQUEST LOCATOR 3	REQUEST STROKE 3
SAMPLE LOCATOR 3	SAMPLE STROKE 3
GET LOCATOR 3	GET STROKE 3

These functions have nearly identical arguments to their 2D counterparts; but, of course, the 2D coordinates (points, echo areas, etc.) are replaced by 3D coordinates. The 2D and 3D functions are 'not quite identical', because the functions REQUEST...3, SAMPLE...3, and GET...3 have an additional parameter, which indicates the 'viewing' transformation being used when mapping DC3 to WC3. See also Section 10.5.

Workstations in GKS-3D are treated primarily as 3D-workstations, and GKS-3D works internally in three dimensions; for these reasons, it makes sense to clarify how LOCATOR and STROKE are handled by GKS-3D. Here, as well, each principle of application that holds true for 2D GKS functions reappears as a special case of its 3D extension.

The course of transforming 2D coordinate input into GKS-3D can be outlined approximately as follows:

1. The value registered on the device is extended to a predefined z-coordinate.
2. The resulting point is transformed exactly like real 3D input from DC3 through NPC, VRC, and NDC3 to WC3.
3. The x- and y-coordinates from the point in WC3 are used as results.

Due to the limited scope of this book, an explicit discussion of this procedure will be avoided. It should be mentioned, however, that GKS-3D offers another function, INQUIRE VIEWING TRANSFORMATION USED, so each additional argument that directly returns LOCATOR 3 and STROKE 3 can be obtained when using conventional coordinate input.

10.3.6 Segments

The only difference between GKS and GKS-3D segments is in the area of the segment transformation matrix. This matrix has three rows and four columns in GKS-3D. Correspondingly, GKS-3D provides the following additional functions:

INSERT SEGMENT 3
SET SEGMENT TRANSFORMATION 3
EVALUATE TRANSFORMATION MATRIX 3
ACCUMULATE TRANSFORMATION MATRIX 3

The 2×3 matrices transferred in the corresponding GKS functions are expanded into 3×4 matrices according to the following description:

Figure 10.3   Mapping GKS to GKS-3D transformation matrices

10.3.7 Metafiles

In this area there is virtually no difference between GKS and GKS-3D. GKS-3D knows the item types for all new functions that affect image generation either directly or indirectly. This implies that GKS metafiles can always be interpreted by a GKS-3D implementation. Things get more complicated with the reverse, because the new item types are coded with numbers greater than 100. However, because GKS does not interpret such item types and considers them to be application items, a call to INTERPRET ITEM simply leads to an error report with such items. It can be said, therefore, that GKS filters out the GKS-3D-specific items from GKS-3D. Clearly, one can say nothing about the reaction of application programs to such metafile items.

Something else that should be considered is that the proposed metafile format in GKS and GKS-3D is not an international standard at this time, but the so-called CGM (Computer Graphics Metafile, ISO 8632 (ISO, 1987) – see Chapter 11) is. However, CGM only partially meets the needs of GKSM. An addendum to the CGM standard is being prepared to fully support the requirements of GKS metafiles (see Section 7.3.2 for further discussion of this topic).

10.3.8 Inquiry Functions and Internal Lists

There is no difference between GKS and GKS-3D except for a series of new inquiry functions and list elements to cover the new capabilities of GKS-3D.

10.3.9 Error Handling

Error handling occurs in GKS-3D in the same way as it does in GKS.

10.4 Primitives and Primitive Attributes

As previously mentioned, GKS-3D has a 3D counterpart for each primitive of GKS. These 3D primitives can be divided into two groups: actual 3D primitives and planar ones. The first group includes POLYLINE 3 and POLYMARKER 3; the second group contains TEXT 3, FILL AREA 3, and CELL ARRAY 3. GDP is associated with one group or the other according to the meaning assigned to the GDP identifier.

   Planar primitives share one (common) rule: they themselves define the planes in which they lie (and these planes can be oriented anywhere in 3-space). This means that their defining points are provided with each call of a planar primitive. These points define the position of the planes in WC3 and the position of the primitives within the planes; these parameters are not present in the corresponding GKS functions.

10.4.1 POLYLINE 3

POLYLINE3

Input: integer   NUMBER OF POINTS
         n*point3 POINTS   (WC3)

or in FORTRAN:

         subroutine GPL3   (N,X,Y,Z)
         integer   N
         real   X(N),Y(N),Z(N)

This function defines a polyline in 3-space and has the same attributes as POLYLINE.

10.4.2 POLYMARKER 3

POLYMARKER 3

Input: integer   NUMBER OF POINTS
         n*point3 POINTS   (WC3)

or in FORTRAN:

>   subroutine GPM3   (N,X,Y,Z)
>   integer   N
>   real   X(N),Y(N),Z(N)

This function defines a set of markers in 3-space and has the same attributes as POLYMARKER. The orientation of polymarkers on the display surface of the workstation is always parallel to the xy-plane and 'upright'.

10.4.3   TEXT 3

TEXT 3 is a planar primitive. It contains two new arguments because two further points are needed to specify the text plane (along with text position).

>   TEXT 3

>   Input: point3   TEXT POSITION   (WC3)
>   2*point3   TEXT DIRECTION VECTORS   (WC3)
>   string   TEXT

or in FORTRAN:

>   subroutine GTX3   (PX,PY,PZ,TDX,TDY,TDZ,STR)
>   real   PX,PY,PZ
>   real   TDX(2),TDY(2),TDZ(2)
>   character*(*)   STR

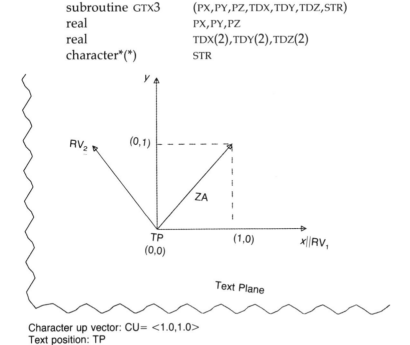

Character up vector: CU= <1.0,1.0>
Text position: TP
Direction vector: DV

Figure 10.4   Text plane

How do the direction vectors determine the text plane and the reference coordinate system in it? Clearly each of them lies in the plane and so establishes it. The positive x-axis is situated parallel to the first direction vector through the text position (which represents the origin of the reference coordinate system), and the positive y-axis can be found on the side of the second direction vector. Character up vector and text path are interpreted relative to this coordinate system. Figure 10.4 demonstrates this situation. The units used in the text planes are the same as in WC3. TEXT 3 has the same attributes as TEXT.

10.4.4   FILL AREA 3

FILL AREA 3 is a planar primitive. In contrast with TEXT 3, however, it implicitly defines the plane in which it lies by itself; namely, by the fill area points. The way this surface will be derived and the way the fill area points will finally be depicted on the workstation is determined in a workstation-specific manner. Fill areas with common edges that have fill area interior styles other than HOLLOW should not intersect or have any space between them.

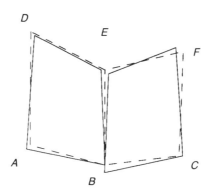

Figure 10.5   Misaligned cube faces

To see this more clearly, consider two normal side surfaces of a cube standing next to one another (see Figure 10.5). Suppose that somehow – because of rounding error, for example – the points A, B, E, and D defining fill area a, on the one hand, and the points B, C, F, and E, defining fill area b, on the other hand, do not lie in the same plane. The solid lines show the two actual planes, while the dashed lines show the intended planar figure abutting along line BE. If, after that, a and b were to be represented with fill area interior style SOLID, this would cause an unwelcome aliasing effect: a and b would no longer abut along a common border, so to speak.

The fill area planes are needed for three reasons:

- in order to be able to implement clipping cleanly;
- in order to be able to apply the inside/outside algorithm described in Section 4.1;
- in order to be able to determine the front side with a fill area interior style PATTERN (and HATCH).

How, then, is FILL AREA 3 filled with PATTERN? First, there is a new function to be learned:

SET PATTERN REFERENCE POINT AND VECTORS

Input: 3*point3   PATTERN REFERENCE POINT AND VECTORS   (wc3)

or in FORTRAN:

                 subroutine GSPRP3   (RFX,RFY,RFZ,RFVX,RFVY,RFVZ)
                 real   RFX,RFY,RFZ,RFVX(2),RFVY(2),RFVZ(2)

The pattern reference point and vectors are now projected along the surface normals onto the fill area plane. The projections are used like text position and text reference points (which determine the text direction vector). If two or more projections of the reference vectors fall together, the result is implementation-dependent.

The coordinate system laid out this way on the fill area plane is used not only to position the fill area pattern (and the hatch) in the way already described, but also to determine the front side of the fill area, which can be used by many algorithms for eliminating hidden lines and surfaces (see Section 10.6).

10.4.5   CELL ARRAY 3

CELL ARRAY 3 is a planar primitive. Because a plane is determined by three points, it looks like this:

CELL ARRAY 3

Input:	3*point3	CELL PARALLELOGRAM	(wc3)
	2*integer	DIMENSIONS OF COLOR MATRIX	
	2*integer	INDICES OF START COLUMN, START ROW	
	2*integer	NUMBER OF COLUMNS, NUMBER OF ROWS	
	DX*DY*integer	COLOR INDEX MATRIX	

or in FORTRAN (see Section 4.1):

> subroutine GCA3   (CXA,CYA,CZA,DX,DY,IDX,IDY,NCS,NRS,
>   COLIA)
> real   CXA(3),CYA(3),CZA(3)
> integer   DX,DY,IDX,IDY,NCS,NRS,COLIA(DIMX,DIMY)

The only difference between CELL ARRAY and CELL ARRAY 3 is the use of the reference points P,Q,R (see Figure 10.6):

> P is the corner point associated with [1,1]
> Q is the corner point associated with [DX,1]
> R is the corner point associated with [1,DY]

This definition implies that 3D cell arrays can be parallelograms (as distinguished from upright, rectangular 2D cell arrays). Because it would be quite costly, however, to force cell arrays to be rectangles (and, in the end, would only mean a reduction of the power of CELL ARRAY 3), this functional extension of CELL ARRAY to CELL ARRAY 3 has been allowed by the drafters of the GKS-3D standard.

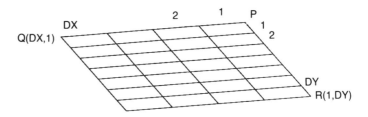

Figure 10.6   Example of CELL ARRAY 3

10.4.6 FILL AREA SET 3

This planar primitive is new in GKS-3D and is created out of any number of fill areas. All rules that hold true for FILL AREA 3 (e.g. determining its planes, inside/outside relationships) are applied similarly here. This means, in particular, that a point in the fill area set is located in the interior of the FILL AREA SET 3 if and only if any of the rays going out from it cuts an odd number of boundaries of the FILL AREA SET.

Figure 10.7 shows a few characteristics of this primitive. First, it is best suited for defining 'holes' in fill areas (C in A), but it is not suitable for defining areas that are to be cut out (like B, for example). In addition, holes should not overlap, because their cross-section would become visible when displayed (like X). The

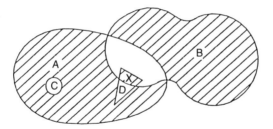

Figure 10.7   FILL AREA SET 3 with four elements

reason for this lies in the set theory equivalent of this primitive, namely the XOR function. (A XOR B is true, if A or B, but not both, are true.) Correspondingly, one point lies within a set of two fill areas if it belongs to one or the other set, but not both. With several fill areas this operation is recursively applied. The set A XOR (b xor (c xor d)) corresponds to the hatched areas in Figure 10.7. This disappearance of areas corresponds to set theory subtraction. Because (A XOR C) = (A−C) is valid only in cases where c is contained in A, one operation (A−C for the definition of 'holes') can be replaced by the geometrically simpler (A XOR C).

    FILL AREA SET 3

    Input: point3list   SET OF POINT LISTS

or in FORTRAN:

                subroutine GFAS3   (NPL,STIXA,XA,YA,ZA)
                integer   NPL
    C   number of point lists
                integer   STIXA(NPL)
    C   array of starting indices
                                            in XA,YA,ZA
                real   XA(*),YA(*),ZA(*)

    In addition to fill area attributes, FILL AREA SET 3 has its own attributes for displaying edges. The following attributes are also valid for FILL AREA SET:

    SET EDGE INDEX

    Input: integer   EDGE INDEX   (>0)

or in FORTRAN:

                subroutine GSEDI   (EDI)
                integer   EDI

SET EDGE REPRESENTATION

Input:	integer	EDGE INDEX	(>0)
	enum	EDGE FLAG	(OFF/ON)
	integer	EDGE TYPE	($\neq 0$)
	real	EDGE WIDTH FACTOR	($\geqslant 0$)
	integer	EDGE COLOR INDEX	($\geqslant 0$)

or in FORTRAN:

```
      subroutine GSEDR    (WKID,EDI,EDFLAG,EDTYPE,EDWSF,COLI)
      integer             WKID,EDI,EDFLAG,EDTYPE
C                                EDFLAG: 0='OFF', 1='ON'
      real                EDWSF
      integer             COLI
```

This function allows edge bundles to be set similarly to line bundles; workstation-specific edge bundle tables can be established. The individual attributes correspond to those of polylines; only 'edge flag' is new. 'Edge flag' shows whether the edges of fill area sets should be displayed or not. In the case of fill area interior style HOLLOW and edge flag = ON, the edge display produced by HOLLOW will be generated first; and, afterwards, each of the edge displays determined by the edge attributes will be generated. (HOLLOW will be treated like any other fill area interior style.)

Like the additional polyline attributes, there are also GKS-3D functions, of course.

    SET EDGE FLAG
    SET EDGE TYPE
    SET EDGE WIDTH FACTOR
    SET EDGE COLOR INDEX
    SET ASPECT SOURCE FLAGS 3

SET ASPECT SOURCE FLAGS 3 sets the aspect source flags for the four new individual attributes.

10.5 Viewing and Projection

If one considers the sets of GKS-3D primitives created by an application program, these primitives, together with their attributes, describe an abstract picture. ('Abstract' in this context means application-independent and device-independent.) The difference from GKS is simply that this image does not exist on a plane but in three-dimensional cartesian space. The image would be easier to discuss in this context as a scene rather than an image.

How can a scene be represented on a workstation display surface? First, the GKS workstation transformation should be extended to three coordinates. This would imply, however, that any cuboid of the unit cube, whose edges are parallel to world coordinate axes, could be chosen as a detail, but its visual display would always correspond to orthogonal parallel projections along the z-axis.

In 3D graphics, however, parallel and perspective projections from any direction and of any distance are of greater importance, and these tasks – as far as possible independent of specific applications – should be provided by a graphical kernel system.

One could object that any views can be realized with the help of segments. That would bring a number of disadvantages with it, however. For one thing, segment transformations in GKS-3D are 3×4 matrices, which do not permit perspective projections. To extend these matrices to 4×4 would contradict two things: on the one hand, the minimal expansion of GKS to GKS-3D, and on the other hand, the segment concept. The reason for this is that segments should be used for image construction, but only minimally for the simulation of different viewpoints. And finally, changing the viewpoint causes all segments to be newly transformed, aside from the fact that the capabilities of any view of a scene are tied to segments and thus to GKS-3D capability levels 1 and 2.

GKS-3D takes another approach. It allows the use of a 'projection transformation', which is conceptually implemented after the segment transformation (and after clipping against the window) and before the workstation transformation. Not only are these projections defined to be workstation-specific, but also several may be active simultaneously. This accomplishes two effects simultaneously: different views can be shown on different workstations; and several views can be displayed simultaneously on one workstation.

How, then, are such projections defined in GKS-3D? In order to understand the methods used, one must visualize how geometric transformations can create the impression of perspective or an oblique viewing angle. If a cuboid perspective is displayed (for example, as suggested in Figure 10.8a), parts closer to the center of projection appear larger than those farther away. Then, if the projection rays are aligned to be parallel and the edges of the cuboid undergo an affine transformation, the result is a perspective impression, as shown in Figure 10.8b.

An affine transformation model is utilized by GKS-3D because projections are determined by the mapping of a so-called projection window onto a projection viewport. Thus, the projection window is always a part of NDC3, and the projection viewport is always an axis-parallel cuboid in a coordinate system that formally corresponds to the NDC3 but is called NPC (normalized projection coordinate system) to distinguish between them conceptually.

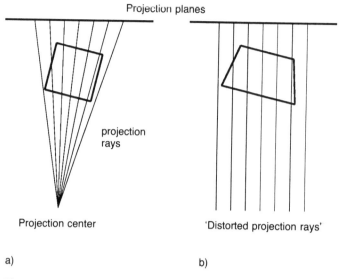

Figure 10.8   Distortion by projection

GKS-3D differentiates between parallel and perspective projections, a useful pragmatic distinction in spite of theoretical non-differentiability obtained by treating parallel as an extreme case of perspective projection. A parallel projection can be defined in GKS-3D by determining the projection window shown in Figure 10.9 (a parallelepiped). First a projection reference point (PRP) and a projection plane (PP) are given. A rectangle on the projection plane is chosen, one that defines the cross-section of the projection window with the projection plane. The ray from the projection reference point through the middle point of this window determines the projection direction. Accordingly, the projection window is a part of that parallelepiped whose edges run in the projection direction through the corner points of this window. The projection window is actually that part of the parallelepiped that lies between the front clipping plane (FP) and rear clipping plane (RP).

In the perspective case, the definition of the projection window is completely similar, but this window (a 'FRUSTRUM') is part of a pyramid whose edges run through the projection reference point and the corners of the window (see Figure 10.10).

Now the only thing left to clarify is how the projection reference point, front clipping plane, rear clipping plane, and projection plane (including the window) are created. To do this, a 'reference coordinate system' is introduced, the so-called VRC (View Reference Coordinate) system. Its origin is described by a VRP (view reference point), and its coordinate axes are described with u,v, and n. The units on u,v, and the normal n are identical to each of the NDC3 units, so

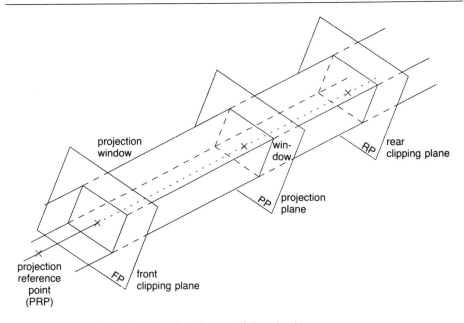

Figure 10.9   Projection window for parallel projection

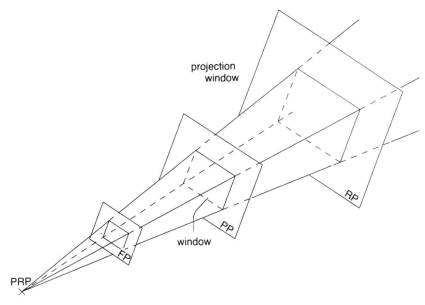

Figure 10.10   Projection window for perspective projection

that the VRC system can be mapped to NDC3 with a twisting motion. The VRC is a right-handed system as are all GKS-3D coordinate systems.

The projection plane, front clipping plane, and rear clipping plane are now parallel to the u,v-plane of the VRC system and are determined by their distances to the plane; the window is an upright rectangle on the projection plane with the borders UMIN, UMAX, VMIN, and VMAX. The projection reference point, likewise given in VRC, must have n$\neq$0.

Depicting the projection window on the projection viewport occurs (see Figure 10.10) so that UMIN is shown on XMIN of the NPC system, VMIN on YMIN, NMIN (value from the rear clipping plane) on ZMIN, etc.

To determine the relationship of VRC to NDC3, GKS-3D provides a general 4×4 matrix for mapping NDC3 into VRC. For simple special cases, a utility function is available, which builds this 4×4 matrix in NDC3 from explicit details about the view reference point position and the location of the VRC system axes.

With the method just described it is possible in GKS-3D to define a specific view of a part of NDC3 and, thus, of the scene to be displayed. GKS-3D allows several such views to remain defined simultaneously on each workstation. It is also possible to specify whether clipping against the projection window or the front or rear clipping plane should occur or not.

Because the workstation transformations determine which portion of the NPC should be displayed on a workstation, it is possible to have several projection viewports within the workstation window and on the display surface. Now, if a primitive is to be generated, through which view should it be seen? This is determined by another primitive attribute, VIEW INDEX, which can be set and, like all attributes, is bound to a primitive at generation time. VIEW INDEX selects the view that should be applied during output on a workstation. Like the clipping rectangle, the function INSERT SEGMENT replaces the view indices that are bound to primitives in the segment being inserted with the current value of the view index.

10.6   Hidden Lines and Surfaces

The previous section discusses an essential concept of GKS-3D – viewing. In this context, a further capability of GKS-3D can be described, namely the suppression of hidden lines and surfaces – the so-called 'hidden line/hidden surface removal' or HL/HSR for short. Included in this term are common methods of displaying objects to look as if they are opaque or transparent. (The similar effects achieved by ray tracing are not counted among these methods, however.) Because HL/HSR is just a method that can be abstracted from specific applications, it is useful to expect this capability from a basic graphics system. One thing should not be overlooked, by the way: there are presently quite a number of HL/HSR methods in use, but hardly any have been generally implemented and most of them are rather specific techniques suitable only for certain visual effects. Ongoing development in this area could be unfavorably influenced by an overly explicit standard at this time.

GKS-3D proceeds in the following way. There is a modal primitive attribute, HL/HSR IDENTIFIER, which can be set and is bound to a primitive at generation time, *though only in an open segment.* (Primitives outside of segments cannot be subjected to HL/HSR.) This non-negative index selects an implementation-specific HL/HSR method that can be applied to it during output on the workstation. The standard specifies that '0' means no HL/HS removal.

In addition, there is an HL/HSR MODE, which can be set to different values on each workstation and which can determine how the different HL/HSR identifiers of overlapping primitives should be handled. INSERT SEGMENT 3 updates the HL/HSR identifier in the same way as it updates VIEW INDEX.

10.7   Supplementary Information

10.7.1   Interpreting GKS Functions in GKS-3D

The following table describes how GKS functions are extended to three dimensions. GKS function calls are listed together with their equivalent GKS-3D call.

POLYLINE	->	POLYLINE 3
n*(x,y) n*(wc)		n*(x,y,0) n*(wc3)
	.	
	.	
	.	
INITIALIZE LOCATOR	->	INITIALIZE LOCATOR 3
INITIALIZE STROKE	->	INITIALIZE STROKE 3

Initial positions are transformed to WC3 by setting the z-coordinates to zero. The echo area is positioned in the z=ZMIN plane (in DC3); ZMIN represents the lower border of the workstation window.

REQUEST LOCATOR	->	REQUEST LOCATOR 3
REQUEST STROKE	->	REQUEST STROKE 3
SAMPLE LOCATOR	->	SAMPLE LOCATOR 3
SAMPLE STROKE	->	SAMPLE STROKE 3
GET LOCATOR	->	GET LOCATOR 3
GET STROKE	->	GET STROKE 3

See Section 10.3.5.

10.7.2 Updating Images

The new GKS-3D capabilities imply a more complex treatment of image change delays as well as implicit and explicit image regeneration than that listed for GKS. To discuss this in detail, however, would go beyond the limits of this book.

10.8 Implementations

At the time of writing this book, no PC-based implementations of GKS-3D were available. This is not surprising since the standard was only published in late 1988. We have included this chapter because we anticipate the availability of more GKS-3D implementations in the near future. The major factors mitigating against this development are the 640kb limitation of PC-DOS and the requirement for floating-point support. Both these factors should become less of an issue on machines based on the Intel 80386 processor running OS/2 and utilizing sophisticated graphics cards.

Chapter 11
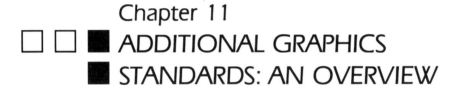
■ ADDITIONAL GRAPHICS
■ STANDARDS: AN OVERVIEW

GKS triggered an avalanche of other graphics standards. Even during its development, ISO undertook various other projects in other areas of computer graphics. One of these projects was GKS-3D. The others were:

- Computer Graphics Metafile (CGM)
- Computer Graphics Interface (CGI)
- Programmer's Hierarchical Interactive Graphics System (PHIGS)
- Programming language environments (the so-called *language bindings*) for GKS, GKS-3D, PHIGS and CGI.

There will be no further discussion here of language bindings, which have been developed for FORTRAN, Pascal, Ada, and C. The three remaining graphics projects will be briefly introduced. Finally, the graphics standards will be discussed in relation to window management systems.

11.1 Computer Graphics Metafile (CGM)

The GKS (and GKS-3D) documents establish the functional capabilities of GKS Metafiles (GKSMs), but not their internal structure. These standards do, in fact, have annexes with proposals suitable for doing that, but these annexes do not have standard status and exist only for clarification purposes.

CGM is the standard that has established the coding and picture representation capability of graphics metafiles. This standard is designated ISO 8632 (ISO, 1987). It consists of four parts. The first part establishes the functional specifications for the CGM. It specifies the data that can be contained in a CGM and, to a certain degree, the meaning of the metafiles and how they should be interpreted (Bono, 1983; Arnold and Bono, 1988). The other parts of ISO 8632 describe three separate encodings:

- *character encoding*: compact and suitable for transmission over networks of heterogeneous computing resources
- *binary encoding*: also compact; easy to generate and manage quickly, but less costly on some environments than others
- *clear text encoding*: verbose, but easy for humans to read and edit

11.1.1 Functional Capability and Structure

The overall structure of a CGM is shown in Figure 11.1. It comprises a series of picture descriptions framed by a header and a trailer. Each picture description itself is composed of a header and a body. In the so-called metafile and picture descriptors, it is possible to establish how specific parameters are coded, whether coordinates are represented by integers or real numbers, etc. CGM supports not only the metrics established in GKS, but also alternatives where it seems sensible. For example, the value of a linewidth is given not only by scale factor (as in GKS), but also in so-called VDC (virtual Device Coordinate) units. In this way, the coordinate area in which pictures can be specified is not exclusively limited to the unit square. A picture description can also establish the coordinate area with the valid VDC for subsequent pictures. A picture body contains the actual picture description ·information. Another example is that the CGM includes both *indexed color* (that is, colors can be determined by their index into a color table as in GKS) or *direct color* (that is, directly specified as an R/G/B triple).

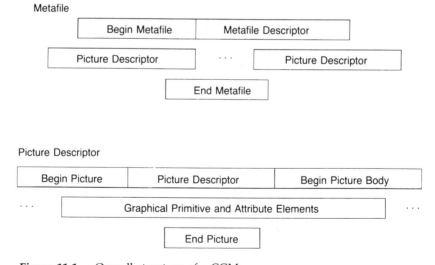

Figure 11.1   Overall structure of a CGM

The CGM BEGIN METAFILE and METAFILE DESCRIPTION elements, like the BEGIN PICTURE element, contain names that allow the identification of CGM files and pictures within the files. Although, in practice, a CGM is often processed sequentially, it need not be. Once the metafile description has been read, any picture in the metafile can then be accessed randomly. There is no need to process all pictures preceding the desired picture.

CGM defines circular and elliptical objects and rectangles as primitives in addition to the GKS primitives. FILL AREA SET is present (to permit easy representation of polygons with holes), as is the so-called DISJOINT POLYLINE, which exists for effectively coding a series of line segments (like the scale marks on an axis or the hatch lines used to shade the interior of a fill area). For the new surface-oriented primitives, there are also attributes for the edge, and the text model is somewhat expanded in comparison with GKS.

CGM item types can be divided into eight classes:

0: delimiter elements
1: metafile descriptor elements
2: control elements
3: picture descriptor elements
4: graphic elements
5: attribute elements
6: escape elements
7: external elements (user data)

When comparing GKSM and CGM, one essential difference stands out: in CGM individual images are completely independent of one another, because at the beginning of each picture all attributes and switches are set back to specific initial values. No segments can be defined in CGM because of this characteristic.

Accordingly, CGM supports only GKSM at output level 0, although CGM contains other capabilities in addition to GKS functionalities. However, development work is underway within ISO to extend the CGM (known as ISO 8632 Addendum 1) by adding elements to permit the CGM to be able to be used as a GKSM at all output levels.

The CGM also does not contain primitives that permit the representation of 3D coordinates. Development work is also under way to extend the CGM (known as ISO 8632 Addendum 2) by adding elements to permit the CGM to function as a GKSM for the GKS-3D standard at all output levels.

11.1.2 Character Encoding

As previously mentioned, several techniques are offered to code CGM. One of them offers the most compact storage of metafiles possible. It is based on a representation of CGM content by the characters of the 7-bit character set

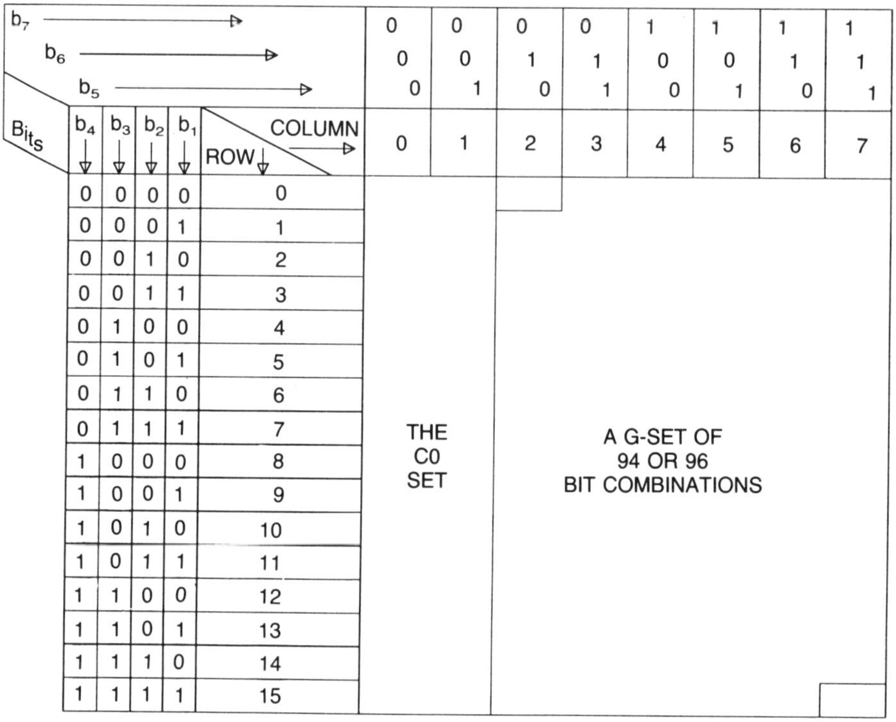

b4	b3	b2	b1	ROW / COLUMN	0	1	2	3	4	5	6	7
			b7→		0	0	0	0	1	1	1	1
			b6→		0	0	1	1	0	0	1	1
			b5→		0	1	0	1	0	1	0	1
0	0	0	0	0								
0	0	0	1	1								
0	0	1	0	2								
0	0	1	1	3								
0	1	0	0	4								
0	1	0	1	5								
0	1	1	0	6								
0	1	1	1	7	THE		A G-SET OF					
1	0	0	0	8	C0		94 OR 96					
1	0	0	1	9	SET		BIT COMBINATIONS					
1	0	1	0	10								
1	0	1	1	11								
1	1	0	0	12								
1	1	0	1	13								
1	1	1	0	14								
1	1	1	1	15								

Figure 11.2   ISO 646 (ASCII) code table

established in ISO 646 or its extension to 8-bit/byte established in ISO 2022 or by two 7-bit/byte coding (two bytes per character) and is therefore called *character encoding*. ISO 646 corresponds to the well-known ASCII character set. A total of 128 characters are represented in this set by the corresponding binary numbers for 0–127. The numbers 0–31 are called control characters and are generally not used; the numbers 32–127 code the displayable or graphic characters. Normally the ISO 646 characters are displayed in a table with 16 rows and 8 columns, as shown in Figure 11.2. As an example, the character in the 5th column and 12th row (/) has the bit combination 1011100. A special notation is often used to show the column and row index; here it would be 5/12. The extension to 8-bit is accomplished by adding columns 8–15 to Figure 11.2, where columns 8 and 9 code another set of control characters.

The character encoding for CGM uses almost exclusively the graphics characters. The following combinations are used as delimiters: 1/11 (ESC), 1/13 (GS), and 1/15 (US). The only other permitted use of control characters is within text strings, where the text control characters (CR, LF, HT, VT, BS, etc.) may appear. Each item type has its own *opcode*, a few examples (see Figure 11.3) of which are discussed in the following.

Opcode for	7-bit Code
METAFILE DESCRIPTOR	2/0
PICTURE DESCRIPTOR	2/1
BEGIN/END METAFILE	2/2
.	.
.	.
POLYLINE	3/0
DISJOINT POLYLINE	3/1
.	.
.	.
LINE BUNDLE INDEX	4/0
.	.
.	.
.	.

Figure 11.3   Character encoding for
CGM item types

When a CGM item is coded, some parameters normally follow the opcode These can be coded in different ways. Optional parameters or those found in infrequently occurring item types are usually introduced by an identifier. The identifier is a whole number that is itself encoded in a fixed manner. The parameter values follow afterwards. Absolute arguments in frequent items, like those of the polyline, are coded only by their values in a predetermined sequence.

To end a parameter list prematurely, the character MPT (metafile parameter terminator) = 1/15 is used. An entire CGM element can be closed prematurely with the MET (metafile element terminator) = 1/13.

Whole numbers, real numbers, and coordinates are encoded according to specific algorithms, which have as their goal the smallest possible number of bytes per value. For example, the number -100 is represented in this way:

1. Write the binary representation of its absolute value: 1100100
2. Group the bits five at a time starting at the right: 00011 00100
3. Add two bits to the left of each group; then code as bytes from left to right. Bits 1 to 5 are kept as they are; bits 7 and 6 are set to '01' in non-final bytes. In the last byte, bit 7 is set to '1', and bit 6 to the sign of the number, here 1 (for a negative number). The coding of -100 is therefore:
      01|00011 and 11|00100 or 2/3 6/4
      B7   B0   B7   B0

With this algorithm, whole numbers in the range $[-31, +31]$ can therefore be encoded with only one byte.

Coding real numbers and coordinates follows a similar approach, but the algorithm will not be illustrated here. For cell arrays there are two coding schemes: one for efficient representation of a long sequence of identical color indices and one for a series of different color indices; both can be used within a cell array.

11.1.3   Binary Encoding

The goal of *binary encoding* is the fastest possible generation and interpretation of the metafile. Compact storage is also a high priority. With these premises in mind, the highest value is placed on choosing number representations that are directly usable for computing in order to minimize the cost of coding and decoding. The units chosen to do that here are the octet with 8 bits and the word comprising 2 octets. CGM elements can be found in 'short form' (up to 30 octets) or in 'long form' (up to 32767 octets). Only exceptionally long elements need to be subdivided (partitioned) into multiple long-form elements.

Each CGM element begins with a header as shown in Figure 11.4. 'Element class' specifies the element class. 0 to 7 correspond to the classes presented in Section 11.1.1; 8 to 15 are reserved for future extensions to the CGM standard. 'Element identification' encodes the elements of the individual classes. Short-form elements contain the lengths of the parameter lists in octets in P.L.length 1 (= parameter list length 1), and no 'word 2' in the header. Long-form elements contain the value 31 in 'P.L.length 1' and the length of the parameter list in 'P.L.length 2'. P indicates whether (P=1) or not (P=0) the last partition of the CGM element has been reached.

For the representation of data (parameter) itself there are a number of data types to be encoded: whole signed numbers with 8-, 16-, 24- or 32-bit accuracy; the same numbers unsigned; fixed point real numbers with 32- or 64-bit accuracy; floating decimal numbers in so-called IEEE format (likewise with 32- or 64-bit resolution) and characters with 8-bit representations.

The precisions of the data types used to encode the CGM parameters are established in the metafile and picture descriptor sections of the CGM.

For cell arrays, there are two alternative formats. In the binary encoding, a cell array is always displayed either in packed format (a fixed number of bytes per row) or in a so-called run-length encoding format, where sequences of like cell values are coded compactly.

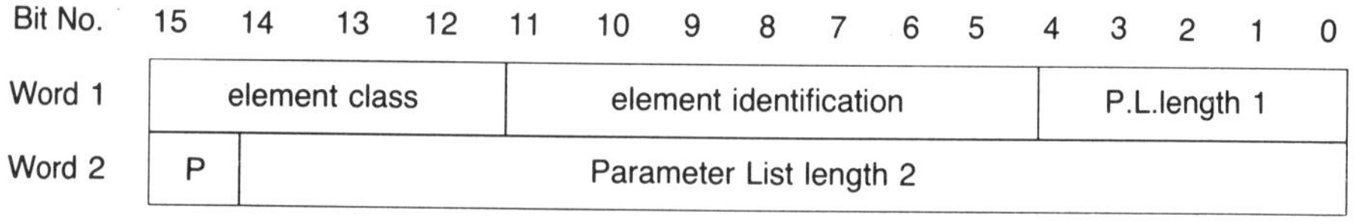

Bit No.	15	14	13	12	11	10	9	8	7	6	5	4	3	2	1	0
Word 1	element class					element identification					P.L.length 1			
Word 2	P	Parameter List length 2													

Figure 11.4   Format of an element header in binary coding

11.1.4   Clear Text Encoding

Clear text encoding offers simple editing capabilities and human readability as well as 'manual' production of CGM files. Correspondingly, the following rules apply to interpreting such encoded files:

- Text formatting characters (CR, LF, ...) are interpreted as empty characters.
- $ and _ are ignored. They can be interspersed at will for readability.
- There is no distinction between lower-case and upper-case letters.
- Numbers are represented as their corresponding ISO 646 character strings.
- Comments are allowed and are bracketed by the percent sign character (%).
- Numbers can be displayed in any base from 2 to 16; the base precedes the # sign (for example, 2 # 1011 = 11 = 10 # 11 = 8 # 13 = 16 # B).
- Text strings are enclosed within a matched pair of single or double quotation marks; quotation marks themselves can be represented in the text string by a double occurrence of the desired quotation mark.

The syntax of individual item types or the entire CGM structure is given in Backus-Naur Form (BNF) as if for a programming language (and this encoding form can also be handled like a programming language).

As an example, consider the derivation of POLYLINE:

```
<POLYLINE>     ::=  LINE<SOFTSEP><P:point>
                    <<SEP><P:point>>+<TERM>
                    |INCRLINE<SOFTSEP><P:point>
                    <<DELTA>+<TERM>>
<SOFTSEP>      ::=  <SEPCHAR>+
<SEPCHAR>      ::=  <SPACE>|<CR>|<LF>|<HT>|<VT>|<FF>
<SEP>          ::=  <SOFTSEP>|<HARDSEP>
<HARDSEP>      ::=  <OPTSEP>, <OPTSEP>
<OPTSEP>       ::=  <SEPCHAR>*
<P>            ::=  <POINTREC>|(<OPTSEP><POINTREC><OPTSEP>)
<POINTREC>     ;;=  <VDC><SEP><VDC>
<VDC>          ::=  <I:integer>|<R:real>
<TERM>         ::=  <OPTSEP> / <OPTSEP>|<OPTSEP>;<OPTSEP>
<DELTA>        ::=  <SEP><DELTAPAIR>|<SEP> (<DELTAPAIR>)
<DELTAPAIR>    ::=  <OPTSEP><VDC:deltax><SEP><VDC:deltay>
                    <OPTSEP>
```

The symbols mean:

<...>*	<...> at least zero times.
<...>+	<...> at least once.
<P:p>	<P> with meaning p.
<lowercase>	no additional derived expressions of corresponding terminal symbols.

The following examples code the same polyline:

(a) LINE 3 7.5 5.5 10 0 4.45;
(b) INCRLINE 3 7.5
     (+2.5,+2.5)(−5.5,−5.55)
(c) LINE (3 7.5),(5.5 10),(0 4.45)

11.2   Computer Graphics Interface (CGI)

GKS standardizes the interface between graphics systems and application programs, but leaves open the question of communication between the graphics system and the workstation or device. It is this graphics workstation interface, however, along with its environment, which is the subject of the Computer Graphics Interface standard currently holding the status of second DP (Draft Proposal) (Arnold and Bono, 1988; ISO, 1988a) within ISO.

CGI overlaps CGM conceptually in a number of ways. CGI contains not only the CGM classes 0, 2, 4, 5, 6, and 7 (see Section 11.1.1) with equivalent capability and power, but also CGI has identical encoding methods as CGM. Consequently, CGI has CGM compatibility, but CGI also supports the GKS workstation interface completely. CGI is a six-part standard, including input, segmentation, and raster, along with the usual control, primitive, and attribute functions. Finally, CGI offers inquiry functions, like GKS, but not appropriate in a CGM setting.

Unlike GKS, CGI standardizes the interface to a single graphics device. A GKS implementation, using CGI to access and support multiple simultaneous workstations, would use multiple instances of a CGI implementation.

11.2.1   Inquiry Functions

With the help of these functions the capabilities of a device can be inquired. Possible requests can be divided into the following classes:

- Output
- Attribute
- Color

- Raster operations
- Input
- Segmentation

The underlying inquiry concept corresponds to that of GKS. For all settable or choosable characteristics of the CGI device, there are inquiry functions through which programs can be adjusted to the capabilities of the device.

11.2.2   Raster Operations

For raster devices (especially raster display screens, which are rapidly becoming the dominant graphics display technology), a collection of specific operations is defined to allow rapid modification of pixel arrays. Such arrays are called bitmaps, and – as already mentioned in Section 1.2 – the operations are called 'raster ops' or 'bitblt'. These operations include the transfer of stored pixel arrays from one bitmap to another, the modification of such image parts by means of any operation on a pixel-by-pixel basis (e.g., Boolean operations like XOR), and other similar operations. Display screens with so-called 'multi-windowing' capabilities make extensive use of such raster operations.

It is beyond the scope of this book to go into more detail here (but see Arnold and Bono, 1988; ISO, 1988a).

11.2.3   Input

The CGI input model is similar, but not identical, to the GKS model. On the one hand, it does not concern itself with EVENT input (because EVENT input is across an entire graphics system, not just on a single device). On the other hand, the CGI echo request model is more extensive than the GKS model. The model according to which input devices operate can be outlined as follows:

- The *measure value* is the last value input by the operator or set by an INITIALIZE function, or the original initial value, until the value is overwritten by successful REQUEST or INQUIRE input.
- A *trigger* can be assigned to several input devices.
- An input device always exists in one of these *states*:
  - □ released;
  - □ idle;
  - □ trigger-armed;
  - □ request-pending.

State transitions take place upon the occurrence of well-specified actions and significant events. The entire CGI input model is described in Arnold and Bono (1988).

11.2.4 Segmentation

The segmentation concept also corresponds closely to that of GKS, but CGI has been designed as well to support the rendering pipeline of PHIGS (after a 3D model has been projected into 2-space).

11.2.5 Summary

CGI is generally considered to be one of the most significant standards in the field of graphics, because it offers the potential of standardizing the graphics device interface. Such an interface, implemented in firmware and hardware, could greatly improve the performance of graphics applications and could greatly reduce the expenses associated with the maintenance of large suites of device drivers. CGI is being awaited with great interest by device manufacturers, in particular. There is hope that CGI's support for GKS will be maintained in the final CGI standard, because it will almost certainly mean that GKS implementations will be significantly easier to realize than they have been until now.

11.3 PHIGS

PHIGS is an acronym for the Programmer's Hierarchical Interactive Graphics System and was originally developed by the US computer graphics standards committee, X3H3, to serve the following purposes:

- Mixed 2D and 3D graphics
- A high degree of interaction
- Real-time manipulation of the image
- Image modification on a more elementary level than that provided by GKS

PHIGS (ISO, 1988b; Brown and Heck, 1985) is designed especially for applications like computer-aided engineering (CAE), molecular modeling, simulation, process control, and data analysis; but it is still not fully adequate for applications that demand higher-quality images or realistic representation, like cartography, animation, pattern recognition, and image processing.

What can PHIGS do, and how does it relate to GKS and GKS-3D? Most basic concepts are carried over from GKS, but PHIGS offers five essential extensions:

- A 3D modeling coordinate system
- Hierarchical structures (more versatile than GKS segments)
- Editing capabilities on structures
- Multiple simultaneous views of 3D modeling space (as in GKS-3D)
- External standardized storage for saving and recalling PHIGS structures

Unfortunately, basing PHIGS on GKS concepts does not mean complete compatibility. It is beyond the scope of this book to discuss these differences at length (see Bettels *et al.*, 1989). However, the expansion of the segment concept is so interesting that it will be presented here in greater detail.

11.3.1   Structure Hierarchies

Segments in PHIGS are called *structures*. PHIGS structures are comparable to GKS-3D segments. Structures can contain primitives, attributes, viewing selections, transformations, application-specific data, references to other structures, and labels. The meaning and interpretation of structures differ significantly from GKS segments.

11.3.1.1   Creating and Displaying Structures

Structures are created like GKS segments. They are, therefore, always handled as a sequence of items or primitives. This does not mean, however, that a structure is automatically displayed on all active workstations. Instead, it must be associated with a workstation to be visible on it: in PHIGS, this is called POST STRUCTURE (TO WORKSTATION). If a structure is associated with a workstation (and is visible), it is displayed there and is sequentially managed and interpreted primitive by primitive. If, as a result, the processing of a structure ends, the process begins anew. If, during that time, a change occurs (see Section 11.3.2), this change is immediately taken into consideration. This concept naturally has a corresponding effect on image delay and updates.

11.3.1.2   Attributes

Attributes in GKS are bound to primitives at the time of generation; binding of attributes occurs in PHIGS only when a structure is traversed during the rendering of the picture. If something like the following sequence is the beginning of a structure to be processed:

     TEXT (x1,Y1,'first text')
     SET CHARACTER HEIGHT (0.17)
     TEXT (x2,Y2,'second text')

then 'first text' is displayed with each attribute that is in effect at the time of its output. In PHIGS this means that each attribute that is set before the beginning of the structure's processing is used for display. However, the attributes set inside the structure are not used for display. 'Second text' is displayed with the same attributes as 'first text', with the exception of character height, which has been changed to 0.17. The way to determine the character height of 'first text' will be described in the next section.

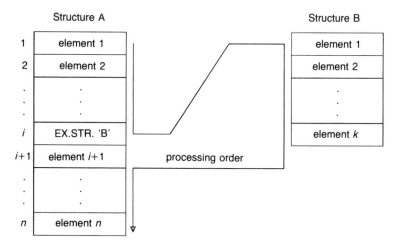

Figure 11.5   Processing a structure hierarchy

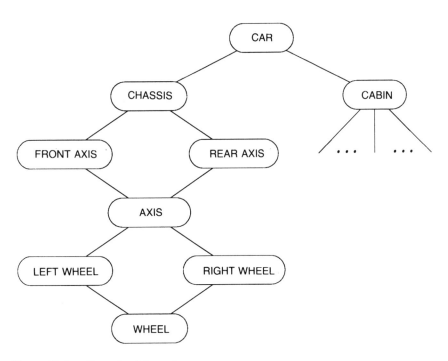

Figure 11.6   Complex hierarchy

11.3.1.3   Hierarchies

One structure can call another by means of EXECUTE STRUCTURE. If, during processing of structure A, an EXECUTE STRUCTURE referencing structure B is encountered, then the processing of structure A is suspended and structure B is processed – like a subroutine call. When the processing of B finishes, processing resumes with the next primitive in A (see Figure 11.5).

Of course, complex hierarchies can also be constructed, as in Figure 11.6. Here is the demonstration of the sense and purpose of the previously introduced rule connecting attributes to processing time. Every structure continues to work with the 'environment' that is current when the structure is processed. Generally, the *Inheritance Rule* applies: each structure inherits the environment that is valid at its processing (either as a set of attributes associated with a workstation or by a call from another structure). Self-effected changes apply to the structure itself as to all structures called by it; this means that after termination of processing the original environment is restored.

11.3.1.4   Viewing and Transformations

The PHIGS viewing model corresponds to that of GKS-3D. Views are not specified in NDC3, of course, but in a so-called *modeling space*. The application itself defines the construction of WC3 in this modeling space with the help of 4×4 *modeling matrices*, which can be inserted at any place within the structures. The modeling matrices can be applied like attributes to the primitive being generated. The essential difference is that a new modeling transformation can be concatenated with the current attributes. This is highly useful for geometric construction of a scene, because it allows individual placement of objects.

11.3.1.5   Primitives Outside of Structures

Unlike GKS, no primitives are permitted to exist or be specified outside of PHIGS structures.

11.3.2   Editing Structures

Structures in PHIGS that have been closed can be reopened and modified. Modification occurs in a very elementary way:

- A so-called ELEMENT POINTER always points to the next (current) primitive that can be edited.
- At the beginning of structure modification, this pointer is located in front of the first element of the structure (pseudo-element with the number 0).

- By calling a PHIGS function, the corresponding element is inserted after the current element, and the pointer is directed at it.
- The current element can be deleted.
- The current element can be inquired.
- The element pointer can be positioned.

Labels whose sole purpose is to facilitate editing can be inserted into structures. That is, element pointers can be set absolutely or relatively not only to element numbers, but also to these labels.

11.3.3   Archiving Structures

PHIGS permits saving structures and structure hierarchies in so-called archive files, in addition to creating and interpreting CGM files. To archive a structure, it is simply stored in a file with the function ARCHIVE STRUCTURE, where all structures referenced by the function are also automatically stored. Structures can be retrieved from archive files and placed in the central structure storage just as easily. The treatment of special cases can be controlled if, for example, structures of the same name already exist in the destination (archive file or central structure storage).

11.3.4   3D Graphics

The entire 3D concept of PHIGS strongly parallels GKS-3D and, consequently, will not be dealt with further.

11.3.5   Error Handling

This concept is also derived from GKS. It is expanded, however, in the sense that PHIGS is specified in such a fashion that no errors can occur during structure processing; accordingly, all errors must be recognized by the corresponding functions when they are called. Whether or not recursions are defined in hierarchies will not be examined (e.g., structure A calls B, and B calls A again). The treatment of such situations is handled by the workstation.

11.3.6   Harmonization with GKS-3D

The previous paragraphs briefly outline the essential differences between PHIGS and GKS-3D. Noll *et al.* 1986; Bettels *et al.*, 1989; and Poller *et al.*, 1989, provide much more detail.

11.4   Window Management Systems

Window management systems are being used in ever-increasing numbers due to a drastic reduction in the cost of (1) high-performance graphic hardware in the area of intelligent workstations, (2) computers with higher computing abilities directly accessible from the workstation, and (3) high-resolution graphics displays. Modern window management systems enable the user to work simultaneously in several work contexts and to do this in such a way as to enhance his or her ideas. The user is free from the constraint of selective information display, which is not the case in conventional interactive systems.

11.4.1   Capabilities and Architecture

Window management systems typically have the following capabilities at their disposal:

- The display of and the change between contexts occurs within a multi-window environment. Each window displays a context, which need not be independent from other contexts.
- Windows on the display screen usually appear as rectangular areas, which either divide the display surface ('tiling') or overlap each other. Overlapping allows the windows to be placed one on top of the other like papers on a desk, somewhat analogous to a 'cluttered desktop'.
- There is a listener window for input functions like keyboard or position input. The user's choice of the listener can occur in different ways, e.g., with the help of a mouse input device.
- The user has operations to enlarge/reduce, shift, and close windows. Opening a window occurs implicitly at the start of a context (e.g., program or process).
- Various menu techniques (e.g., pop-up, drop-down, pull-down menus) are used to select functions at a decision branch and to select from among alternatives.
- Graphics symbols (icons) are used for object-oriented representation of facts.
- The classical limitation 'one display screen – one context' disappears. It is replaced by extensions of the 'several (virtual) screens per context' type.
- The principle of direct manipulation is realized; that is, manipulation of the image causes a direct effect, and the changed image represents the new state of the system.

Figure 11.7 shows a general architecture model for window management systems. In the lowest layer, basic input/output, transformation of

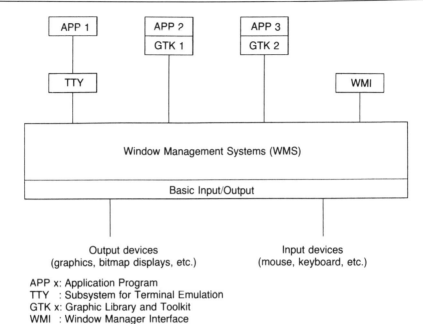

APP x: Application Program
TTY : Subsystem for Terminal Emulation
GTK x: Graphic Library and Toolkit
WMI : Window Manager Interface

Figure 11.7   General architecture model for window management systems
(Hopgood *et al.*, 1986a)

device-specific functions, and hardware properties on a device-independent
level occur. The realization of this basic layer could occur, for example, with the
standard proposal CGI (Computer Graphics Interface) (Arnold and Bono, 1988;
ISO, 1988a).

Building upon these basic functions, window management systems can
manage overlapping screen areas, tile input results in this area, output basic
primitives, handle output in hidden areas, and restore windows.

The graphics library and toolkit and the window manager interface (that is,
the human–computer interface) comprise the upper layer. The graphics library
and toolkit provide:

■ Menus (different types)
■ Icons
■ Dialog boxes
■ Mask functions
■ Systems based on graphics standard (e.g., GKS)

to use within the windows. The window manager interface is a special
application program and manages the user interaction and the display surface
by using window management system functions.

11.4.2 GKS and Window Management Systems

There is a significant reason to include the standardized GKS (ISO, 1985) in a window management system. The openness of such a system is strengthened by integrating a common graphics standard. Existing application programs that use GKS can then work with the system without problems. However, integrating GKS into a multi-window environment raises the following problems:

- GKS wants sole control over physical input and output devices. This contradicts the window management system concept of shared output resources.
- Representation on the output surface is determined by GKS application programs. A change of the visual appearance caused by the user on the screen can occur only by informing the application program, which then initiates the change.
- The maximum size that can be displayed for output is fixed to the extent of the output device and is not dynamically alterable as the current window size changes.

Any solution to these problems should attempt to maintain the GKS concept largely unchanged; it should not damage the standard and should guarantee that a standard-conforming program will run successfully.

ISO is now studying revisions to GKS that might include modifications to the definition of GKS that would allow a GKS application to run within a window. ISO is also now studying whether a standard for the low-level windowing interface is needed. Within the United States, the computer graphics standards committee, X3H3, is in the process of standardizing the data-stream protocol to the X Version 11 windowing system, a *de facto* standard developed by the Massachusetts Institute of Technology and supported by many UNIX workstation vendors.

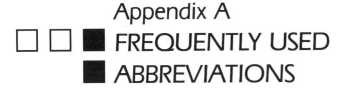

Appendix A
■ FREQUENTLY USED
■ ABBREVIATIONS

In order to save the reader the need to go to great lengths to find the meaning of abbreviations that are unfamiliar, we list here those abbreviations frequently used along with their meaning.

Abbreviation	Meaning
ANSI	American National Standardization Institute
ASF	Aspect Source Flag
CGI	Computer Graphics Interface
CGM	Computer Graphics Metafile
CS	Coordinate System
DC	Device Coordinates
DIN	Deutsches Institut für Normung (German Institute for Standardization)
EGA	Extended Graphics Adaptor
GDP	Generalized Drawing Primitive
GKS	Graphical Kernel System
GKS-3D	GKS Extensions for Three Dimensions
GKSM	GKS Metafile
IRG	Implicit Regeneration
ISO	International Standardization Organization
NDC	Normalized Device Coordinates
NPC	Normalized Projection Coordinates
NT	Normalization Transformation
PHIGS	Programmer's Hierarchical Interactive Graphics System
VDC	Virtual Device Coordinates
VRC	View Reference Coordinates
WC	World Coordinates
WDSS	Workstation-Dependent Segment Storage
WISS	Workstation-Independent Segment Storage
WK	Workstation
WKID	Workstation Identifier
WMS	Window Management System
WT	Workstation Transformation

Appendix B
SUMMARY OF
GKS FUNCTIONS

The tables on the following pages summarize all GKS functions in the same order as they are presented in the ISO GKS standard. For each function, the following information is provided:

- Name
- FORTRAN77 subroutine name
- C procedure name
- GKS states in which the function can be used
- GKS level at which the function must be supported
- Section of this book that discusses the function
- Reference to the example programs demonstrating the function

In order to maintain the usefulness of the tables by keeping them compact, it was unfortunately necessary to use abbreviations for some of the function names.

Please note that the C procedure names for the GKS functions are those provided in the GSS*GKS implementation and, in general, are not identical to those likely to be standardized by ISO and ANSI. These names were selected by GSS in late 1983, in the absence of any guidance from the standards committees. Even now (1989), there is not yet any official C language binding of GKS, principally because the programming language C itself has not been officially standardized, although a detailed working draft has been prepared for approval as soon as the work on C is completed (ISO, 1988c; 1988d; 1988e; 1988f; 1988h; 1989a; 1989b; 1989c; 1989d; 1989e; 1989f; 1989g; 1989h; 1989i).

Where the GSS*GKS implementation does not provide a level 2c function, we show the C procedure name from the ISO GKS C language binding working draft. These procedure names are marked with a plus (+) in the table.

Full Function Name	Fortran-Name	C-Name	GKS-State	Level	Sect.	Example Programs
CONTROL FUNCTIONS						
OPEN GKS	GOPKS	gopn_ks	GKCL	0a	3.1	spiral.for,tree.c
CLOSE GKS	GCLKS	gcls_ks	GKOP	0a	3.1	spiral.for,tree.c
OPEN WORKSTATION	GOPWK	gopn_wk	GKOP-SGOP	0a	3.1	spiral.for,tree.c
CLOSE WORKSTATION	GCLWK	gcls_wk	WSOP-SGOP	0a	3.1	spiral.for,tree.c
ACTIVATE WORKSTATION	GACWK	gact_wk	WSOP-WSAC	0a	3.1	spiral.for,tree.c
DEACTIVATE WORKSTATION	GDAWK	gdct_wk	WSAC-SGOP	0a	3.1	spiral.for,tree.c
CLEAR WORKSTATION	GCLRWK	gclear_wk	WSOP-WSAC	0a	4.2	
REDRAW ALL SEGMENTS ON WORKSTATION	GRSGWK	g_redraw	WSOP-SGOP	1a	6.1	segredwk.for
UPDATE WORKSTATION	GUWK	gupdate_wk	WSOP-SGOP	0a	4.2	loc.for
SET DEFERRAL STATE	GSDS	gs_defer	WSOP-SGOP	1a	4.2	
MESSAGE	GMSG(S)	g_message	WSOP-SGOP	1a	4.2	
ESCAPE	GESC	g_escape	GKOP-SGOP	0a	4.2	
OUTPUT FUNCTIONS						
POLYLINE	GPL	g_pline	WSAC-SGOP	0a	3.2	lines.for,tree.c
POLYMARKER	GPM	g_pmarker	WSAC-SGOP	0a	4.1	marker.for
TEXT	GTX(S)	g_text	WSAC-SGOP	0a	4.1	txtfonts.for
FILL AREA	GFA	g_fillarea	WSAC-SGOP	0a	4.1	areas.for,tree.c
CELL ARRAY	GCA	g_cell	WSAC-SGOP	0a	4.1	cell.c
GENERALIZED DRAWING PRIMITIVE	GGDP	g_gdp	WSAC-SGOP	0a	4.1	stattemp.*,statstop.for
ATTRIBUTE FUNCTIONS						
SET POLYLINE INDEX	GSPLI	gsl_bindex	GKOP-SGOP	0a	3.2	
SET LINETYPE	GSLN	gsl_type	GKOP-SGOP	0a	5.3.1	lines.for
SET LINEWIDTH SCALE FACTOR	GSLWSC	gsl_scale	GKOP-SGOP	0a	5.3.1	
SET POLYLINE COLOUR INDEX	GSPLCI	gsl_color	GKOP-SGOP	0a	5.3.1	lines.for
SET POLYMARKER INDEX	GSPMI	gsm_bindex	GKOP-SGOP	0a	4.1	
SET MARKER TYPE	GSMK	gsm_type	GKOP-SGOP	0a	5.3.2	marker.for
SET MARKER SIZE SCALE FACTOR	GSMKSC	gsm_scale	GKOP-SGOP	0a	5.3.2	markwid.for
SET POLYMARKER COLOUR INDEX	GSPMCI	gsm_color	GKOP-SGOP	0a	5.3.2	marker.for
SET TEXT INDEX	GSTXI	gst_bindex	GKOP-SGOP	0a	4.1	
SET TEXT FONT AND PRECISION	GSTXFP	gst_ftpr	GKOP-SGOP	0a	5.3.4	txtfonts.for
SET CHARACTER EXPANSION FACTOR	GSCHXP	gsc_expan	GKOP-SGOP	0a	5.3.4	
SET CHARACTER SPACING	GSCHSP	gsc_space	GKOP-SGOP	0a	5.3.4	
SET TEXT COLOUR INDEX	GSTXCI	gst_color	GKOP-SGOP	0a	5.3.4	txtcolup.for
SET CHARACTER HEIGHT	GSCHH	gsc_height	GKOP-SGOP	0a	5.3.4	txthght.for
SET CHARACTER UP VECTOR	GSCHUP	gsc_upvec	GKOP-SGOP	0a	5.3.4	txtcolup.for
SET TEXT PATH	GSTXP	gst_path	GKOP-SGOP	0a	5.3.4	
SET TEXT ALIGNMENT	GSTXAL	gst_align	GKOP-SGOP	0a	5.3.4	txtalign.for
SET FILL AREA INDEX	GSFAI	gsf_bindex	GKOP-SGOP	0a	4.1	
SET FILL AREA INTERIOR STYLE	GSFAIS	gsf_inter	GKOP-SGOP	0a	5.3.3	areas.for
SET FILL AREA STYLE INDEX	GSFASI	gsf_style	GKOP-SGOP	0a	5.3.3	areas.for
SET FILL AREA COLOUR INDEX	GSFACI	gsf_color	GKOP-SGOP	0a	5.3.3	areas.for
SET PATTERN SIZE	GSPA	gsp_size	GKOP-SGOP	0a	5.3.3	
SET PATTERN REFERENCE POINT	GSPARF	gsp_rfpnt	GKOP-SGOP	0a	5.3.3	
SET ASPECT SOURCE FLAGS	GSASF	gs_asf	GKOP-SGOP	0a	5.2.3	
SET PICK IDENTIFIER	GSPKID	gs_pickid	GKOP-SGOP	1b	8.11	pick.for
WORKSTATION ATTRIBUTE FUNCTIONS						
SET POLYLINE REPRESENTATION	GSPLR	gsl_rep	WSOP-SGOP	1a	5.4	
SET POLYMARKER REPRESENTATION	GSPMR	gsm_rep	WSOP-SGOP	1a	5.4	
SET TEXT REPRESENTATION	GSTXR	gst_rep	WSOP-SGOP	1a	5.4	
SET FILL AREA REPRESENTATION	GSFAR	gsf_rep	WSOP-SGOP	1a	5.4	
SET PATTERN REPRESENTATION	GSPAR	gsp_rep	WSOP-SGOP	1a	5.4	
SET COLOUR REPRESENTATION	GSCR	gscl_rep	WSOP-SGOP	0a	5.4	

Full Function Name	Fortran-Name	C-Name	GKS-State	Level	Sect.	Example Programs
TRANSFORMATION FUNCTIONS						
SET WINDOW	GSWN	gs_wind	GKOP-SGOP	0a	3.3	multnt.*
SET VIEWPORT	GSVP	gs_view	GKOP-SGOP	0a	3.3	multnt.*
SET VIEWPORT INPUT PRIORITY	GSVPIP	gsview_pri	GKOP-SGOP	0b	8.6	pick.for,loc.*
SELECT NORMALIZATION TRANSFORMATION	GSELNT	g_seltrn	GKOP-SGOP	0a	3.3	multnt.*
SET CLIPPING INDICATOR	GSCLIP	gs_clip	GKOP-SGOP	0a	3.3	clip.for
SET WORKSTATION WINDOW	GSWKWN	gswk_wind	WSOP-SGOP	0a	3.3	wkwn.for,dsurf.*
SET WORKSTATION VIEWPORT	GSWKVP	gswk_view	WSOP-SGOP	0a	3.3	wkwn.for,dsurf.*
SEGMENT FUNCTIONS						
CREATE SEGMENT	GCRSG	gcreat_seg	WSAC	1a	6.1	segcrdel.*
CLOSE SEGMENT	GCLSG	gcls_seg	SGOP	1a	6.1	segcrdel.*
RENAME SEGMENT	GRENSG	gren_seg	WSOP-SGOP	1a	6.1	
DELETE SEGMENT	GDSG	gdelet_seg	WSOP-SGOP	1a	6.1	segcrdel.*
DELETE SEGMENT FROM WORKSTATION	GDSGWK	gwkdel_seg	WSOP-SGOP	1a	6.1	
ASSOCIATE SEGMENT WITH WORKSTATION	GASGWK	gassoc_seg	WSOP-WSAC	2a	6.2	segassoc.for
COPY SEGMENT TO WORKSTATION	GCSGWK	gcopy_seg	WSOP-WSAC	2a	6.2	segcopwk.for,clock.c
INSERT SEGMENT	GINSG	ginsrt_seg	WSAC-SGOP	2a	6.?	segins.for,rectrot.c
SET SEGMENT TRANSFORMATION	GSSGT	gs_stran	WSOP-SGOP	1a	6.3	segacc.for,clock.c
SET VISIBILITY	GSVIS	gs_svisi	WSOP-SGOP	1a	6.3	segvis.for,clock.c
SET HIGHLIGHTING	GSHLIT	gs_shigh	WSOP-SGOP	1a	6.3	seghlit.for
SET SEGMENT PRIORITY	GSSGP	gs_sprior	WSOP-SGOP	1a	6.3	segprior.for
SET DETECTABILITY	GSDTEC	gs_sdetec	WSOP-SGOP	1a	6.3	pick.for
INPUT FUNCTIONS						
INITIALIZE LOCATOR	GINLC	g_loc_ini	WSOP-SGOP	0b		loc.*
INITIALIZE STROKE	GINSK	g_srk_ini	WSOP-SGOP	0b		
INITIALIZE VALUATOR	GINVL	g_val_ini	WSOP-SGOP	0b		
INITIALIZE CHOICE	GINCH	g_chc_ini	WSOP-SGOP	0b	8.9	choice.for
INITIALIZE PICK	GINPK	g_pck_ini	WSOP-SGOP	1b		pick.for
INITIALIZE STRING	GINST	g_str_ini	WSOP-SGOP	0b		string.for
SET LOCATOR MODE	GSLCM	gsloc_mode	WSOP-SGOP	0b		
SET STROKE MODE	GSSKM	gssrk_mode	WSOP-SGOP	0b		
SET VALUATOR MODE	GSVLM	gsval_mode	WSOP-SGOP	0b		
SET CHOICE MODE	GSCHM	gschc_mode	WSOP-SGOP	0b		
SET PICK MODE	GSPKM	gspck_mode	WSOP-SGOP	1b		
SET STRING MODE	GSSTM	gsstr_mode	WSOP-SGOP	0b		
REQUEST LOCATOR	GRQLC	grq_loc	WSOP-SGOP	0b	8.6	loc.*
REQUEST STROKE	GRQSK	grq_srk	WSOP-SGOP	0b	8.7	
REQUEST VALUATOR	GRQVL	grq_val	WSOP-SGOP	0b	8.8	
REQUEST CHOICE	GRQCH	grq_chc	WSOP-SGOP	0b	8.9	choice.for
REQUEST PICK	GRQPK	grq_pck	WSOP-SGOP	1b	8.11	pick.for
REQUEST STRING	GRQST	grq_str	WSOP-SGOP	0b	8.10	string.for
SAMPLE LOCATOR	GSMLC	gsm_loc	WSOP-SGOP	0c		
SAMPLE STROKE	GSMSK	gsm_srk	WSOP-SGOP	0c		
SAMPLE VALUATOR	GSMVL	gsm_val	WSOP-SGOP	0c		
SAMPLE CHOICE	GSMCH	gsm_chc	WSOP-SGOP	0c		
SAMPLE PICK	GSMPK	gsm_pck	WSOP-SGOP	1c		
SAMPLE STRING	GSMST	gsm_str	WSOP-SGOP	0c		
AWAIT EVENT	GWAIT	gawait_ev[+]	WSOP-SGOP	0c		
FLUSH DEVICE EVENTS	GFLUSH	gflush_ev[+]	WSOP-SGOP	0c		
GET LOCATOR	GGTLC	gget_loc[+]	WSOP-SGOP	0c		
GET STROKE	GGTSK	gget_stroke[+]	WSOP-SGOP	0c		
GET VALUATOR	GGTVL	gget_val[+]	WSOP-SGOP	0c		
GET CHOICE	GGTCH	gget_choice[+]	WSOP-SGOP	0c		
GET PICK	GGTPK	gget_pick[+]	WSOP-SGOP	1c		
GET STRING	GGTST	gget_string[+]	WSOP-SGOP	0c		

Full Function Name	Fortran-Name	C-Name	GKS-State	Level	Sect.	Example Programs
METAFILE FUNCTIONS						
WRITE ITEM TO GKSM	GWITM	gwr_gksm	WSAC-SGOP	0a	7.2	
GET ITEM TYPE FROM GKSM	GGTITM	gget_gksm	WSOP-SGOP	0a	7.2	
READ ITEM FROM GKSM	GRDITM	grd_gksm	WSOP-SGOP	0a	7.2	
INTERPRET ITEM	GIITM	gint_gksm	GKOP-SGOP	0a	7.2	
INQUIRY FUNCTIONS						
INQUIRE OPERATING STATE VALUE	GQOPS	gqop_state	GKCL-SGOP	0a		
INQUIRE LEVEL OF GKS	GQLVKS	gq_level	GKOP-SGOP	0a		
INQUIRE LIST OF AVAILABLE WS TYPES	GQEWK	gq_wt_lst	GKOP-SGOP	0a		
INQUIRE WORKSTATION MAXIMUM NUMBERS	GQWKM	gq_maxwks	GKOP-SGOP	1a		
INQUIRE MAXIMUM NT NUMBER	GQMNTN	gq_mtran	GKOP-SGOP	0a		
INQUIRE SET OF OPEN WORKSTATIONS	GQOPWK	gqopn_wks	GKOP-SGOP	0a		
INQUIRE SET OF ACTIVE WORKSTATIONS	GQZCWK	gqact_wks	GKOP-SGOP	1a		
INQUIRE CURRENT PRIM. ATTRIBUTE VALUE	GQPLI	gql_bindex	GKOP-SGOP	0a		
(split into several functions)	GQPMI	gqm_bindex				
	GQTXI	gqt_bindex				
	GQCHH	gqc_height				
	GQCHUP	gqc_upvec				
	GQCHW	gqc_width				
	GQCHB	gqc_basevec				
	GQTXP	gqt_path				
	GQTXAL	gqt_align				
	GQFAI	gqf_bindex				
	GQPA	gqp_size				
	GQPARF	gqp_rep				
	GQPKID	gq_pickid				
INQUIRE CURRENT INDIV. ATTRIBUTE VALUE	GQLN	gql_type	GKOP-SGOP	0a		
(split into several functions)	GQLWSC	gql_scale				
	GQPLCI	gql_color				
	GQMK	gqm_type				
	GQMKSC	gqm_scale				
	GQPMCI	gqm_color				
	GQTXFP	gqt_ftpr				
	GQCHXP	gqc_upvec				
	GQCHSP	gqc_space				
	GQTXCI	gqt_color				
	GQFAIS	gqf_inter				
	GQFASI	gqf_style				
	GQFACI	gqf_color				
	GQASF	gq_asf				
INQUIRE CURRENT NT NUMBER	GQCNTN	gq_ctrn_no	GKOP-SGOP	0a		
INQUIRE LIST OF NT NUMBERS	GQENTN	gq_tran_lst	GKOP-SGOP	0a		
INQUIRE NORMALIZATION TRANSFORMATION	GQNT	gq_ntran	GKOP-SGOP	0a		
INQUIRE CLIPPING INDICATOR	GQCLIP	gq_clip	GKOP-SGOP	0a		
INQUIRE NAME OF OPEN SEGMENT	GQOPSG	gqopen_seg	SGOP	1a		
INQUIRE SET OF SEGMENT NAMES IN USE	GQSGUS	gqsg_inuse	SGOP	1a		
INQUIRE MORE SIMULTANEOUS EVENTS	GQSIM	gq_more_simult_ev[+]	WSOP-SGOP	0c		
INQUIRE WS CONNECTION AND TYPE	GQWKC	gq_wk_type	WSOP-SGOP	0a		
INQUIRE WORKSTATION STATE	GQWKS	gqw_state	WSOP-SGOP	0a		
INQUIRE WS DEFERRAL AND UPDATE STATE	GQWKDU	gqw_defer	WSOP-SGOP	0a		
INQUIRE LIST OF POLYLINE INDICES	GQEPLI	gq_li_lst	WSOP-SGOP	1a		
INQUIRE POLYLINE REPRESENTATION	GQPLR	gql_rep	WSOP-SGOP	1a		
INQUIRE LIST OF POLYMARKER INDICES	GQEPMI	gq_mi_lst	WSOP-SGOP	1a		
INQUIRE POLYMARKER REPRESENTATION	GQPMR	gqm_rep	WSOP-SGOP	1a		
INQUIRE LIST OF TEXT INDICES	GQETXI	gq_ti_lst	WSOP-SGOP	1a		
INQUIRE TEXT REPRESENTATION	GQTXR	gqt_rep	WSOP-SGOP	1a		
INQUIRE TEXT EXTENT	GQTXX(S)	gqt_extent	WSOP-SGOP	0a		
INQUIRE LIST OF FILL AREA INDICES	GQEFAI	gq_fi_lst	WSOP-SGOP	1a		

Full Function Name	Fortran-Name	C-Name	GKS-State	Level	Sect.	Example Programs
INQUIRE PATTERN REPRESENTATION	GQPAR	gqp_rep	WSOP-SGOP	1a		
INQUIRE LIST OF COLOUR INDICES	GQECI	gq_ci_lst	WSOP-SGOP	0a		
INQUIRE COLOUR REPRESENTATION	GQCR	gqcl_rep	WSOP-SGOP	0a	5.5	
INQUIRE WORKSTATION TRANSFORMATION	GQWKT	gq_wtran	WSOP-SGOP	0a		
INQUIRE SET OF SEGMENT NAMES ON WS	GQSGWK	gqsg_nmwk	WSOP-SGOP	1a		
INQUIRE LOCATOR DEVICE STATE	GQLCS	gq_loc_st	WSOP-SGOP	0b		
INQUIRE STROKE DEVICE STATE	GQSKS	gq_srk_st	WSOP-SGOP	0b		
INQUIRE VALUATOR DEVICE STATE	GQVLS	gq_val_st	WSOP-SGOP	0b		
INQUIRE CHOICE DEVICE STATE	GQCHS	gq_chc_st	WSOP-SGOP	0b		
INQUIRE PICK DEVICE STATE	GQPKS	gq_pck_st	WSOP-SGOP	1b		
INQUIRE STRING DEVICE STATE	GQSTS(S)	gq_str_st	GKOP-SGOP	0b		
INQUIRE WORKSTATION CATEGORY	GQWKCA	gqw_cat	GKOP-SGOP	0b		
INQUIRE WORKSTATION CLASSIFICATION	GQWKCL	gqw_class	GKOP-SGOP	0a		
INQUIRE MAXIMUM DISPLAY SURFACE SIZE	GQDSP	gqmax_dsp	GKOP-SGOP	0a		wkwn.for,dsurf.*
INQUIRE DYNAMIC MODIF. OF WS ATTRIBUTES	GQDWKA	gqw_dmod	GKOP-SGOP	1a		
INQUIRE DEFAULT DEFERRAL STATE VALUE	GQDDS	gq_defer	GKOP-SGOP	1a		
INQUIRE POLYLINE FACILITIES	GQPLF	gql_facil	GKOP-SGOP	0a		
INQUIRE PREDEFINED POLYLINE REPR.	GQPPLR	gql_prep	GKOP-SGOP	0a		
INQUIRE POLYMARKER FACILITIES	GQPMF	gqm_facil	GKOP-SGOP	0a		
INQUIRE PREDEFINED POLYMARKER REPR.	GQPPMR	gqm_prep	GKOP-SGOP	0a		
INQUIRE TEXT FACILITIES	GQTXF	gqt_facil	GKOP-SGOP	0a		
INQUIRE PREDEFINED TEXT REPR.	GQPTXR	gqt_prep	GKOP-SGOP	0a		
INQUIRE FILL AREA FACILITIES	GQFAF	gqf_facil	GKOP-SGOP	0a		
INQUIRE PREDEFINED FILL AREA REPR.	GQPFAR	gqf_prep	GKOP-SGOP	0a		
INQUIRE PATTERN FACILITIES	GQPAF	gqp_facil	GKOP-SGOP	0a		
INQUIRE PREDEFINED PATTERN REPR.	GQPPAR	gqp_prep	GKOP-SGOP	0a		
INQUIRE COLOUR FACILITIES	GQCF	gqcl_facil	GKOP-SGOP	0a	5.5	
INQUIRE PREDEFINED COLOUR REPR.	GQPCR	gqcl_prep	GKOP-SGOP	0a	5.5	
INQUIRE LIST OF AVAILABLE GDP	GQEGDP	gq_gdp_lst	GKOP-SGOP	0a		
INQUIRE GENERALIZED DRAWING PRIMITIVE	GQGDP	gq_gdp	GKOP-SGOP	0a		
INQUIRE MAX. LENGTH OF WS STATE TABLE	GQLWK	gq_tables	GKOP-SGOP	1a		
INQUIRE NO. OF SEGMENT PRIORITIES SUPP.	GQSGP	gq_nprior	GKOP-SGOP	1a		
INQUIRE DYNAMIC MODE OF SEGMENT ATTR.	GQDSGA	gqdyn_seg	GKOP-SGOP	1a		
INQUIRE NO. OF AVAILABLE INPUT DEVICE	GQLI	gq_ninput	GKOP-SGOP	0b		
INQUIRE DEFAULT LOCATOR DEVICE DATA	GQDLC	gqloc_data	GKOP-SGOP	0b		
INQUIRE DEFAULT STROKE DEVICE DATA	GQDSK	gqsrk_data	GKOP-SGOP	0b		
INQUIRE DEFAULT VALUATOR DEVICE DATA	GQDVL	gqval_data	GKOP-SGOP	0b		
INQUIRE DEFAULT CHOICE DEVICE DATA	GQDCH	gqchc_data	GKOP-SGOP	0b		
INQUIRE DEFAULT PICK DEVICE DATA	GQDPK	gqpck_data	GKOP-SGOP	1b		
INQUIRE DEFAULT STRING DEVICE DATA	GQDST	gqstr_data	GKOP-SGOP	0b		
INQUIRE SET OF ASSOCIATED WORKSTATIONS	GQASWK	gqsg_wks	WSOP-SGOP	1a *		
INQUIRE SEGMENT ATTRIBUTES	GQSGA	gqsg_attr	WSOP-SGOP	1a		
INQUIRE PIXEL ARRAY DIMENSIONS	GQPXAD	gqpx_dim	WSOP-SGOP	0a		
INQUIRE PIXEL ARRAY	GQPXA	gqpx_array	WSOP-SGOP	0a		
INQUIRE PIXEL	GQPX	gqpixel	WSOP-SGOP	0a		
INQUIRE INPUT QUEUE OVERFLOW	GQIQOV	ginq_in_que_overf+	WSOP-SGOP	0c		
UTILITY FUNCTIONS						
EVALUATE TRANSFORMATION MATRIX	GEVTM	gev_stran	GKOP-SGOP	1a	6.3	segshift.for,rectrot.c
ACCUMULATE TRANSFORMATION MATRIX	GACTM	gac_stran	GKOP-SGOP	1a	6.3	segacc.for,clock.c
PACK DATA RECORD	GPREC(S)	gpack_rec	GKCL-SGOP	0a	App.C	loc.for,cell.c
UNPACK DATA RECORD	GUREC(S)	gupack_rec	GKCL-SGOP	0a	App.C	
ERROR HANDLING FUNCTIONS						
EMERGENCY CLOSE GKS	GECLKS	gecls_gks	GKCL-SGOP	0a	9.2	
ERROR HANDLING	GERHND	gerr_hnd	GKCL-SGOP	0a		
ERROR LOGGING	GERLOG	gerr_log	GKCL-SGOP	0a		

Appendix C
 PACKING AND UNPACKING
DATA RECORDS

There are currently two GKS functions defined exclusively in the FORTRAN language shell: PACK DATA RECORD and UNPACK DATA RECORD. These functions, described in the following, support the preparation and use of parameters of the type *data record*.

PACK DATA RECORD

subroutine GPREC(IL,IA,RL,RA,SL,LSTR,STR,
                       MLDR,ERRIND,LDR,DATREC)

Input:

    integer IL

C   Number of integer values

    integer IA(*)

C   Array of integer values

    integer RL

C   Number of real values

    real RA(*)

C   Array of real values

    integer SL

C   Number of character strings

    integer LSTR(*)

C   Array of lengths of each character string

    character*(*) STR(*)

C   Array of character strings

    integer MLDR

C   Maximum length of the data record into which all these data are to be packed

Output:

    integer ERRIND

C   Error indicator

```
            integer LDR
C                           Number of 80-character entries in the data record
            character*80 DATREC(MLDR)
C                           Data record
```

Here, the data given in fields IA, RA, and STR are packed together in DATREC so that this field can be used as a parameter of the type data record in GKS functions like WRITE ITEM TO GKSM or INITIALIZE LOCATOR. LDR contains the number of DATREC elements used. For the FORTRAN subset language binding, the type STR(*) is changed to character*80 STR(*).

UNPACK DATA RECORD

subroutine GUREC(LDR,DATREC,IIL,IRL,ISL,ERRIND,
                            IL,IA,RL,RA,SL,LSTR,STR)

Input:
```
            integer LDR
C                           Length of data record (in 80-character blocks)
            character*80 DATREC(LDR)
C                           Data record
            integer IIL
C                           dimension of the integer array IA
            integer IRL
C                           dimension of the real array RA
            integer ISL
C                           dimension of the character array STR
                            and the length array LSTR
```

Output:
```
            integer ERRIND
C                           Error indicator
            integer IL
C                           Number of integer values placed in array IA
            integer IA(IIL)
C                           integer array
            integer RL
C                           Number of real values placed in array RA
            real RL(IRL)
C                           real array
            integer SL
C                           Number of character strings placed in array STR
```

        integer LSTR(ISL)
C   Array of lengths of each character string in STR
        character*(*) STR(ISL)
C   Array of character strings

Here the data record is unpacked so that the arrays IA, RA, and STR receive the integer, real, and character values contained in the data record. Thus, UNPACK DATA RECORD can be considered as the inverse of PACK DATA RECORD.

Appendix D
□ □ ■ MAPPING THE CALCOMP
■ INTERFACE ONTO GKS

```
            subroutine    PLOTS (IBUF,NLOC,LDEV)
            integer       IBUF(NLOC), NLOC, LDEV
C
C Goal:
C       previously:       -initializing the plotter
C                         -preparing the buffer area
C       now:              -initializing /CALGKS/
C
C Parameters:
C       IBUF, NLOC:       Buffer area to be used for interim
C                         storage of previously-coded plotter
C                         commands. It is now ignored because our
C                         implementation does not need to use it.
C       LDEV:             Corresponds to CONID (connection ID) in
C                         GKS.
C
            integer       ERRFIL, WKTYPE, CONID, PLIND, IND
            real          XMIN, XMAX, YMIN, YMAX, FACT, X(100), Y(100)
            logical       CLOSED
            common        /CALGKS/ ERRFIL, WKTYPE, CONID, PLIND, IND
            common        /CALGKS/ XMIN, XMAX, YMIN, YMAX, FACT, X, Y
            common        /CALGKS/ CLOSED
C
            CONID         = LDEV
            PLIND         = 1
            ND            = 1
            X(1)          = 0.0
            Y(1)          = 0.0
            FACT          = 1.0
            CLOSED        = .true.
            return
            end
```

```
          subroutine     CALSWN    (XMINEW,XMANEW,YMINEW, YMANEW)
          real                     XMINEW,XMANEW,YMINEW,YMANEW,
C
C Goal:                   Change workstation window
C                         Operation is carried out only if WK is closed!
C
C Parameters:
C        XMINEW,...,XMANEW: new window borders
C
          integer        ERRFIL, WKTYPE, CONID, PLIND, IND
          real           XMIN, XMAX, YMIN, YMAX, FACT, X(100), Y(100)
          logical        CLOSED
          common         /CALGKS/ ERRFIL, WKTYPE, CONID, PLIND, IND
          common         /CALGKS/ XMIN, XMAX, YMIN, YMAX, FACT, X, Y
          common         /CALGKS/ CLOSED
C
          if (CLOSED) then
          XMIN    =    XMINEW
          XMAX    =    XMANEW
          YMIN    =    YMINEW
          YMAX    =    YMANEW
          else
                write (ERRFIL,1000)
1000            format('CALSWN: GKS in wrong state.')
          endif
          return
          end

          subroutine     PLOT (XP,YP,IPEN)
          real           XP,YP
          integer        IPEN
C
C Goal:
C        previously:          move the drawing pen to position (XP,YP).
C        now:                 interim storage of (XP,YP) and call GPL
C                             if the buffer is full (max 100 points).
C
C Parameters:
C        XP,YP: coordinates of the point to which a line
C                             should be drawn.
C        IPEN:                controls pen movement:
C                             = 2   ==> pen down (visible line)
C                             = 3   ==> pen up (invisible line)
```

```
C                              = −2 or −3 ==> like 2 and 3 but (XP,YP)
C                                         becomes the new origin
C                              = 999    ==> like −3 but (XP,YP) is the last
C                                         point of the drawing
C                                         (this ends the drawing).
C

      integer          ERRFIL, WKTYPE, CONID, PLIND, IND
      real             XMIN, XMAX, YMIN, YMAX, FACT, X(100), Y(100)
      logical          CLOSED
      common           /CALGKS/ ERRFIL, WKTYPE, CONID, PLIND, IND
      common           /CALGKS/ XMIN, XMAX, YMIN, YMAX, FACT, X, Y
      common           /CALGKS/ CLOSED
C
      real             YTOX, XNK, YNK
      integer          IPABS
C          BUFSIZ should be set according to the needs of
C                        the installation.
      integer          BUFSIZ
      data             BUFSIZ /64/
C
C      if(CLOSED) then
C                     .      open and activate GKS
      call GOPKS (ERRFIL,BUFSIZ)
      call GOPWK (1,CONID,WKTYPE)
      call GACWK (1)
C                     initialize NT and WT
      call GSELNT(1)
      call GSWN(1,XMIN/FACT,XMAX/FACT,YMIN/FACT,YMAX/FACT)
      YTOX = (YMAX−YMIN)/(XMAX−XMIN)
      XNK = AMIN1 (1.0, 1.0/YTOX)
      YNK = AMIN1 (1.0, YTOX)
      call GSVP (1,0.0,XNK,0.0,YNK)
      call GSWKWN (1,0.0,XNK,0.0,YNK)
      CLOSED = .false.
      endif
C
      IPABS = IABS(IPEN)
C
      if (IPABS .eq.2) then
C                          visible line
          IND = IND + 1
          X(IND) = XP
          Y(IND) = YP
          if((IND.eq.100) .or. (IPEN.It.0)) then
```

```
C                              buffer full or new origin:
C                              empty and begin new polyline
                 call GPL (IND,X,Y)
                 X(1) = XP
                 Y(1) = YP
                 IND = 1
            endif
       elseif ((IPABS.eq.3) .or. (IPABS.eq.999)) then
C                              invisible line
            if (IND .gt. 1) then
C                              output buffered polyline
                 call GPL (IND,X,Y)
            endif
C                              begin new polyline with (XP,YP)
            X(1) = XP
            Y(1) = YP
            IND = 1
       else
            write(ERRFIL,1000) IPEN
1000        format('PLOT:'I7,'is invalid IPEN parameter')
            return
       endif
C
       if(IPEN.It.0) then
C                              new origin-> shift window
            XMIN = XMIN−XP
            MAX = XMAX−XP
            YMIN = YMIN−YP
            YMAX = YMAX−YP
            call GWSN(1,XMIN/FACT,XMAX/FACT,YMIN/FACT,YMAX/FACT)
            X(1) = 0.0
            Y(1) = 0.0
            IND = 1
       endif
C
       if(IPEN.eq. 999) then
C                              drawing finished -> close WK and GKS
            call GDAWK (1)
            call GCLWK (1)
            call GCLKS
            CLOSED = .true.
       endif
```

```
C
        return
        end

        subroutine      NEWPEN (INP)
        integer         INP
C
C Goal:
C       previously:             change drawing pen
C       now:                    change polyline index
C
C Input:
C       INP: new PLIND
C
        integer         ERRFIL, WKTYPE, CONID, PLIND, IND
        read            XMIN, XMAX, YMIN, YMAX, FACT, X(100), Y(100)
        logical         CLOSED
        common          /CALGKS/ ERRFIL, WKTYPE, CONID, PLIND, IND
        common          /CALGKS/ XMIN, XMAX, YMIN, YMAX, FACT, X, Y
        common          /CALGKS/ CLOSED
C
        if (IND .gt.1) then
C                               close polyline with old window
                call GPL (IND,X,Y)
                X(1) = X(IND)
                Y(1) = Y(IND)
                IND = 1
        endif
        PLIND = IND
        call GSPLI (PLIND)
        return
        end

        subroutine      FACTOR (FACNEW)
        real            FACNEW
C
C Goal:
C       previously:             reset scale factor
C       now:                    update WC window
C
C Input:
C       FACNEW: new scale factor
```

```
C
         integer         ERRFIL, WKTYPE, CONID, PLIND, IND
         real            XMIN, XMAX, YMIN, YMAX, FACT, X(100), Y(100)
         logical         CLOSED
         common          /CALGKS/ ERRFIL, WKTYPE, CONID, PLIND, IND
         common          /CALGKS/ XMIN, XMAX, YMIN, YMAX, FACT, X, Y
         common          /CALGKS/ CLOSED
C
         if (IND .gt. 1) then
C                                      close polyline with old index
             call GPL (IND,X,Y)
             X(1) = X(IND)
             Y(1) = Y(IND)
             IND = 1
         endif
         FACT = FACNEW
         call GSWN(1,XMIN/FACT,XMAX/FACT,YMIN/FACT,YMAX/FACT)
         return
         end

         subroutine      WHERE (XP,YP,FACTP)
         real            XP,YP,FACTP
C
C Goal: Return current drawing pen position and scale factor
C
C Output:
C        XP, YP: current drawing pen position in WC
C        FACTP: current scale factor
C
         integer         ERRFIL, WKTYPE, CONID, PLIND, IND
         real            XMIN, XMAX, YMIN, YMAX, FACT, X(100), Y(100)
         logical         CLOSED
         common          /CALGKS/ ERRFIL, WKTYPE, CONID, PLIND, IND
         common          /CALGKS/ XMIN, XMAX, YMIN, YMAX, FACT, X, Y
         common          /CALGKS/ CLOSED
C
         XP              = X(IND)
         YP              = Y(IND)
         FACTP           = FACT
         return
         end
```

Appendix E
# GKS FORTRAN PROGRAMMING
EXAMPLES FOR THE IBM PC/AT

E.1   Device Environment

E.1.1   Recommended Hardware

The following hardware was used to check out the examples and produce the pictures. Other combinations of computer and display hardware may work as well. For example, the math co-processor is highly recommended because GKS uses a floating point world coordinate system. Furthermore, GSS does support many other graphics display devices. Contact them for the latest details regarding supported devices.

- IBM-compatible Personal Computer AT with 512 kbytes of RAM.
- 1 floppy disk drive with 360 kbytes capacity.
- 1 hard disk drive with at least 10 Mbytes capacity.
- EGA-compatible graphics card.
- Math co-processor.
- Microsoft Mouse.

E.1.2   Recommended Software

The following software was used to check out the examples and produce the pictures. Other combinations of IBM and GSS software may work as well. In addition, GSS does support other combinations of FORTRAN compilers and linkers. Contact them for the latest details regarding supported environments.

- Graphic Software Systems Graphical Kernel System (GSS*GKS Version 2.10 or later), which uses the GSS*CGI Virtual Device Interface software.
- GSS*CGI Device Driver for the IBM Extended Graphics Adaptor (IBMEGA.SYS).

- GSS*CGI Device Driver for the Microsoft Mouse (MSMOUSE.SYS).
- Microsoft Personal Computer Disk Operating System (MS-DOS) Version 2.1 or later.
- Microsoft Personal Computer Linker Version 5.01.02 or appropriate substitute (e.g., MS-Linker Version 3.61).
- Microsoft FORTRAN Version 4.1 or later.
- Microsoft Mouse Device Driver Version 6.0 or appropriate substitute.

E.1.3 Comments

- Microsoft Version 4.0 FORTRAN cannot be used, due to a bug in that version of the product.
- Differences between what you see in this book and what you see on your display are to be expected if you use different hardware and software.
- In all the examples, it is assumed that the initial values of the aspect source flags are set to INDIVIDUAL.
- For a rigorous GKS program seeking maximum portability, each 'read(5,*)' should be replaced by 'call GRQST (...)'.
- For clarity and to keep the examples self-contained, the use of previously-defined subroutines has been avoided in the introductory programs (Chapters 3, 4 and 5).
- The example programs are terminated by pressing the RETURN or ENTER key after you have finished viewing the picture on the display.
- The names of the program examples do not necessarily agree with the corresponding file names.
- The use of 'common/gracom/size,intary' is specific to the GSS*GKS and IBM GKS implementations.
- The color descriptions used are specific to the EGA device.

Your AUTOEXEC.BAT file should contain at least:

- SET KERNEL=<path to a subdirectory where your KERNEL.SYS file will reside.>

Your CONFIG.SYS file should contain at least:

- device=[path]IBMEGA.SYS
- device=[path]GSSCGI.SYS
- files=20
- buffers=16

if possible, in that order.

E.2   Use of the Microsoft Fortran Compiler

Compile your PROG.FOR program by typing

> [path]FL /AL /FPc87 /c prog.for

at the command line. Refer to your Microsoft C Compiler manual to find the appropriate options for your program.

E.3   Use of the Microsoft Linker

There are two possibilities:

1. type LINK;
   input the files requested;
   %%this procedure is awkward with frequent use%%
2. create a .BAT file with changeable parameters;
   start the .BAT file with the desired program name and parameters.

For example, the TEST.OBJ program compiled with MSFOR should be connected to the subroutine SUB.OBJ and the required GKS and FORTRAN libraries; the result should be filed under TEST.EXE, and a listing should be created under the name TEXT.MAP. (In the following, [path] stands for the respective path entries.)
Creating L.BAT:

> [path]LINK [path]MFGKS %1 %2 /SEG:1024,%1,%1,[path]MFGKS
> > [path]FORTRAN [path]LLIBFOR7 [path]MSGKS /STACK:5000/NOD

(must be written on one line)

MFGKS.OBJ	: GKS error handler for Microsoft FORTRAN,
MFGKS.LIB	: GKS language binding for Microsoft FORTRAN 4.1
FORTRAN.LIB	: MS-FORTRAN 4.1 runtime library,
LLIBFOR7.LIB	: MS-FORTRAN 4.1 library,
MSGKS.LIB	: GKS library for MS-FORTRAN 4.1

To link, type:

> L [path]TEST [path]SUB

If you want to link the example programs you have to type:

> L [path]<prog>
> or
> L [path]<prog> [path]DSURF

where <prog> is the name of the FORTRAN program taken from the table below. (See the comments in the header of the program listing to determine whether you need to link with the subroutine DSURF.)

Index of GKS FORTRAN Programs on the IBM PC/AT

The headers of these files contain references to the chapters of the book where the functions illustrated by the programs are explained.

Include Files

The FORTRAN programs share several include files and subroutine DSURF, which are listed following the listing of program E.35.

```
c*****************************************************************
c* E.1 SPIRAL : Drawing a Polyline whose Control Points lie on a *
c*                Spiral Curve                                   *
c*****************************************************************
c* Refers to chapter : 3.1                                      *
c* Used external subroutines :                                  *
c*****************************************************************
c
          program spiral
c
          integer*4 size,intary(12500)
          integer*2 gerrnr, gfctid
c
          common /gracom/size,intary
          common /gercom/gerrnr, gfctid
c
$INCLUDE:'gdefines.def'
$INCLUDE:'devices.def'
c
          integer unit1

          real xdc, ydc, xndc, yndc
          real x(100),y(100),s,t
          integer i
c
$INCLUDE:'gdefines.dat'
$INCLUDE:'devices.dat'
c
          data unit1 /14/
c
          size = 12500
          open (unit1,file='errors.lst',status='new')

c*===============================================================
c
c *** OPEN GKS
c
          call GOPKS (unit1, 1024)
c
c *** OPEN WORKSTATION
c
          call GOPWK (crtdev, 0, crtdev)
c
c *** ACTIVATE WORKSTATION
c
          call GACWK (crtdev)
c
c *** SET NORMALIZATION TRANSFORMATION
c
          call GSWN (1,-1.5,1.5,-1.5,1.5)
          call GSVP (1,0.0,1.0,0.0,1.0)
c
          call GSELNT (1)
c
c *** Initialize Control Points
c
          do 100 i=1,100
          t = 0.2 * (i-1)
          s = t / 20.0
          x(i) = s * cos(t)
          y(i) = s * sin(t)
  100     continue
c
```

```
c
c *** DRAW POLYLINE
c
            call GPL (100,x,y)
c
c *** DEACTIVATE WORKSTATION
c
            call GDAWK (crtdev)
c
c *** Wait for Input
c
            read (5,*)
c
c *** CLOSE WORKSTATION
c
            call GCLWK (crtdev)
c
c *** CLOSE GKS
c
            call GCLKS
            close (unit1)
c
            end
```

See Plate 9(a).

```
c*******************************************************************
c* E.2 SPIRAL3 : Drawing three different Spirals using the      *
c*               Polyline Output Primitive                      *
c*******************************************************************
c* Refers to chapter : 3.2                                      *
c* Used external subroutines :                                  *
c*******************************************************************
      program spiral3
c
      integer*4 size,intary
      integer*2 gerrnr, gfctid
c
      common /gracom/size,intary
      common /gercom/gerrnr, gfctid
c
$INCLUDE:'gdefines.def'
$INCLUDE:'devices.def'
c
      real x(100),y(100),s,t
      integer i,j
      integer unit1
      data unit1 /14/
c
$INCLUDE:'gdefines.dat'
$INCLUDE:'devices.dat'
c
      size = 12500
c
      open (unit1,file='errors.lst',status='new')
c
c*=================================================================
c
      call GOPKS (unit1, size)
      call GOPWK (crtdev, 0, crtdev)
      call GACWK (crtdev)
c
      call GSWN (1,-1.5,1.5,-1.5,1.5)
      call GSVP (1,0.0,1.0,0.0,1.0)
c
      call GSELNT (1)
c
c
c *** Initialize Control Points
c
      do 100 i=1,100
          t = 0.2 * (i-1)
          s = t / 20.0
          x(i) = s * cos(t)
          y(i) = s * sin(t)
 100  continue
c
c
      do 200 i = 1,3
c
c    *** SET POLYLINE TYPE
c
          call GSLN (i)
c
c       **+ Draw Polyline
c
          call GPL (100,x,y)
c
          if (i.ne.3) then
```

```
c
c               *** Shift Spiral down
c
               do 180 j = 1,100
                  y(j) = y(j) - 0.1
 180           continue
c
          endif
 200  continue
c
      call GDAWK (crtdev)
c
      read (5,*)
c
      call GCLWK (crtdev)
c
c *** Close GKS
c
      call GCLKS
      close (unit1)
c
      end
```

See Plate 9(b).

```
c*****************************************************************
c* E.3 COORD : Displaying an Object (Roe) from the "World Coordi-*
c*              nate System " into the "Normalized Coordinate    *
c*              System" by a Normalization Transformation        *
c*****************************************************************
c* Refers to chapter : 3.3                                       *
c* Used external subroutines :                                   *
c*****************************************************************
          program coord
c
          integer*4 size,intary(12500)
          integer*2 gerrnr, gfctid
c
          common /gracom/size,intary
          common /gercom/gerrnr, gfctid
c
$INCLUDE:'gdefines.def'
$INCLUDE:'devices.def'
$INCLUDE:'hatch.def'
$INCLUDE:'roe.def'
c
          integer unit1
          real xcoord(3), ycoord(3)
c
$INCLUDE:'gdefines.dat'
$INCLUDE:'devices.dat'
$INCLUDE:'hatch.dat'
$INCLUDE:'roe.dat'
c
          data unit1 /14/
          data xcoord /  0.0, 0.0, 200.0/
          data ycoord / 200.0, 0.0,  0.0/
c
          size = 12500
c
          open (unit1,file='errors.lst',status='new')
c
c*===============================================================
c
          call GOPKS (unit1, 1024)
          call GOPWK (crtdev, 0, crtdev)
          call GACWK (crtdev)
c
c *** SET NORMALIZATION TRANSFORMATION
c
c          ** SET WORKSTATION WINDOW (WORLD COORDINATES)
c
          call GSWN (1,0.0,200.0,0.0,200.0)
c
c          ** SET WORKSTATION VIEWPORT (NORMALIZED COORDINATES)
c
          call GSVP (1,0.0,1.0,0.0,1.0)
c
c          ** SELECT NORMALIZATION TRANSFORMATION
c
          call GSELNT (1)
c
c
c *** Drawing the two Coordinate Axes
c
          call GSLN (gldot)
          call GPL (3,xcoord,ycoord)
c
```

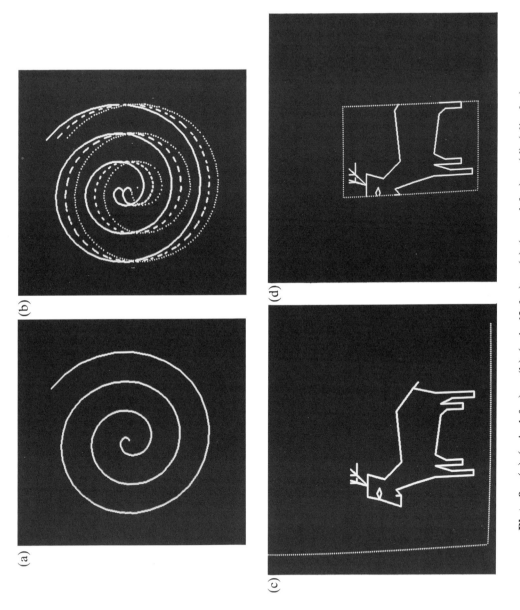

Plate 9 (a) (spiral.for); (b) (spiral3.for); (c) (coord.for); (d) (clip.for)

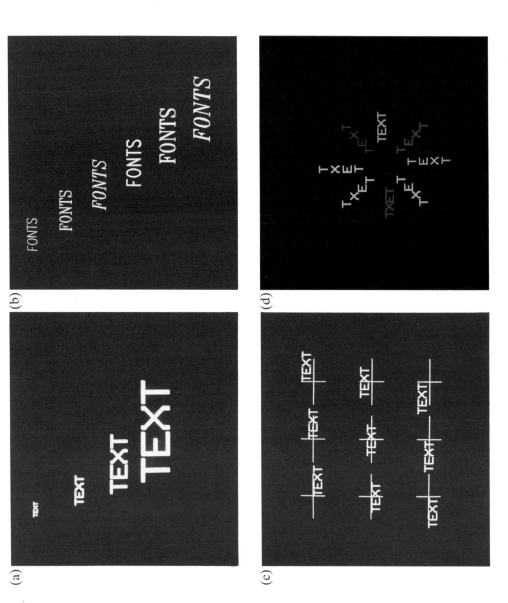

Plate 10 (a) (txthght.for); (b) (txtfonts.for); (c) (txtalign.for); (d) (txtcolup.for)

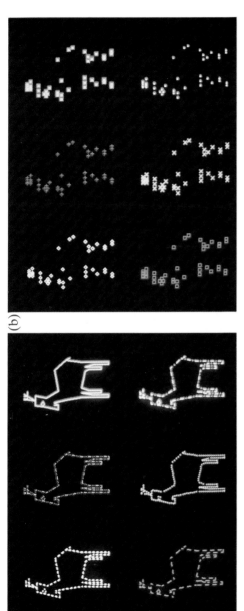

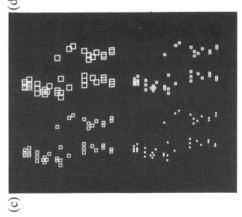

Plate 11 (a) (lines.for); (b) (marker.for); (c) (markwid.for); (d) (areas.for)

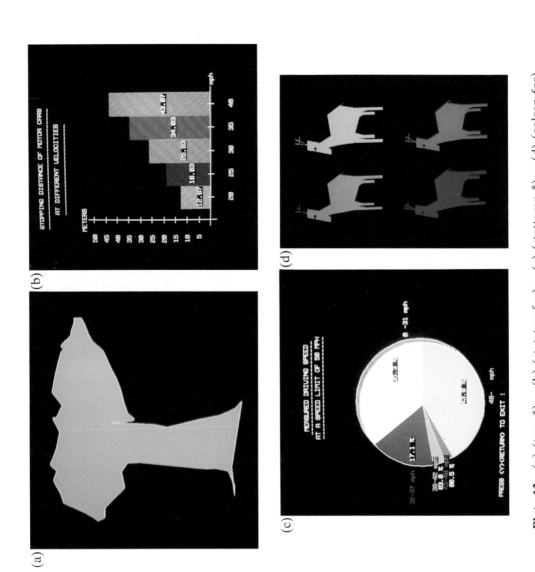

Plate 12 (a) (tree.*);   (b) (statstop.for);   (c) (stattemp.*);   (d) (colrep.for)

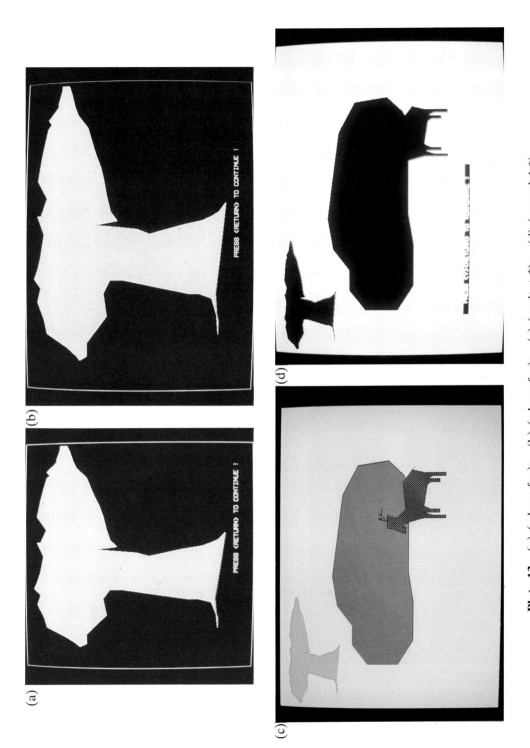

Plate 13 (a) (wkwn.for); (b) (wkwn.for); (c) (multnt.*); (d) (segcrdel.*)

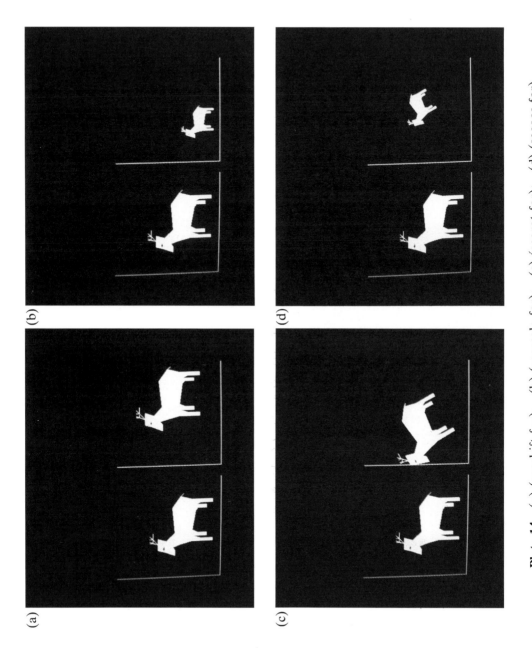

(a)

(b)

(c)

(d)

Plate 14 (a) (segshift.for); (b) (segscale.for); (c) (segrot.for); (d) (segacc.for)

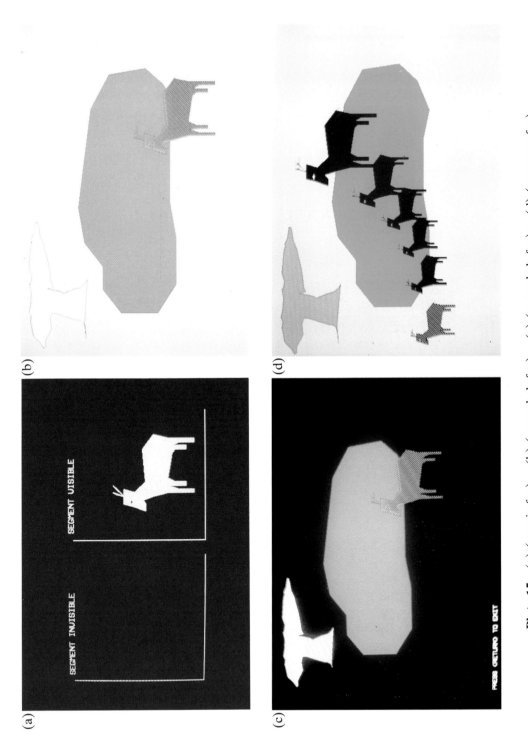

(a) SEGMENT INVISIBLE   SEGMENT VISIBLE

(b)

(c) PRESS <RETURN> TO EXIT

(d)

Plate 15 (a) (segvis.for); (b) (segredwk.for); (c) (segredwk.for); (d) (segassoc.for).

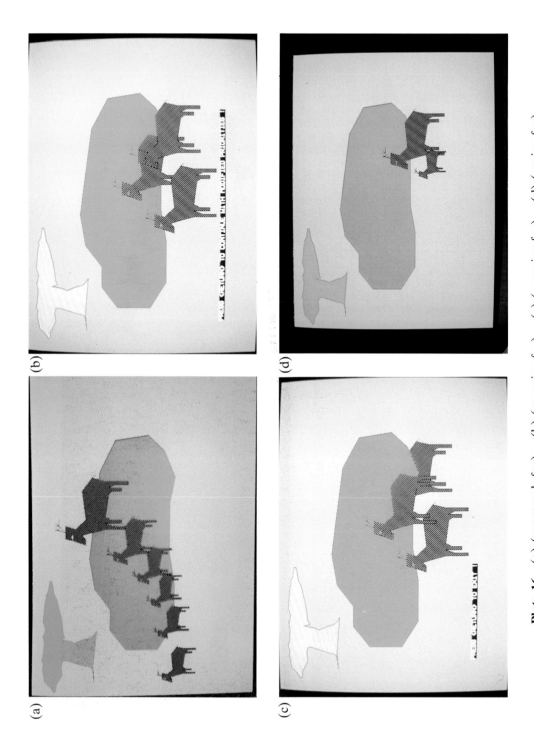

Plate 16 (a) (segcopwk.for); (b) (segprior.for); (c) (segprior.for); (d) (segins.for)

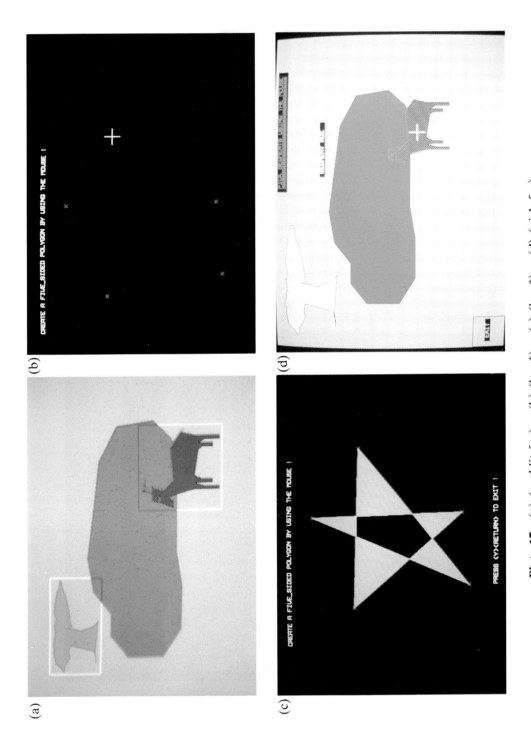

(a) (b) (c) (d)

Plate 17 (a) (seghlit.for); (b) (loc.*); (c) (loc.*); (d) (pick.for)

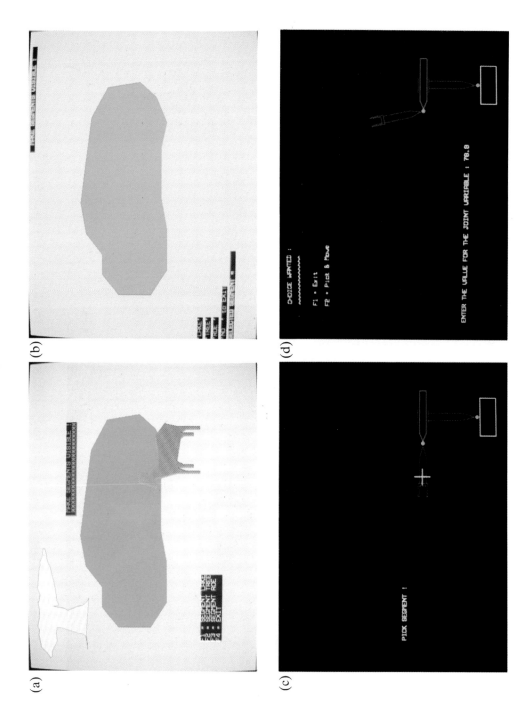

Plate 18 (a) (choice.for); (b) (string.for); (c) (robot.for); (d) (robot.for)

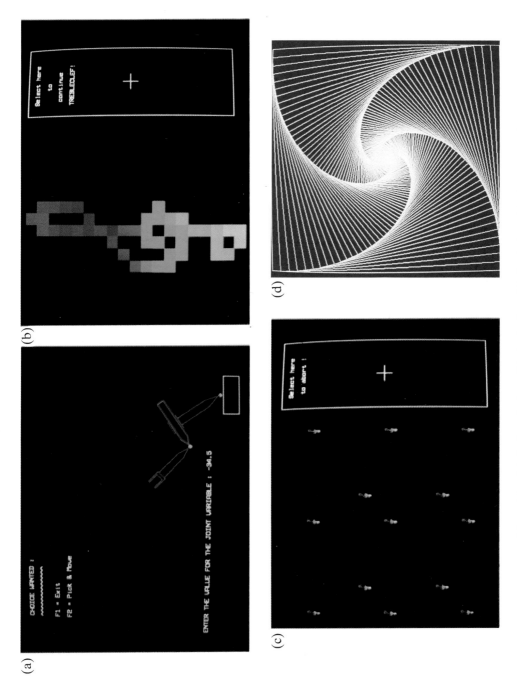

Plate 19 (a) (robot.for); (b) (cell.c); (c) (cell.c); (d) (rectrot.for)

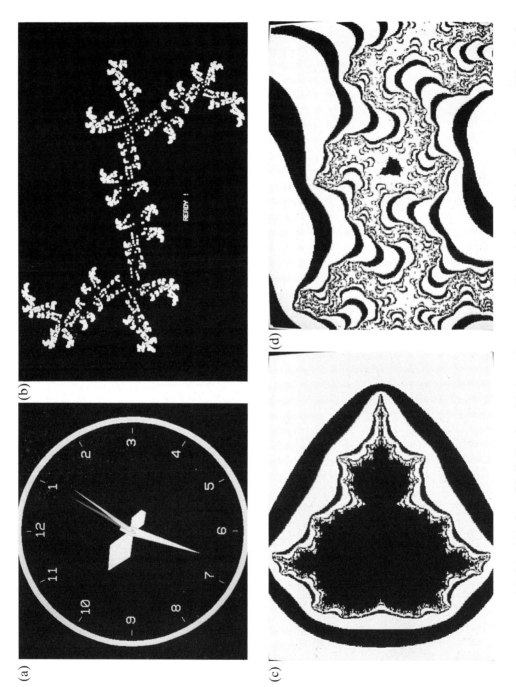

Plate 20 (a) (clock.for); (b) (julia.c); (c) (mandbrot.c,mandlbro.dat); (d) (mandbrot.c,mand2bro.dat)

```
c *** Create Object "Roe"
c
          call GSLN (glsoli)
          call GPL (53,xroe,yroe)
c
          call GDAWK (crtdev)
c
          read (5,*)
c
          call GCLWK (crtdev)
          call GCLKS
          close (unit1)
c
          end
```

See Plate 9(c).

```
c********************************************************************
c* E.4 CLIP : Clipping an Object (roe) at the Viewport           *
c*                (in the Normalized Coordinate System)          *
c********************************************************************
c* Refers to chapter : 3.3                                       *
c* Used external subroutines :                                   *
c********************************************************************
c
      program clip
c
      integer*4 size,intary(12500)
      integer*2 gerrnr, gfctid
c
      common /gracom/size,intary
      common /gercom/gerrnr, gfctid
c
$INCLUDE:'gdefines.def'
$INCLUDE:'devices.def'
$INCLUDE:'roe.def'
c
      real xcoord(5), ycoord(5)
      integer unit1
      data unit1 /14/
c
$INCLUDE:'gdefines.dat'
$INCLUDE:'devices.dat'
$INCLUDE:'roe.dat'
c
      data xcoord / 50.0, 50.0, 130.0, 130.0, 50.0/
      data ycoord / 130.0, 10.0, 10.0, 130.0, 130.0/
c
      size = 12500
c
      open (unit1,file='errors.lst',status='new')
c
c*==================================================================
c
      call GOPKS (unit1, size)
      call GOPWK (crtdev, 0, crtdev)
      call GACWK (crtdev)
c
      call GSWN (1,50.0,130.0,10.0,130.0)
      call GSVP (1,0.25,0.65,0.05,0.65)
      call GSELNT (1)
c
c *** Drawing a Frame around the Window
c
      call GSLN (gldot)
      call GPL (5,xcoord,ycoord)
c
c
c *** SET THE CLIPPING INDICATOR TO "CLIP"
c
      call GSCLIP (gclip)
c
c *** Create the Object "Roe"
c
      call GSLN (glsoli)
      call GPL (53,xroe,yroe)
c
c
      call GDAWK (crtdev)
c
```

```
      read (5,*)
c
      call GCLWK (crtdev)
      call GCLKS
      close (unit1)
c
      end
```

See Plate 9(d).

```
C************************************************************AAAAAA
c* E.5 TXTHGHT : Drawing a word ("Text") four times with      *
c*                   different Character Heights               *
C****************************************************************
c* Refers to chapter : 5.1.5                                   *
c* Used external subroutines :                                 *
C****************************************************************
          program txthght
c
          integer*4 size,intary(12500)
          integer*2 gerrnr, gfctid
c
          common /gracom/size,intary
          common /gercom/gerrnr, gfctid
c
$INCLUDE:'devices.def'
c
          integer unit1
          real px, py, r
c
$INCLUDE:'devices.dat'
c
          data unit1 /14/
c
          size = 12500
c
          open (unit1,file='errors.lst',status='new')
          call GOPKS (unit1, 1024)
          call GOPWK (crtdev, 0, crtdev)
          call GACWK (crtdev)
c
          call GSWN. (1,0.0,100.0,0.0,100.0)
          call GSVP (1,0.0,1.0,0.0,1.0)
          call GSELNT (1)
c
c *** Initialize Start Coordinates
c
          px = 10.0
          py = 90.0
          r  = 0.0
c
          do 100 i = 2,5
            r = i*1.0 + r
c
c            *** SET CHARACTER HEIGHT
c
            call GSCHH (r)
c
c            *** DISPLAY TEXT
c
            call GTX (px,py,'TEXT')
c
            px = px + 5.0
            py = py - 20.0
 100      continue
c
          call GDAWK (crtdev)
          read (5,*)
          call GCLWK (crtdev)
          call GCLKS
          close (unit1)
c
          end
```

See Plate 10(a).

```
c****************************************************************
c* E.6 TXTFONTS : Depicting some Text Fonts using the          *
c*                "Set Text Font And Precision" Function        *
c****************************************************************
c* Refers to chapter : 5.1.5                                    *
c* Used external subroutines :                                  *
c****************************************************************
          program txtfonts
c
          integer*4 size,intary(12500)
          integer*2 gerrnr, gfctid
c
          common /gracom/size,intary
          common /gercom/gerrnr, gfctid
c
$INCLUDE:'devices.def'
$INCLUDE:'gdefines.def'
c
          integer unit1
          real px(6), py(6)
c
$INCLUDE:'devices.dat'
$INCLUDE:'gdefines.dat'
c
          data unit1 /14/
c
          data px /10, 20, 30, 40, 50, 60/
          data py /90, 75, 60, 45, 30, 15/
c
          size = 12500
c
          open (unit1,file='errors.lst',status='new')
c
c*================================================================
c
          call GOPKS (unit1, 1024)
          call GOPWK (crtdev, 0, crtdev)
          call GACWK (crtdev)
c
          call GSWN (1,0.0,100.0,0.0,100.0)
          call GSVP (1,0.0,1.0,0.0,1.0)
c
          call GSELNT (1)
c
          do 100 i = 1,6
c
c            ** Set Character Height
c
             call GSCHH (4.0+(i*0.5))
c
c            *** SET TEXT FONT AND PRECISION (Fonts:-101..-106,
c                                            Precision: Stroke)
             call GSTXFP (-100-i,gstrkp)
c
c            *** DISPLAY TEXT
c
             call GTX (px(i),py(i),'FONTS')
c
  100     continue
c
c
          call GDAWK (crtdev)
c
```

```
          read (5,*)
c
          call GCLWK (crtdev)
          call GCLKS
          close (unit1)
c
          end
```

See Plate 10(b).

```
c*******************************************************************
c* E.7 TXTALIGN : Depicting a word ("Text") with different      *
c*                Text Alignments without changing the Character *
c*                Height and Character Up Vector                 *
c*******************************************************************
c* Refers to chapter : 5.1.5                                    *
c* Used external subroutines :                                  *
c*******************************************************************
      program txtalign
c
      integer*4 size,intary(12500)
      integer*2 gerrnr, gfctid
c
      common /gracom/size,intary
      common /gercom/gerrnr, gfctid
c
$INCLUDE:'gdefines.def'
$INCLUDE:'devices.def'
c
      real px, py, lhx(2), lhy(2), lvx(2), lvy(2)
      integer i, j, k(3)
      integer unit1
c
$INCLUDE:'gdefines.dat'
$INCLUDE:'devices.dat'
c
      data unit1 /14/
c
      data k /1, 3, 5/
c
      size = 12500
c
      open (unit1,file='errors.lst',status='new')
c
c*================================================================
c
      call GOPKS (unit1, 1024)
      call GOPWK (crtdev, 0, crtdev)
      call GACWK (crtdev)
c
      call GSWN (1,0.0,100.0,0.0,100.0)
      call GSVP (1,0.0,1.0,0.0,1.0)
c
      call GSELNT (1)
c
c   ** Set Character Height
c
      call GSCHH (4.0)
c
      do 100 i = 1,3
        py = 100.0 - i*25.0
        lhy(1) = py
        lhy(2) = py
        lvy(1) = py - 5.0
        lvy(2) = py + 5.0
c
        do 200 j = 1,3
          px = j*25.0
          lhx(1) = px - 10.0
          lhx(2) = px + 10.0
          lvx(1) = px
          lvx(2) = px
c
```

```
c            *** SET TEXT ALIGNMENT
c
             call GSTXAL (i,k(j))
c
c             ** Display Text
c
             call GTX (px,py,'TEXT')
c
c             ** Mark Alignment Point with horizontal and vertical lines
c
             call GPL (2,lhx,lhy)
             call GPL (2,lvx,lvy)
c
 200    continue
c
 100  continue
c
c
      call GDAWK (crtdev)
c
      read (5,*)
c
      call GCLWK (crtdev)
      call GCLKS
      close (unit1)
c
      end
```

See Plate 10(c).

```
c******************************************************************
c* E.8 TXTCOLUP : Depicting a word ("Text") eight times with    *
c*                different Character Up Vector and Text Color   *
c*                Indices and the default Text Precision "String"*
c******************************************************************
c* Refers to chapter : 5.1.5                                     *
c* Used external subroutines :                                   *
c******************************************************************
          program txtcolup
c
          integer*4 size,intary(12500)
          integer*2 gerrnr, gfctid
c
          common /gracom/size,intary
          common /gercom/gerrnr, gfctid
c
$INCLUDE:'devices.def'
c
          integer unit1
          real px(8), py(8), xaw(8), yaw(8)
c
$INCLUDE:'devices.dat'
c
          data unit1 /14/
c
          data px /50, 55, 60, 55, 50, 45, 40, 45/
          data py /60, 55, 50, 45, 40, 45, 50, 55/
          data xaw /-1, -0.5, 0, 0.5, 1,  0.5,  0, -0.5/
          data yaw / 0,  0.5, 1, 0.5, 0, -0.5, -1, -0.5/
c
          size = 12500
c
          open (unit1,file='errors.1st',status='new')
c
c*================================================================
c
          call GOPKS (unit1, 1024)
          call GOPWK (crtdev, 0, crtdev)
          call GACWK (crtdev)
c
          call GSWN (1,0.0,100.0,0.0,100.0)
          call GSVP (1,0.0,1.0,0.0,1.0)
          call GSELNT (1)
c
c     ** Set Character Height
c
          call GSCHH (4.0)
c
          do 100 i = 1,8
c
c        *** SET TEXT COLOR INDEX
c
             call GSTXCI (i)
c
c        *** SET CHARACTER UP VECTOR
c
             call GSCHUP (xaw(i),yaw(i))
c
c        *** DISPLAY TEXT
c
             call GTX (px(i),py(i),'TEXT')
c
 100      continue
```

```
c
c
          call GDAWK (crtdev)
c
          read (5,*)
c
          call GCLWK (crtdev)
          call GCLKS
          close (unit1)
c
          end
```

See Plate 10(d).

```
c******************************************************************
c* E.9 LINES : Depicting an Object ("Roe") using the Polyline   *
c*             Output Primitive, changing Line Type and Line     *
c*             Color Index                                        *
c******************************************************************
c* Refers to chapter : 5.1.2                                     *
c* Used external subroutines : dsurf                             *
c******************************************************************
          program lines
c
          integer*4 size,intary(12500)
          integer*2 gerrnr, gfctid
c
          common /gracom/size,intary
          common /gercom/gerrnr, gfctid
c
$INCLUDE:'devices.def'
$INCLUDE:'roe.def'
c
          integer unit1
          real xdc, ydc, xndc, yndc
          integer i
c
$INCLUDE:'devices.dat'
$INCLUDE:'roe.dat'
c
          data unit1 /14/
c
          size = 12500
c
          open (unit1,file='errors.lst',status='new')
c
c*================================================================
c
          call GOPKS (unit1, 1024)
          call GOPWK (crtdev, 0, crtdev)
          call GACWK (crtdev)
c
          call dsurf (crtdev, xdc, ydc, xndc, yndc)
c
c         ** Set Normalization Transformations
c
          call GSWN (1,0.0,   200.0,    0.0,   150.0)
          call GSVP (1,0.0,0.3*xndc,0.5*yndc,1.0*yndc)
c
          call GSWN (2,   0.0,   200.0,    0.0,   150.0)
          call GSVP (2,0.3*xndc,0.6*xndc,0.5*yndc,1.0*yndc)
c
          call GSWN (3,   0.0,   200.0,    0.0,   150.0)
          call GSVP (3,0.6*xndc,0.9*xndc,0.5*yndc,1.0*yndc)
c
          call GSWN (4,0.0,   200.0,0.0,   150.0)
          call GSVP (4,0.0,0.3*xndc,0.0,0.5*yndc)
c
          call GSWN (5,   0.0,   200.0,0.0,   150.0)
          call GSVP (5,0.3*xndc,0.6*xndc,0.0,0.5*yndc)
c
          call GSWN (6,   0.0,   200.0,0.0,   150.0)
          call GSVP (6,0.6*xndc,0.9*xndc,0.0,0.5*yndc)
c
c
```

```
                  do 100 i = 1,6
    c
                    call GSELNT (i)
    c
    c               *** SET LINE TYPE
    c
                    if (i .lt. 3) then
                        call GSLN    (-i)
                    else
                        call GSLN    (i-2)
                    endif
    c
    c               *** SET POLYLINE COLOR INDEX
    c
                    call GSPLCI (i)
    c
    c               *** DISPLAY POLYLINE
    c
                    call GPL (53,xroe,yroe)
    c
    c
     100          continue
    c
    c
                  call GDAWK (crtdev)
    c
                  read (5,*)
    c
                  call GCLWK (crtdev)
                  call GCLKS
                  close (unit1)
    c
                  end
```

See Plate 11(a).

```
c******************************************************************
c* E.10 MARKER : Depicting an Object ("Roe") using the Polymarker*
c*              Output Primitive, changing Marker Type and      *
c*              Polymarker Color Index                          *
c******************************************************************
c* Refers to chapter : 5.1.3                                    *
c* Used external subroutines : dsurf                            *
c******************************************************************
          program marker
c
          integer*4 size,intary(12500)
          integer*2 gerrnr, gfctid
c
          common /gracom/size,intary
          common /gercom/gerrnr, gfctid
c
$INCLUDE:'devices.def'
$INCLUDE:'roe.def'
c
          integer unit1
          real xdc, ydc, xndc, yndc
          integer i
c
$INCLUDE:'devices.dat'
$INCLUDE:'roe.dat'
c
          data unit1 /14/
c
          size = 12500
c
          open (unit1,file='errors.lst',status='new')
c
c*================================================================
c
          call GOPKS (unit1, 1024)
          call GOPWK (crtdev, 0, crtdev)
          call GACWK (crtdev)
c
          call dsurf (crtdev, xdc, ydc, xndc, yndc)
c
c         *** Set Normalization Transformations
c
          call GSWN (1,0.0,   200.0,    0.0,   150.0)
          call GSVP (1,0.0,0.3*xndc,0.5*yndc,1.0*yndc)
c
          call GSWN (2,    0.0,   200.0,    0.0,   150.0)
          call GSVP (2,0.3*xndc,0.6*xndc,0.5*yndc,1.0*yndc)
c
          call GSWN (3,    0.0,   200.0,    0.0,   150.0)
          call GSVP (3,0.6*xndc,0.9*xndc,0.5*yndc,1.0*yndc)
c
          call GSWN (4,0.0,   200.0,0.0,   150.0)
          call GSVP (4,0.0,0.3*xndc,0.0,0.5*yndc)
c
          call GSWN (5,    0.0,   200.0,0.0,   150.0)
          call GSVP (5,0.3*xndc,0.6*xndc,0.0,0.5*yndc)
c
          call GSWN (6,    0.0,   200.0,0.0,   150.0)
          call GSVP (6,0.6*xndc,0.9*xndc,0.0,0.5*yndc)
c
c
```

```
                  do 100 i = 1,6
      c
                  call GSELNT (i)
      c
      c           *** SET MARKER TYPE
      c
                  if (i .eq. 1) then
                     call GSMK    (-1)
                  else
                     call GSMK    (i)
                  endif
      c
      c           *** SET POLYMARKER COLOR INDEX
      c
                  call GSPMCI (i)
      c
      c           *** DISPLAY POLYMARKER
      c
                  call GPM (53,xroe,yroe)
      c
      c
       100        continue
      c
      c
                  call GDAWK (crtdev)
      c
                  read (5,*)
      c
                  call GCLWK (crtdev)
                  call GCLKS
                  close (unit1)
      c
                  end
```

See Plate 11(b).

```
c****************************************************************
c* E.11 MARKWID : Depicting an Object ("Roe") using the        *
c*               Polymarker Output Primitive changing the      *
c*               Marker Size Scale Factor                      *
c****************************************************************
c* Refers to chapter : 5.1.3                                   *
c* Used external subroutines :                                 *
c****************************************************************
          program markwid
c
          integer*4 size,intary(12500)
          integer*2 gerrnr, gfctid
c
          common /gracom/size,intary
          common /gercom/gerrnr, gfctid
c
$INCLUDE:'gdefines.def'
$INCLUDE:'devices.def'
$INCLUDE:'roe.def'
c
     ,    integer unit1
          integer i
c
$INCLUDE:'gdefines.dat'
$INCLUDE:'devices.dat'
$INCLUDE:'roe.dat'
c
          data unit1 /14/
c
          size = 12500
c
          open (unit1,file='errors.lst',status='new')
          call GOPKS (unit1, 1024)
          call GOPWK (crtdev, 0, crtdev)
          call GACWK (crtdev)
c
c         *** Set Normalization Transformations
c
          call GSWN (1,0.0,250.0,0.0,200.0)
          call GSVP (1,0.0,0.5,0.0,0.5)
c
          call GSWN (2,0.0,250.0,0.0,200.0)
          call GSVP (2,0.5,1.0,0.0,0.5)
c
          call GSWN (3,0.0,250.0,0.0,200.0)
          call GSVP (3,0.0,0.5,0.5,1.0)
c
          call GSWN (4,0.0,250.0,0.0,200.0)
          call GSVP (4,0.5,1.0,0.5,1.0)
c
          call GSELNT (1)
c
c
c         *** SET MARKER TYPE TO "POINT"
c
          call GSMK (gpoint)
c
          do 100 i = 1,4
c
             call GSELNT (i)
```

```
c
c                ***  SET MARKER SIZE SCALE FACTOR
c
                 call GSMKSC (i*1.0)
c
c                ***  DISPLAY POLYMARKER
c
                 call GPM (53,xroe,yroe)
c
 100             continue
c
c
                 call GDAWK (crtdev)
c
                 read (5,*)
c
                 call GCLWK (crtdev)
                 call GCLKS
                 close (unit1)
c
                 end
```

See Plate 11(c).

```
c*******************************************************************
c* E.12 AREAS : Depicting an Object ("Roe") using the Fill Area  *
c*              Output Primitive with all Fill Area Interior      *
c*              Styles and different Fill Area Style- and Color-  *
c*              Indices                                           *
c*******************************************************************
c* Refers to chapter : 5.1.4                                      *
c* Used external subroutines : dsurf                              *
c*******************************************************************
          program areas
c
          integer*4 size,intary(12500)
          integer*2 gerrnr, gfctid
c
          common /gracom/size,intary
          common /gercom/gerrnr, gfctid
c
$INCLUDE:'gdefines.def'
$INCLUDE:'devices.def'
$INCLUDE:'roe.def'
c
          integer unit1
          real  xdc, ydc, xndc, yndc
          integer i
          real  k
c
$INCLUDE:'gdefines.dat'
$INCLUDE:'devices.dat'
$INCLUDE:'roe.dat'
c
          data unit1 /14/
c
          size = 12500
c
          open (unit1,file='errors.lst',status='new')
c
c*================================================================
c
          call GOPKS (unit1, 1024)
          call GOPWK (crtdev, 0, crtdev)
          call GACWK (crtdev)
c
          call dsurf (crtdev, xdc, ydc, xndc, yndc)
c
c         *** Set Normalization Transformations
c
          do 50 i=1,4
            k = (i-1)*0.25*xndc
            call GSWN (i,0.0,  200.0,        0.0,130.0)
            call GSVP (i,  k, k+0.25, 0.75*yndc, yndc)
c
            call GSWN (i+5,0.0,  200.0,        0.0,     130.0)
            call GSVP (i+5,  k, k+0.25, 0.25*yndc, 0.5*yndc)
  50      continue
c
          call GSWN (5,      0.0,     200.0,      0.0,      130.0)
          call GSVP (5, 0.3*xndc, 0.6*xndc, 0.5*yndc, 0.75*yndc)
c
          call GSWN (10,     0.0,     200.0, 0.0,       130.0)
          call GSVP (10, 0.3*xndc, 0.6*xndc, 0.0, 0.25*yndc)
c
```

```
c
            do 100 i = 1,4
c
            call GSELNT (i)
c
c     *** SET FILL AREA INTERIOR STYLE TO "HATCHED"
c
            call GSFAIS (ghatch)
c
c     *** SET FILL AREA STYLE INDEX (-1..-7, STEP -2)
c
            call GSFASI (-(i*2)+1)
c
c     *** SET FILL AREA COLOR INDEX
c
            call GSFACI (i)
c
c     *** DISPLAY FILL AREA
c
            call GFA (52,xroe,yroe)
c
c     -----------------------------------------------------------
c
            call GSELNT (i+5)
c
c     *** SET FILL AREA INTERIOR STYLE TO "PATTERN"
c
            call GSFAIS (gpattr)
c
c     *** SET FILL AREA STYLE INDEX
c
            call GSFASI (i)
c
c     *** SET FILL AREA COLOR INDEX
c
            call GSFACI (i)
c
c     *** DISPLAY FILL AREA
c
            call GFA (52,xroe,yroe)
c
  100       continue
c
c     -----------------------------------------------------------
c
            call GSFACI (6)
c
c
            call GSELNT (5)
c
c     *** SET FILL AREA INTERIOR STYLE TO "HOLLOW"
c                          (NO STYLE INDEX AVAILABLE)
c
            call GSFAIS (ghollo)
c
c     *** DISPLAY FILL AREA
c
            call GFA     (52,xroe,yroe)
c
c     -----------------------------------------------------------
c
```

```
          call GSELNT (10)
c
c         *** SET FILL AREA INTERIOR STYLE TO "SOLID"
c                              (NO STYLE INDEX AVAILABLE)
c
          call GSFAIS (gsolid)
c
c         *** DISPLAY FILL AREA
c
          call GFA    (52,xroe,yroe)
c
c*---------------------------------------------------------------
c
          call GDAWK (crtdev)
c
          read (5,*)
c
          call GCLWK (crtdev)
          call GCLKS
          close (unit1)
c
          end
```

See Plate 11(d).

```
c*******************************************************************
c* E.13 TREE : Depicting an Object ("Tree") using different      *
c*             Output Primitives (Polyline and Fill Area) and    *
c*             their Attributes                                  *
c*             (Compare with Tree.c)                             *
c*******************************************************************
c* Refers to chapter : 5.1                                       *
c* Used external subroutines :                                   *
c*******************************************************************
          program tree
c
          integer*4 size,intary(12500)
          integer*2 gerrnr, gfctid
c
          common /gracom/size,intary
          common /gercom/gerrnr, gfctid
c
$INCLUDE:'gdefines.def'
$INCLUDE:'devices.def'
$INCLUDE:'tree.def'
c
          integer xdc, ydc, xras, yras
c
          integer unit1
          data unit1 /14/
c
$INCLUDE:'gdefines.dat'
$INCLUDE:'devices.dat'
$INCLUDE:'tree.dat'
c
          size = 12500
c
          open (unit1,file='errors.lst',status='new')
c
c*=================================================================
c
          call GOPKS (unit1, size)
          call GOPWK (crtdev, 0, crtdev)
          call GACWK (crtdev)
c
c         *** Set Normalization Transformation
c
          call GSWN (1,0.0,70.0,0.0,70.0)
          call GSVP (1,0.0,1.0,0.0,1.0)
c
          call GSELNT (1)
c
c    *** Construction of Object "Tree"
c
c         *** SET FILL AREA INTERIOR STYLE AND COLOR INDEX
c
          call GSFAIS (gsolid)
          call GSFACI (3)
c
c         *** DISPLAY FILL AREA
c
          call GFA (59,xtree,ytree)
c
c
c         *** SET LINETYPE AND POLYLINE COLOR INDEX
c
          call GSLN (glsoli)
          call GSPLCI (1)
```

```
c
c          *** DISPLAY POLYLINE
c
           call GPL (60,xtree,ytree)
c
c*----------------------------------------------------------------
c
           call GDAWK (crtdev)
c
           read (5,*)
c
           call GCLWK (crtdev)
           call GCLKS
           close (unit1)
c
           end
```

See Plate 12(a).

```
c*****************************************************************
c* E.14 STATSTOP : Displaying Statistics using the Generalized   *
c*                 Drawing Primitive "Bar"                       *
c*****************************************************************
c* Refers to chapter : 5.1.6                                     *
c* Used external subroutines :                                   *
c*****************************************************************
          program statstop
c
          integer*4 size,intary(12500)
          integer*2 gerrnr, gfctid
c
          common /gracom/size,intary
          common /gercom/gerrnr, gfctid
c
$INCLUDE:'gdefines.def'
$INCLUDE:'devices.def'
$INCLUDE:'hatch.def'
c
          integer unit1
c
          real xax1(2), yax1(2), xax2(2), yax2(2)
          real xpnt1(2), ypnt1(2), xpnt2(2), ypnt2(2)
          real xnum1, ynum1, xnum2, ynum2, xtxt, ytxt
          real xbar(2), ybar(2), ybdiff(5)
          character*3 num1(10)
          character*2 num2(5)
          character*5 value(5)
          character*80 datrec(1)
          integer i, k
c
$INCLUDE:'gdefines.dat'
$INCLUDE:'devices.dat'
$INCLUDE:'hatch.dat'
c
          data unit1 /14/
c
          data xax1 /20,20/
          data yax1 /20,130/
          data xax2 /15,135/
          data yax2 /25,25/
          data xpnt1 /17.5,22.5/
          data ypnt1 /125,125/
          data xpnt2 /40,40/
          data ypnt2 /27.5,22.5/
          data num1 /'50 ','45 ','40 ','35 ','30 ','25 ','20','15'
     $                    '10 ',' 5 '/
          data num2 /'20','25','30','35','40'/
c
          data xbar /30, 50/
          data ybar /25.0, 50.34/
          data ybdiff /0.0, 12.32, 14.2, 16.2, 18.08/
c
          data value /'12.67','18.83','25.93','34.03','43.07'/
c
          size = 12500
c
          open (unit1,file='errors.1st',status='new')
c
c*===============================================================
```

```
c
              call GOPKS (unit1, 1024)
              call GOPWK (crtdev, 0, crtdev)
              call GACWK (crtdev)
c
              call GSWN (1,-20.0,180.0,-20.0,180.0)
              call GSVP (1,0.0,1.0,0.0,1.0)
c
              call GSELNT (1)
c
c         *** Initialize Polyline and Fill Area Attributes
c
              call GSPLCI (1)
              call GSLN (glsoli)
              call GSFAIS (ghatch)
              call GSFASI (nhatch)
c
c
c         *** Generate Title
c
              call GTX (0.0,170.0,
     $ '    STOPPING DISTANCE OF MOTOR CARS')
              call GTX (0.0,165.0,
     $ ' _____ ')
              call GTX (0.0,155.0,
     $ '    AT DIFFERENT VELOCITIES')
              call GTX (0.0,150.0,
     $ '    _____ ')
c
c
c         *** Generate Unit Inscription of Axes
c
              call GSTXAL (gacent,gavnor)
              call GTX (20.0,132.0,'METERS')
              call GSTXAL (gahnor,gahalf)
              call GTX (137.0,25.0,'mph')
c
c
c
c         *** SELECTING AND DEPICTING GENERALIZED DRAWING PRIMITIVE
c
              do 10 i = 1,5
                call GSFACI (i)
c
c           ** Positions for Bars
c
                ybar(2) = ybar(2) + ybdiff(i)
c
c           ** Positions for Values in Bars
c
                xtxt = xbar(1) + 2.0
                ytxt = ybar(2)/2 + 10.0
c
c           *** SELECT AND DISPLAY GENERALIZED DRAWING PRIMITIVE "BAR"
C
                call GGDP (2,xbar,ybar, gbar ,0,datrec)
c
```

```
c
c                  ** Display Values in Bars
c
                   call GTX (xtxt,ytxt,value(i))
c
                   do 5 k = 1,2
                     xbar(k) = xbar(k) + 20.0
      5            continue
c
     10          continue
c
c
c
c                  *** Generate Coordinate Axes with Inscription
c
                   call GPL (2,xax1,yax1)
                   call GPL (2,xax2,yax2)
c
                   xnum1 = 0.0
                   ynum2 = 10.0
c
c                  ** Inscription of Y - Axis
c
                   call GSTXAL (gahnor,gahalf)
c
                   do 100 i = 1,10
                     ynum1 = ypnt1(1)
c
                     call GPL (2,xpnt1,ypnt1)
                     call GTX (xnum1,ynum1,num1(i))
c                              .
                     do 50 k = 1,2
                       ypnt1(k) = ypnt1(k) - 10.0
     50              continue
c
    100          continue
c
c
c                  ** Inscription of X - Axis
c
                   call GSTXAL (galeft,gatop)
c
                   do 200 i = 1,5
                     xnum2 = xpnt2(1) - 2.5
c
                     call GPL (2,xpnt2,ypnt2)
                     call GTX (xnum2,ynum2,num2(i))
c
                     do  60 k = 1,2
                       xpnt2(k) = xpnt2(k) + 20.0
     60            continue
c
    200          continue
c*-----------------------------------------------------------------
                   call GDAWK (crtdev)
c
                   read (5,*)
c
                   call GCLWK (crtdev)
                   call GCLKS
                   close (unit1)
c
                   end
```

See Plate 12(b).

```
c*****************************************************************
c* E.15 STATTEMP : Displaying Statistics using the Generalized  *
c*                 Drawing Primitives "Circle","Pie Slice" and  *
c*                 "Arc"                                         *
c*                 (Compare with Stattemp.c)                     *
c*****************************************************************
c* Refers to chapter : 5.1.6                                    *
c* Used external subroutines : dsurf                            *
c*****************************************************************
          program stattemp
c
          integer*4 size,intary(12500)
          integer*2 gerrnr, gfctid
c
          common /gracom/size,intary
          common /gercom/gerrnr, gfctid
c
$INCLUDE:'gdefines.def'
$INCLUDE:'devices.def'
$INCLUDE:'hatch.def'
c
          integer unit1
c
          real xpsl(3), ypsl(3), xdiff(5), ydiff(5)
          real xcirc(3),ycirc(3),xtemp(5),ytemp(5),xproz(5),yproz(5)
          integer i, j
          character*9 temp(5)
          character*6 proz(5)
          character*80 datrec(1)
c
$INCLUDE:'gdefines.dat'
$INCLUDE:'devices.dat'
$INCLUDE:'hatch.dat'

          data unit1 /14/
c
          data xpsl /90.0, 145.0, 55.5/
          data ypsl /75.0, 75.0, 117.5/
          data xdiff /-19.0, 3.0, 3.0, 107.0, 0.0/
          data ydiff /-52.0, -10.0, -7.5, 25.0, 0.0/
          data temp /'0 -31 mph','32-37 mph','38-42 km/h','43-48 mph',
     $              '49-   mph'/
          data proz /'35.3 %','17.1 %','03.0 %','00.5 %','43.0 %'/
          data xtemp /150.0, 0.0, 12.5, 14.0, 90.0/
          data ytemp /90.0, 85.0, 65.0, 55.0, 15.0/
          data xproz /110.0, 40.0, 14.0, 16.0, 90.0/
          data yproz /100, 85.0, 60.0, 50.0, 40.0/
c
          size = 12500
c
          open (unit1,file='errors.lst',status='new')
c
c*================================================================
c
          call GOPKS (unit1, 1024)
          call GOPWK (crtdev, 0, crtdev)
          call GACWK (crtdev)
c
          call dsurf (crtdev, xdc, ydc, xndc, yndc)
c
          call GSWN (1,0.0,280.0,0.0,280.0)
          call GSVP (1,0.0,1.0,0.0,1.0)
c
```

```
                  call GSELNT (1)
c
c         *** Initialize Fill Area Attributes
c
                  call GSFACI (1)
                  call GSFAIS (ghatch)
c
c         *** Initialize Polyline Attributes
c
                  call GSLN (glsoli)
                  call GSPLCI (1)
c
c         *** Generate Title
c
                  call GTX (60.0,175.0,'  MEASURED DRIVING SPEED')
                  call GTX (60.0,170.0,' -----------------------')
                  call GTX (60.0,165.0,'AT A SPEED LIMIT OF 50 MPH')
                  call GTX (60.0,160.0,'-------------------------')
c
c
c         *** SELECT AND DISPLAY GENERALIZED DRAWING PRIMITIVE "CIRCLE"
c
                  do 10 i = 1,2
                    xcirc(i) = xpsl(i) + 3.0
                    ycirc(i) = ypsl(i) + 3.0
        10        continue
c
                  call GGDP (2,xcirc,ycirc, gcircl,0,datrec)
c
                  call GSFAIS (ghollo)
                  call GGDP (2,xcirc,ycirc,gcircl,0,datrec)
c
c
c
c         *** SELECT AND DISPLAY GENERALIZED DRAWING PRIMITIVES
c                      "PIE SLICE" AND "ARC"
c
                  call GSFAIS (gsolid)
c
                  do 100 i = 1,5
                    call GSFACI (i)
c
c           ** DISPLAY GGDP "PIE SLICE"
c
                    call GGDP (3,xpsl,ypsl,gpie,0,datrec)
c
c           ** DISPLAY GGDP "ARC"
c
                    call GGDP (3,xpsl,ypsl,garc,0,datrec)
c
c
c           ** Display Inscription Values
c
                    call GSTXAL (gahnor,gahalf)
c
                    call GSTXCI (i)
                    call GTX (xtemp(i),ytemp(i),temp(i))
c
                    call GSTXCI (1)
                    call GTX (xproz(i),yproz(i),proz(i))
c
```

```
c
            xpsl(2) = xpsl(3)
            xpsl(3) = xpsl(3) + xdiff(i)
            ypsl(2) = ypsl(3)
            ypsl(3) = ypsl(3) + ydiff(i)
c
  100       continue
c
            call GTX (5.0, 5.0,'PRESS <Y><RETURN> TO EXIT !')
c
c*----------------------------------------------------------------
c
            call GDAWK (crtdev)
c
            read (5,*)
c
            call GCLWK (crtdev)
            call GCLKS
            close (unit1)
c
            end
```

See Plate 12(c).

```
C********************************************************************
c* E.16 COLREP : Depicting an Object ("Roe") using the Fill Area *
c*               Output Primitive in four program-defined Colors *
C********************************************************************
c* Refers to chapter : 5.5                                        *
c* Used external subroutines :                                    *
C********************************************************************
           program colrep
c
           integer*4 size,intary(12500)
           integer*2 gerrnr, gfctid
c
           common /gracom/size,intary
           common /gercom/gerrnr, gfctid
c
$INCLUDE:'gdefines.def'
$INCLUDE:'devices.def'
$INCLUDE:'roe.def'
c
           integer unit1
c
           integer i
c
$INCLUDE:'gdefines.dat'
$INCLUDE:'devices.dat'
$INCLUDE:'roe.dat'
c
           data unit1 /14/
c
           size = 12500
c
c
           open (unit1,file='errors.lst',status='new')
c
c*=================================================================
c
           call GOPKS (unit1, 1024)
           call GOPWK (crtdev, 0, crtdev)
           call GACWK (crtdev)
c
c
c          *** Set Normalization Transformations
c
           call GSWN (1,0.0,200.0,0.0,200.0)
           call GSVP (1,0.0,0.5,0.5,1.0)
c
           call GSWN (2,0.0,200.0,0.0,200.0)
           call GSVP (2,0.5,1.0,0.5,1.0)
c
           call GSWN (3,0.0,200.0,0.0,200.0)
           call GSVP (3,0.0,0.5,0.0,0.5)
c
           call GSWN (4,0.0,200.0,0.0,200.0)
           call GSVP (4,0.5,1.0,0.0,0.5)
c
           call GSELNT (1)
c
```

```
c
c          *** SET COLOR REPRESENTATIONS (PC-AT DEPENDENT)
c
c          ** blue
c
           call GSCR (crtdev,1,0.0,0.0,0.6)
c
c          ** light red
c
           call GSCR (crtdev,2,1.0,0.4,0.4)
c
c          ** brown
c
           call GSCR (crtdev,3,0.6,0.6,0.0)
c
c          ** light grey
c
           call GSCR (crtdev,4,0.6,0.6,0.6)
c
c
c          *** Set Fill Area Interior Style to "Solid"
c
           call GSFAIS (gsolid)
c
           do 100 i = 1,4
c
             call GSELNT (i)
c
c            *** SET FILL AREA COLOR INDEX TO DEFINED COLORS
c
             call GSFACI (i)
c
c            *** DISPLAY FILL AREA
c
             call GFA (52,xroe,yroe)
c
c
 100         continue
c
c
c
           call GDAWK (crtdev)
c
           read (5,*)
c
           call GCLWK (crtdev)
           call GCLKS
           close (unit1)
c
           end
```

See Plate 12(d).

```
c******************************************************************
c* E.17 WKWN : Depicting an Object ("Tree") without and with    *
c*             previous Workstation Transformation              *
c******************************************************************
c* Refers to chapter : 3.3                                      *
c* Used external subroutines :                                  *
c******************************************************************
          program wkwn
c
          integer*4 size,intary(12500)
          integer*2 gerrnr, gfctid
c
          common /gracom/size,intary
          common /gercom/gerrnr, gfctid
c
$INCLUDE:'gdefines.def'
$INCLUDE:'devices.def'
$INCLUDE:'tree.def'
c
          integer unit1,errind
          real xdc, ydc, xndc, yndc, xras, yras, now
          real xcoord(5), ycoord(5)
c
$INCLUDE:'gdefines.dat'
$INCLUDE:'devices.dat'
$INCLUDE:'tree.dat'
c
          data unit1 /14/
c
          data xcoord /0.0, 70.0, 70.0, 0.0, 0.0/
          data ycoord /0.0, 0.0, 70.0, 70.0, 0.0/
c
          size = 12500
c
c
          open (unit1,file='errors.lst',status='new')
c
c*===============================================================
c
          call GOPKS (unit1, 1024)
          call GOPWK (crtdev, 0, crtdev)
          call GACWK (crtdev)
c
c
c         *** SET NORMALIZATION TRANSFORMATION
c
          call GSWN (1,0.0,70.0,0.0,70.0)
          call GSVP (1,0.0,1.0,0.0,1.0)
c
c
          do 100 i = 1,2
c
             call GSELNT (i)
c
```

```
c          *** Construction of Object "Tree"
c
           call GSFAIS (gsolid)
           call GSFACI (1)
           call GFA (59,xtree,ytree)
c
           call GSLN (glsoli)
           call GSPLCI (1)
           call GPL (5,xcoord,ycoord)
           call GPL (60,xtree,ytree)
c
c
           call GTX (30.0,5.0,'PRESS <RETURN> TO CONTINUE !')
c
c          ** Wait for Input
c
           read (5,*)
c
c*----------------------------------------------------------------
c
           if (i .eq. 2) goto 1000
c
c
c          ** Clear Workstation
c
           call GCLRWK (crtdev,galway)
c
c
c          *** SET WORKSTATION TRANSFORMATION
c              (the following function calls to adjust the
c               workstation transformation for differences in
c               display space size are also available as
c               subroutine "dsurf")
c
c
c              ** INQUIRE DISPLAY SPACE SIZE
c
               call GQDSP (crtdev,errind,dcunit,xdc,ydc,xras,yras)
c
c              ** CALCULATE WORKSTATION TRANSFORMATION
c
               now = xdc
               if (xdc .LT. ydc) now = ydc
               xndc = xdc / now
               yndc = ydc / now
c
c              ** SET WORKSTATION TRANSFORMATION
c
               call GSWKWN (crtdev,0.0,xndc,0.0,yndc)
               call GSWKVP (crtdev,0.0,xdc,0.0,ydc)
c
c          *** SET NORMALIZATION TRANSFORMATION
c
           call GSWN (2,0.0,70.0,0.0,70.0)
           call GSVP (2,0.0,xndc,0.0,yndc)
c
c
 100       continue
c
 1000      continue
c
c*----------------------------------------------------------------
c
```

```
            call GDAWK (crtdev)
            call GCLWK (crtdev)
            call GCLKS
            close (unit1)
c
            end
```

See Plates 13(a) and (b).

```
c*****************************************************************
c* E.18 MULTNT : Displaying Objects using different        *
c*               Normalization Transformations             *
c*               (Compare with Multnt.c)                   *
c*****************************************************************
c* Refers to chapter : 3.3                                 *
c* Used external subroutines : dsurf                       *
c*****************************************************************
          program multnt
c
          integer*4 size,intary(12500)
          integer*2 gerrnr, gfctid
c
          common /gracom/size,intary
          common /gercom/gerrnr, gfctid
c
$INCLUDE:'gdefines.def'
$INCLUDE:'devices.def'
$INCLUDE:'hatch.def'
$INCLUDE:'roe.def'
$INCLUDE:'lake.def'
$INCLUDE:'tree.def'
c
          integer unit1
c
          real xback(5),yback(5)
c
$INCLUDE:'gdefines.dat'
$INCLUDE:'devices.dat'
$INCLUDE:'hatch.dat'
$INCLUDE:'roe.dat'
$INCLUDE:'lake.dat'
$INCLUDE:'tree.dat'
c
          data unit1 /14/
c
          data xback /0, 10, 10, 0, 0/
          data yback /0, 0, 10, 10, 0/
c
          size = 12500
c
c
          open (unit1,file='errors.lst',status='new')
c
c*===============================================================
c
          call GOPKS (unit1, 1024)
          call GOPWK (crtdev, 0, crtdev)
          call GACWK (crtdev)
c
          call dsurf (crtdev, xdc, ydc, xndc, yndc)
c
c
c         *** SET NORMALIZATION TRANFORMATIONS
c
          call GSWN (1,0.0,10.0,0.0,10.0)
          call GSVP (1,0.0,1.0,0.0,1.0)
c
          call GSWN (2,0.0,250.0,0.0,150.0)
          call GSVP (2,0.1,0.9,0.1,0.6)
c
          call GSWN (3,0.0,70.0,0.0,70.0)
          call GSVP (3,0.0,0.4,0.5,0.7)
```

```
c
            call GSWN (4,0.0,200.0,0.0,200.0)
            call GSVP (4,0.5,0.9,0.15,0.55)
c
c
c       *** Set Color Representations
c
            call GSCR (crtdev,8,0.6,0.6,0.0)
            call GSCR (crtdev,9,0.6,0.6,0.6)
c
c       *** Initialize Polymarker Attributes
c
            call GSLN (glsoli)
            call GSPLCI (0)
c
c
c
c
c       *** SELECT NORMALIZATION TRANSFORMATIONS
c            ... and Create Objects
c
c                              Object "Background"
            call GSELNT (1)
            call GSFAIS (gsolid)
            call GSFACI (9)
            call GFA (4,xback,yback)
c
c                              Object "Lake"
            call GSELNT (2)
            call GSFAIS (gsolid)
            call GSFACI (4)
            call GFA (15,xlake,ylake)
            call GPL (16,xlake,ylake)
c
c                              Object "Tree"
            call GSELNT (3)
            call GSFAIS (gsolid)
            call GSFACI (3)
            call GFA (59,xtree,ytree)
            call GPL (60,xtree,ytree)
c
c                              Object "Roe"
            call GSELNT (4)
            call GSFAIS (ghatch)
            call GSFASI (nhatch)
            call GSFACI (8)
            call GFA (52,xroe,yroe)
            call GPL (53,xroe,yroe)
c
c*----------------------------------------------------------------
c
            call GDAWK (crtdev)
c
            read (5,*)
c
            call GCLWK (crtdev)
            call GCLKS
            close (unit1)
c
            end
```

See Plate 13(c).

```
c*****************************************************************
c* E.19 SEGCRDEL : Creating and Deleting Segments                *
c*                                                               *
c*                  (Compare with Segcrdel.c)                    *
c*****************************************************************
c* Refers to chapter : 6.1                                       *
c* Used external subroutines : dsurf                             *
c*****************************************************************
            program segcrdel
c
            integer*4 size,intary(12500)
            integer*2 gerrnr, gfctid
c
            common /gracom/size,intary
            common /gercom/gerrnr, gfctid
c
$INCLUDE:'gdefines.def'
$INCLUDE:'devices.def'
$INCLUDE:'hatch.def'
$INCLUDE:'roe.def'
$INCLUDE:'lake.def'
$INCLUDE:'tree.def'
c
            integer unit1
            real xdc, ydc, xndc, yndc
c
            real xback(5),yback(5)
c
$INCLUDE:'gdefines.dat'
$INCLUDE:'devices.dat'
$INCLUDE:'hatch.dat'
$INCLUDE:'roe.dat'
$INCLUDE:'lake.dat'
$INCLUDE:'tree.dat'
c
            data unit1 /14/
c
            data xback /0, 10, 10, 0, 0/
            data yback /0, 0, 10, 10, 0/
c
            size = 12500
c
c
            open (unit1,file='errors.lst',status='new')
c
c*===============================================================
c
            call GOPKS (unit1, 1024)
            call GOPWK (crtdev, 0, crtdev)
            call GACWK (crtdev)
c
            call gdsurf (crtdev, xdc, ydc, xndc, yndc)
c
c                    Normalization Transformations for Objects
c
c                                             ... Background
            call GSWN (1,0.0,10.0,0.0,10.0)
            call GSVP (1,0.0,1.0,0.0,1.0)
c
c                                             ... Segment Lake
            call GSWN (2,0.0,250.0,0.0,150.0)
            call GSVP (2,0.1,0.9,0.1,0.6)
```

```
c
c                                                          ... Segment Tree
         call GSWN (3,0.0,70.0,0.0,70.0)
         call GSVP (3,0.0,0.4,0.5,0.7)
c
c                                                          ... Segment Roe
         call GSWN (4,0.0,200.0,0.0,200.0)
         call GSVP (4,0.5,0.9,0.15,0.55)
c
c
         call GSCR (crtdev,8,0.6,0.6,0.0)
         call GSCR (crtdev,9,0.6,0.6,0.6)
c
         call GSLN (glsoli)
         call GSPLCI (0)
c
         call GSFAIS (gsolid)
c
         call GSELNT (1)
         call GSFACI (9)
         call GFA (4,xback,yback)
c
c
c
c        *** CREATE SEGMENTS
c
c          ** Segment Lake
c
         call GCRSG (1)
           call GSELNT (2)
           call GSFACI (4)
           call GFA (15,xlake,ylake)
           call GPL (16,xlake,ylake)
         call GCLSG
c
c
c          ** Segment Tree
c
         call GCRSG (2)
           call GSELNT (3)
           call GSFACI (3)
           call GFA (59,xtree,ytree)
           call GPL (60,xtree,ytree)
         call GCLSG
c
c
c          ** Segment Roe
c
         call GCRSG (3)
           call GSELNT (4)
           call GSFAIS (ghatch)
           call GSFASI (nhatch)
           call GSFACI (8)
           call GFA (52,xroe,yroe)
           call GPL (53,xroe,yroe)
         call GCLSG
c
c
c        *** Wait for Input
c
         call GSELNT (1)
         call GTX (0.5,0.5,'PRESS <RETURN> TO DELETE SEGMENTS !')
         read (5,*)
```

```
c
c
c          *** DELETE SEGMENTS
c
           do 100 i = 1,3
             call GDSG (i)
 100       continue
c
c
           call GTX (0.5,0.5,'    PRESS <RETURN> TO EXIT !      ')
c
c*----------------------------------------------------------------
c
           call GDAWK (crtdev)
c
           read (5,*)
c
           call GCLWK (crtdev)
           call GCLKS
           close (unit1)
c
           end
```

See Plate 13(d).

```
c*******************************************************************
c* E.20 SEGSHIFT : Shifting a Segment using the                    *
c*                 Evaluate Transformation Matrix Function          *
c*                 and the Set Segment Transformation Function      *
c*******************************************************************
c* Refers to chapter : 6.3                                         *
c* Used external subroutines :                                     *
c*******************************************************************
          program segshift
c
          integer*4 size,intary(12500)
          integer*2 gerrnr, gfctid
c
          common /gracom/size,intary
          common /gercom/gerrnr, gfctid
c
$INCLUDE:'gdefines.def'
$INCLUDE:'devices.def'
$INCLUDE:'roe.def'
c
          integer unit1
c
          real xcoord(3), ycoord(3) ,transmat(2,3)
          integer i
c
$INCLUDE:'gdefines.dat'
$INCLUDE:'devices.dat'
$INCLUDE:'roe.dat'
c
          data unit1 /14/
c
          data xcoord /  0.0, 0.0, 180.0/
          data ycoord / 180.0, 0.0,  0.0/
c
          size = 12500
c
c
          open (unit1,file='errors.lst',status='new')
c
c*================================================================
c
          call GOPKS (unit1, 1024)
          call GOPWK (crtdev, 0, crtdev)
          call GACWK (crtdev)
c
          call GSWN (1,0.0,200.0,0.0,200.0)
          call GSVP (1,0.0,0.5,0.2,0.7)
c
          call GSWN (2,0.0,200.0,0.0,200.0)
          call GSVP (2,0.5,1.0,0.2,0.7)
c
c
c         *** Draw Coordinate System twice
c
          call GSELNT (1)
          call GPL (3,xcoord,ycoord)
c
          call GSELNT (2)
          call GPL (3,xcoord,ycoord)
```

```
c
c           *** CREATE SEGMENT ROE TWICE
c
            do 100 i = 1,2
              call GCRSG (i)
                call GSELNT (i)
                call GSFAIS (gsolid)
                call GSFACI (1)
                call GFA (52,xroe,yroe)
              call GCLSG
  100       continue
c
c
            call GSELNT (2)
c
c           *** EVALUATE TRANSFORMATION MATRIX FOR SHIFTING
c
            call GEVTM (0.0,0.0, 0.0556,0.0556,0, 1.0,1.0,gndc,transmat)
c
c           *** SET SEGMENT TRANSFORMATION
c            ** for second Segment Roe
c
            call GSSGT (2,transmat)
c
c*----------------------------------------------------------------
c
            call GDAWK (crtdev)
c
            read (5,*)
c
            call GCLRWK (crtdev,galway)
            call GCLWK (crtdev)
            call GCLKS
            close (unit1)
c
            end
```

See Plate 14(a).

```
c********************************************************************
c* E.21 SEGSCALE : Scaling a Segment using the                    *
c*                 Evaluate Transformation Matrix Function         *
c*                 and the Set Segment Transformation Function     *
c********************************************************************
c* Refers to chapter : 6.3                                        *
c* Used external subroutines :                                    *
c********************************************************************
          program segscale
c
          integer*4 size,intary(12500)
          integer*2 gerrnr, gfctid
c
          common /gracom/size,intary
          common /gercom/gerrnr, gfctid
c
$INCLUDE:'gdefines.def'
$INCLUDE:'devices.def'
$INCLUDE:'roe.def'
c
          integer unit1
c
          real xcoord(3), ycoord(3) ,transmat(2,3)
          integer i
c
$INCLUDE:'gdefines.dat'
$INCLUDE:'devices.dat'
$INCLUDE:'roe.dat'
c
          data unit1 /14/
c
          data xcoord /  0.0, 0.0, 180.0/
          data ycoord / 180.0, 0.0,  0.0/
c
          size = 12500
c
c
          open (unit1,file='errors.lst',status='new')
c
c*================================================================
c
          call GOPKS (unit1, 1024)
          call GOPWK (crtdev, 0, crtdev)
          call GACWK (crtdev)
c
          call GSWN (1,0.0,200.0,0.0,200.0)
          call GSVP (1,0.0,0.5,0.2,0.7)
c
          call GSWN (2,0.0,200.0,0.0,200.0)
          call GSVP (2,0.5,1.0,0.2,0.7)
c
c
c         *** Draw Coordinate System twice
c
          call GSELNT (1)
          call GPL (3,xcoord,ycoord)
c
          call GSELNT (2)
          call GPL (3,xcoord,ycoord)
```

```
c
c          *** CREATE SEGMENT ROE TWICE
c
           do 100 i = 1,2
             call GCRSG (i)
               call GSELNT (i)
               call GSFAIS (gsolid)
               call GSFACI (1)
               call GFA (52,xroe,yroe)
               call GCLSG
 100       continue
c
c
           call GSELNT (2)
c
c          *** EVALUATE TRANSFORMATION MATRIX FOR SCALING
c
           call GEVTM (0.61,0.22, 0.0,0.0, 0, 0.5,0.5, gndc, transmat)
c
c          *** SET SEGMENT TRANSFORMATION
c           ** for second Segment Roe
c
           call GSSGT (2,transmat)
c
c*----------------------------------------------------------------
c
           call GDAWK (crtdev)
c
           read (5,*)
c
           call GCLRWK (crtdev,galway)
           call GCLWK (crtdev)
           call GCLKS
           close (unit1)
c
           end
```

See Plate 14(b).

```
c*******************************************************************
c* E.22 SEGROT  :  Rotating a Segment using the              *
c*                 Evaluate Transformation Matrix Function   *
c*                 and the Set Segment Transformation Function *
c*******************************************************************
c* Refers to chapter : 6.3                                   *
c* Used external subroutines :                               *
c*******************************************************************
          program segrot
c
          integer*4 size,intary(12500)
          integer*2 gerrnr, gfctid
c
          common /gracom/size,intary
          common /gercom/gerrnr, gfctid
c
$INCLUDE:'gdefines.def'
$INCLUDE:'devices.def'
$INCLUDE:'roe.def'
c
          integer unit1
c
          real xcoord(3), ycoord(3) ,transmat(2,3)
          integer i
c
$INCLUDE:'gdefines.dat'
$INCLUDE:'devices.dat'
$INCLUDE:'roe.dat'
c
          data unit1 /14/
c
          data xcoord /  0.0, 0.0, 180.0/
          data ycoord / 180.0, 0.0,  0.0/
c
          size = 12500
c
c
          open (unit1,file='errors.lst',status='new')
c
c*=================================================================
c
          call GOPKS (unit1, 1024)
          call GOPWK (crtdev, 0, crtdev)
          call GACWK (crtdev)
c
          call GSWN (1,0.0,200.0,0.0,200.0)
          call GSVP (1,0.0,0.5,0.2,0.7)
c
          call GSWN (2,0.0,200.0,0.0,200.0)
          call GSVP (2,0.5,1.0,0.2,0.7)
c
c
c         *** Draw Coordinate System twice
c
          call GSELNT (1)
          call GPL (3,xcoord,ycoord)
c
          call GSELNT (2)
          call GPL (3,xcoord,ycoord)
c
c
c         *** CREATE SEGMENT ROE TWICE
c
```

```
            do 100 i = 1,2
              call GCRSG (i)
                call GSELNT (i)
                call GSFAIS (gsolid)
                call GSFACI (1)
                call GFA (52,xroe,yroe)
              call GCLSG
  100       continue
c
c
            call GSELNT (2)
c
c           *** EVALUATE TRANSFORMATION MATRIX FOR ROTATING
c
            call GEVTM (0.75,0.45,0.0,0.0, 0.5236, 1.0,1.0,gndc,transmat)
c
c           *** SET SEGMENT TRANSFORMATION
c            ** for second Segment Roe
c
            call GSSGT (2,transmat)
c
c*----------------------------------------------------------------
c
            call GDAWK (crtdev)
c
            read (5,*)
c
            call GCLRWK (crtdev,galway)
            call GCLWK (crtdev)
            call GCLKS
            close (unit1)
c
            end
```

See Plate 14(c).

```
C******************************************************************
c* E.23 SEGACC  :  Shifting, scaling and rotating a Segment    *
c*                 simultaneously using the                    *
c*                 Evaluate Transformation Matrix Function, the *
c*                 Accumulate Transformation Matrix Function    *
c*                 and the Set Segment Transformation Function  *
C******************************************************************
c* Refers to chapter : 6.3                                      *
c* Used external subroutines :                                  *
C******************************************************************
          program segacc
c
          integer*4 size,intary(12500)
          integer*2 gerrnr, gfctid
c
          common /gracom/size,intary
          common /gercom/gerrnr, gfctid
c
$INCLUDE:'gdefines.def'
$INCLUDE:'devices.def'
$INCLUDE:'roe.def'
c
          integer unit1
c
          real xcoord(3), ycoord(3) ,tmat1(2,3),tmat2(2,3),tmat3(2,3)
          integer i
c
$INCLUDE:'gdefines.dat'
$INCLUDE:'devices.dat'
$INCLUDE:'roe.dat'
c
          data unit1 /14/
c
          data xcoord /  0.0, 0.0, 180.0/
          data ycoord / 180.0, 0.0,  0.0/
c
          size = 12500
c
c
          open (unit1,file='errors.lst',status='new')
c
c*================================================================
c
          call GOPKS (unit1, 1024)
          call GOPWK (crtdev, 0, crtdev)
          call GACWK (crtdev)
c
          call GSWN (1,0.0,200.0,0.0,200.0)
          call GSVP (1,0.0,0.5,0.2,0.7)
c
          call GSWN (2,0.0,200.0,0.0,200.0)
          call GSVP (2,0.5,1.0,0.2,0.7)
c
c         *** Draw Coordinate System twice
c
          call GSELNT (1)
          call GPL (3,xcoord,ycoord)
c
          call GSELNT (2)
          call GPL (3,xcoord,ycoord)
```

```
c
c                *** CREATE SEGMENT ROE TWICE
c
                 do 100 i = 1,2
                   call GCRSG (i)
                     call GSELNT (i)
                     call GSFAIS (gsolid)
                     call GSFACI (1)
                     call GFA (52,xroe,yroe)
                   call GCLSG
  100            continue
c
c
                 call GSELNT (2)
c
c
c                *** EVALUATE TRANSFORMATION MATRIX FOR SCALING
c
                 call GEVTM (0.0,0.0, 50.0,50.0, 0, 1.0,1.0,gwc,tmat1)
c
c
c                *** ACCUMULATE TRANSFORMATION MATRIX WITH ROTATION
c
                 call GACTM (tmat1,0.75,0.45, 0.0,0.0,0.5236,1.0,1.0,gndc,tmat2)
c
c
c                *** ACCUMULATE TRANSFORMATION MATRIX WITH SCALING
c
                 call GACTM (tmat2,0.61,0.22, 0.0,0.0, 0.0, 0.5,0.5,gndc,tmat3)
c
c
c                *** SET ACCUMULATED SEGMENT TRANSFORMATION
c                 ** for second Segment Roe
c
                 call GSSGT (2,tmat3)
c
c*----------------------------------------------------------------
c
                 call GDAWK (crtdev)
c
                 read (5,*)
c
                 call GCLRWK (crtdev,galway)
                 call GCLWK (crtdev)
                 call GCLKS
                 close (unit1)
c
                 end
```

See Plate 14(d).

```
c*******************************************************************
c* E.24 SEGVIS  :  Depicting the same Segment ("Roe") with     *
c*                 different values of Segment Visibility        *
c*******************************************************************
c* Refers to chapter : 6.3                                      *
c* Used external subroutines :                                  *
c*******************************************************************
          program segvis
c
          integer*4 size,intary(12500)
          integer*2 gerrnr, gfctid
c
          common /gracom/size,intary
          common /gercom/gerrnr, gfctid
c
$INCLUDE:'gdefines.def'
$INCLUDE:'devices.def'
$INCLUDE:'roe.def'
c
          integer unit1
c
          real xkoord(3), ykoord(3)
c
$INCLUDE:'gdefines.dat'
$INCLUDE:'devices.dat'
$INCLUDE:'roe.dat'
c
          data unit1 /14/
c
          data xkoord /  0.0, 0.0, 180.0/
          data ykoord / 180.0, 0.0,  0.0/
c
          size = 12500
c
c
          open (unit1,file='errors.lst',status='new')
c
c*=================================================================
c
          call GOPKS (unit1, 1024)
          call GOPWK (crtdev, 0, crtdev)
          call GACWK (crtdev)
c                                            .
          call GSWN (1,0.0,200.0,0.0,200.0)
          call GSVP (1,0.0,0.5,0.2,0.7)
c
          call GSWN (2,0.0,200.0,0.0,200.0)
          call GSVP (2,0.5,1.0,0.2,0.7)
c
c
c         *** Draw Coordinate System twice
c
          call GSELNT (1)
          call GPL (3,xkoord,ykoord)
c
          call GSELNT (2)
          call GPL (3,xkoord,ykoord)
c
```

```
c
c            *** CREATE SEGMENT ROE TWICE
c
             do 100 i = 1,2
               call GCRSG (i)
                 call GSELNT (i)
                 call GSFAIS (1)
                 call GSFACI (1)
                 call GFA (52,xroe,yroe)
c
c                *** SET SEGMENT VISIBILITY
c
                 call GSVIS (i,i-1)
c
               call GCLSG
 100         continue
c
c
c            *** Display Text
c
             call GSTXCI (1)
c
             call GSELNT (1)
             call GTX (10.0,180.0,'SEGMENT INVISIBLE')
c
             call GSELNT (2)
             call GTX (10.0,180.0,'SEGMENT VISIBLE')
c
c*----------------------------------------------------------------
c
             call GDAWK (crtdev)
c
             read (5,*)
c
             call GCLRWK (crtdev,galway)
             call GCLWK (crtdev)
             call GCLKS
             close (unit1)
c
             end
```

See Plate 15(a).

```
C*****^*^************************************************************
c* E.25 SEGREDWK : Creating some Objects and Redrawing the       *
c*                  Segments on the current Workstation          *
C******************************************************************
c* Refers to chapter : 6.1                                       *
c* Used external subroutines : dsurf                             *
C******************************************************************
            program segredwk
c
            integer*4 size,intary(12500)
            integer*2 gerrnr, gfctid
c
            common /gracom/size,intary
            common /gercom/gerrnr, gfctid
c
$INCLUDE:'gdefines.def'
$INCLUDE:'devices.def'
$INCLUDE:'hatch.def'
$INCLUDE:'roe.def'
$INCLUDE:'lake.def'
$INCLUDE:'tree.def'
c
            integer unit1
            real xdc, ydc, xndc, yndc
c
            real xback(5),yback(5)
c
$INCLUDE:'gdefines.dat'
$INCLUDE:'devices.dat'
$INCLUDE:'hatch.dat'
$INCLUDE:'roe.dat'
$INCLUDE:'lake.dat'
$INCLUDE:'tree.dat'
c
            data unit1 /14/
c
            data xback /0, 10, 10, 0, 0/
            data yback /0, 0, 10, 10, 0/
c
            size = 12500
c
c
            open (unit1,file='errors.lst',status='new')
c
c*================================================================
c
            call GOPKS (unit1, 1024)
            call GOPWK (crtdev, 0, crtdev)
            call GACWK (crtdev)
c
            call dsurf (crtdev, xdc, ydc, xndc, yndc)
c
            call GSWN (1,0.0,10.0,0.0,10.0)
            call GSVP (1,0.0,1.0,0.0,1.0)
c
            call GSWN (2,0.0,250.0,0.0,150.0)
            call GSVP (2,0.1,0.9,0.1,0.6)
c
            call GSWN (3,0.0,70.0,0.0,70.0)
            call GSVP (3,0.0,0.4,0.5,0.7)
c
            call GSWN (4,0.0,200.0,0.0,200.0)
            call GSVP (4,0.5,0.9,0.15,0.55)
```

```
c
            call GSCR (crtdev,8,0.6,0.6,0.0)
            call GSCR (crtdev,9,0.6,0.6,0.6)
c
            call GSLN (glsoli)
            call GSPLCI (0)
c
c       *** Create Objects
c
            call GSFAIS (gsolid)
c
            call GSELNT (1)
            call GSFACI (9)
            call GFA (4,xback,yback)
c
c        ** Create Segments
c
            call GCRSG (1)
              call GSELNT (2)
              call GSFACI (4)
              call GFA (15,xlake,ylake)
              call GPL (16,xlake,ylake)
            call GCLSG
c
            call GCRSG (2)
              call GSELNT (3)
              call GSFACI (3)
              call GFA (59,xtree,ytree)
              call GPL (60,xtree,ytree)
            call GCLSG
c
            call GCRSG (3)
              call GSELNT (4)
              call GSFAIS (ghatch)
              call GSFASI (nhatch)
              call GSFACI (8)
              call GFA (52,xroe,yroe)
              call GPL (53,xroe,yroe)
            call GCLSG
c
            call GSELNT (1)
            call GTX (0.2,0.2,'PRESS <RETURN> TO REDRAW SEGMENTS')
            read (5,*)
c
c
c       *** REDRAW ALL SEGMENTS ON WORKSTATION
c
            call GRSGWK (crtdev)
c
            call GTX (0.2,0.2,'PRESS <RETURN> TO EXIT')
c
c*----------------------------------------------------------------
c
            call GDAWK (crtdev)
c
            read (5,*)
c
            call GCLRWK (crtdev,galway)
            call GCLWK (crtdev)
            call GCLKS
            close (unit1)
c
            end
```

See Plates 15(b) and 15(c).

```
c*******************************************************************
c* E.26 SEGASSOC : Sending a Segment ("Roe") from the Workstation*
c*                 Independent Segment Storage (WISS) to the      *
c*                 Workstation "Crtdev" (=DISPLAY) and storing    *
c*                 the Segment there                              *
c*                 (Compare the result with the result of        *
c*                 Segcopwk)                                      *
c*******************************************************************
c* Refers to chapter : 6.2                                        *
c* Used external subroutines : dsurf                              *
c*******************************************************************
            program segassoc
c
            integer*4 size,intary(12500)
            integer*2 gerrnr, gfctid
c
            common /gracom/size,intary
            common /gercom/gerrnr, gfctid
c
$INCLUDE:'gdefines.def'
$INCLUDE:'devices.def'
$INCLUDE:'hatch.def'
$INCLUDE:'roe.def'
$INCLUDE:'lake.def'
$INCLUDE:'tree.def'
c
            integer unit1
            real xdc, ydc, xndc, yndc
c
            real xback(5),yback(5), tmat1(2,3),tmat2(2,3),k
            integer i, l, j
c
$INCLUDE:'gdefines.dat'
$INCLUDE:'devices.dat'
$INCLUDE:'hatch.dat'
$INCLUDE:'roe.dat'
$INCLUDE:'lake.dat'
$INCLUDE:'tree.dat'
c
            data unit1 /14/
c
            data xback /0, 10, 10, 0, 0/
            data yback /0, 0, 10, 10, 0/
c
            size = 12500
c
c
            open (unit1,file='errors.lst',status='new')
c
c*=================================================================
c
            call GOPKS (unit1, 1024)
            call GOPWK (crtdev, 0, crtdev)
            call GACWK (crtdev)
c
            call dsurf (crtdev, xdc, ydc, xndc, yndc)
c
            call GSWN (1,0.0,10.0,0.0,10.0)
            call GSVP (1,0.0,1.0,0.0,1.0)
c
            call GSWN (2,0.0,250.0,0.0,150.0)
            call GSVP (2,0.1,0.9,0.1,0.6)
c
```

```
        call GSWN (3,0.0,70.0,0.0,70.0)
        call GSVP (3,0.0,0.4,0.5,0.7)
c
        call GSWN (4,-200.0,300.0,-200.0,300.0)
        call GSVP (4,0.0,1.0,0.0,1.0)
c
        call GSCR (crtdev,8,0.6,0.6,0.0)
        call GSCR (crtdev,9,0.6,0.6,0.6)
c
        call GSLN (glsoli)
        call GSPLCI (0)
        call GSFAIS (gsolid)
c
c       ** Create Objects on Workstation "Crtdev"
c
        call GSELNT (1)
        call GSFACI (9)
        call GFA (4,xback,yback)
c
        call GSELNT (2)
        call GSFACI (4)
        call GFA (15,xlake,ylake)
        call GPL (16,xlake,ylake)
c
        call GSELNT (3)
        call GSFACI (3)
        call GFA (59,xtree,ytree)
        call GPL (60,xtree,ytree)
c
c
        call GDAWK (crtdev)
c
c
c       *** OPEN AND ACTIVATE WISS
c
        call GOPWK (wssdev,0,wssdev)
        call GACWK (wssdev)
c
c
c       *** CREATE SEGMENT "ROE"
c
        call GCRSG (1)
          call GSELNT (4)
          call GSFAIS (ghatch)
          call GSFASI (nhatch)
          call GSFACI (8)
          call GFA (52,xroe,yroe)
          call GPL (53,xroe,yroe)
        call GCLSG
c
c
c       *** ASSOCIATE SEGMENT "ROE" WITH WORKSTATION "CRTDEV"
c
        call GASGWK (crtdev,1)
c
c
c       *** DEACTIVATE AND CLOSE WISS
c
        call GDAWK (wssdev)
        call GCLWK (wssdev)
```

```
c
c
c               *** ACTIVATE DISPLAY
c
                call GACWK (crtdev)
c
                call GEVTM (0.0,0.0, 0.0,0.0, 0.0, 1.0,1.0, gndc, tmat1)
                call GSSGT (1,tmat1)
c
c
c               ** Transform the Segment five times
c
                do 100 i = 7,11
                  k = i*0.1
c
                  call GACTM (tmat1,0.61,0.22,-0.1,-0.025,0,k,k,gndc,tmat2)
                  call GSSGT (1,tmat2)
c
                  do 20 l = 1,2
                    do 10 j = 1,3
                      tmat1(l,j) = tmat2(l,j)
                      tmat2(l,j) = 0
10                  continue
20                continue
c
100             continue
c
c
c               *** DEACTIVATE DISPLAY
c
                call GDAWK (crtdev)
c
                read (5,*)
c
                call GCLWK (crtdev)
                call GCLKS
                close (unit1)
c
                end
```

See Plate 15(d).

```
c*****************************************************************
c* E.27 SEGCOPWK : Copying a Segment ("Roe") from the Workstation*
c*                 Independant Segment Storage (WISS) to the      *
c*                 Workstation "Crtdev" (=DISPLAY) without        *
c*                 storing the Segment there                      *
c*                 (Compare the result with the result of         *
c*                 Segassoc)                                      *
c*****************************************************************
c* Refers to chapter : 6.2                                        *
c* Used external subroutines : dsurf                              *
c*****************************************************************
          program segcopwk
c
          integer*4 size,intary(12500)
          integer*2 gerrnr, gfctid
c
          common /gracom/size,intary
          common /gercom/gerrnr, gfctid
c
$INCLUDE:'gdefines.def'
$INCLUDE:'devices.def'
$INCLUDE:'hatch.def'
$INCLUDE:'roe.def'
$INCLUDE:'lake.def'
$INCLUDE:'tree.def'
c
          integer unit1
          real xdc, ydc, xndc, yndc
c
          real xback(5),yback(5), tmat1(2,3),tmat2(2,3),k
          integer i, l, j
c
$INCLUDE:'gdefines.dat'
$INCLUDE:'devices.dat'
$INCLUDE:'hatch.dat'
$INCLUDE:'roe.dat'
$INCLUDE:'lake.dat'
$INCLUDE:'tree.dat'
c
          data unit1 /14/
c
          data xback /0, 10, 10, 0, 0/
          data yback /0, 0, 10, 10, 0/
c
          size = 12500
c
c
          open (unit1,file='errors.lst',status='new')
c
c*================================================================
c
          call GOPKS (unit1, 1024)
          call GOPWK (crtdev, 0, crtdev)
          call GACWK (crtdev)
c
          call dsurf (crtdev, xdc, ydc, xndc, yndc)
c
          call GSWN (1,0.0,10.0,0.0,10.0)
          call GSVP (1,0.0,1.0,0.0,1.0)
c
          call GSWN (2,0.0,250.0,0.0,150.0)
          call GSVP (2,0.1,0.9,0.1,0.6)
c
```

```
            call GSWN (3,0.0,70.0,0.0,70.0)
            call GSVP (3,0.0,0.4,0.5,0.7)
c
            call GSWN (4,-200.0,300.0,-200.0,300.0)
            call GSVP (4,0.0,1.0,0.0,1.0)
c
            call GSCR (crtdev,8,0.6,0.6,0.0)
            call GSCR (crtdev,9,0.6,0.6,0.6)
c
            call GSLN (glsoli)
            call GSPLCI (0)
            call GSFAIS (gsolid)
c
c           ** Create Objects on Workstation "Crtdev"
c
            call GSELNT (1)
            call GSFACI (9)
            call GFA (4,xback,yback)
c
            call GSELNT (2)
            call GSFACI (4)
            call GFA (15,xlake,ylake)
            call GPL (16,xlake,ylake)
c
            call GSELNT (3)
            call GSFACI (3)
            call GFA (59,xtree,ytree)
            call GPL (60,xtree,ytree)
c
c
            call GDAWK (crtdev)
c
c
c           *** OPEN AND ACTIVATE WISS
c
            call GOPWK (wssdev,0,wssdev)
            call GACWK (wssdev)
c
c           *** CREATE SEGMENT "ROE"
c
            call GCRSG (1)
              call GSELNT (4)
              call GSFAIS (ghatch)
              call GSFASI (nhatch)
              call GSFACI (8)
              call GFA (52,xroe,yroe)
              call GPL (53,xroe,yroe)
            call GCLSG
c
c
c           *** COPY SEGMENT "ROE" FROM WISS TO DISPLAY
c
            call GCSGWK (crtdev,1)
c
c
            call GEVTM (0.0,0.0, 0.0,0.0, 0.0, 1.0,1.0, gndc, tmat1)
            call GSSGT (1,tmat1)
```

```
c
c            *** Transform the Segment five times
c
             do 100 i = 7,11
               k = i*0.1
c
               call GACTM (tmat1,0.61,0.22,-0.1,-0.025,0,k,k,gndc,tmat2)
               call GSSGT (1,tmat2)
c
c
c            *** COPY SEGMENT "ROE" FROM WISS TO DISPLAY
c
               call GCSGWK (crtdev,1)
c
               do 20 l = 1,2
                 do 10 j = 1,3
                   tmat1(l,j) = tmat2(l,j)
                   tmat2(l,j) = 0
 10              continue
 20            continue
c
 100         continue
c
c
c            *** DEACTIVATE AND CLOSE WISS
c
             call GDAWK (wssdev)
             call GCLWK (wssdev)
c
             read (5,*)
c
             call GCLWK (crtdev)
             call GCLKS
             close (unit1)
c
             end
```

See Plate 16(a).

```
C*****************************************************************
c* E.28 SEGPRIOR : Creating Segments with different values of   *
c*               Segment Priority                               *
C*****************************************************************
c* Refers to chapter : 6.3                                      *
c* Used external subroutines : dsurf                            *
C*****************************************************************
                program segprior
c
                integer*4 size,intary(12500)
                integer*2 gerrnr, gfctid
c
                common /gracom/size,intary
                common /gercom/gerrnr, gfctid
c
$INCLUDE:'gdefines.def'
$INCLUDE:'devices.def'
$INCLUDE:'hatch.def'
$INCLUDE:'roe.def'
$INCLUDE:'lake.def'
$INCLUDE:'tree.def'
c
                integer unit1
                real xdc, ydc, xndc, yndc
c
                real xback(5),yback(5)
                integer i
c
$INCLUDE:'gdefines.dat'
$INCLUDE:'devices.dat'
$INCLUDE:'hatch.dat'
$INCLUDE:'roe.dat'
$INCLUDE:'lake.dat'
$INCLUDE:'tree.dat'
c
                data unit1 /14/
c
                data xback /0, 10, 10, 0, 0/
                data yback /0, 0, 10, 10, 0/
c
                size = 12500
c
c
                open (unit1,file='errors.lst',status='new')
c
c*================================================================
c
                call GOPKS (unit1, 1024)
                call GOPWK (crtdev, 0, crtdev)
                call GACWK (crtdev)
c
                call dsurf (crtdev, xdc, ydc, xndc, yndc)
c
                call GSWN (1,0.0,10.0,0.0,10.0)
                call GSVP (1,0.0,1.0,0.0,1.0)
c
                call GSWN (2,0.0,250.0,0.0,150.0)
                call GSVP (2,0.1,0.9,0.1,0.6)
c
                call GSWN (3,0.0,70.0,0.0,70.0)
                call GSVP (3,0.0,0.4,0.5,0.7)
c
                call GSWN (4,0.0,200.0,0.0,200.0)
```

```
            call GSVP (4,0.4,0.8,0.2,0.6)
c
            call GSWN (5,0.0,200.0,0.0,200.0)
            call GSVP (5,0.5,0.9,0.15,0.55)
c
            call GSWN (6,0.0,200.0,0.0,200.0)
            call GSVP (6,0.3,0.7,0.1,0.5)
c
            call GSCR (crtdev,8,0.6,0.6,0.0)
            call GSCR (crtdev,9,0.6,0.6,0.6)
c
            call GSLN (glsoli)
            call GSPLCI (0)
c
c           *** CREATE SEGMENTS

            call GSFAIS (gsolid)
c
c            ** Segment "Background"
c
            call GCRSG (1)
              call GSELNT (1)
              call GSFACI (9)
              call GFA (4,xback,yback)
            call GCLSG
c
c            ** Segment "Lake"
c
            call GCRSG (2)
              call GSELNT (2)
              call GSFACI (4)
              call GFA (15,xlake,ylake)
              call GPL (16,xlake,ylake)
            call GCLSG
c
c            ** Segment "Tree"
c
            call GCRSG (3)
              call GSELNT (3)
              call GSFACI (3)
              call GFA (59,xtree,ytree)
              call GPL (60,xtree,ytree)
            call GCLSG
c
c
            call GSFAIS (ghatch)
            call GSFASI (nhatch)
c
c            ** 3 Segments "Roe"
c
            do 100 i = 4,6
              call GCRSG (i)
                call GSELNT (i)
                call GSFACI (8)
                call GFA (52,xroe,yroe)
                call GPL (53,xroe,yroe)
              call GCLSG
  100       continue
c
c
            call GSELNT (2)
            call GTX (2.0,2.0,'PRESS <RETURN> TO CONTINUE WITH MODIFIED PRIOR
      $ITIES !')
```

```
              read (5,*)
c
c
c          *** SET SEGMENT PRIORITIES
c
c             ** Segment "Lake" gets second lowest Priority
              call GSSGP (2,0.2)
c
c             ** Segment "Roe1" gets highest Priority
              call GSSGP (4,0.4)
c
c             ** Segment "Roe2" gets lowest Priority
              call GSSGP (5,0.1)
c
c             ** Segment "Roe3" gets second highest Priority
              call GSSGP (6,0.3)
c
c
c          *** Redraw all Segments on Workstation
c
              call GRSGWK (crtdev)
c
              call GTX (2.0,2.0,'PRESS <RETURN> TO EXIT !')
c
c*----------------------------------------------------------------
c
              call GDAWK (crtdev)
c
              read (5,*)
c
              call GCLWK (crtdev)
              call GCLKS
              close (unit1)
c
              end
```

See Plates 16(b) and 16(c).

```
c*****************************************************************
c* E.29 SEGINS : Inserting a Segment ("Roe") in a currently     *
c*                  opened Segment after storing it in the      *
c*                  Workstation Independant Segment Storage (WISS) *
c*****************************************************************
c* Refers to chapter : 6.2                                      *
c* Used external subroutines : dsurf                            *
c*****************************************************************
          program segins
c
          integer*4 size,intary(12500)
          integer*2 gerrnr, gfctid
c
          common /gracom/size,intary
          common /gercom/gerrnr, gfctid
c
$INCLUDE:'gdefines.def'
$INCLUDE:'devices.def'
$INCLUDE:'hatch.def'
$INCLUDE:'roe.def'
$INCLUDE:'lake.def'
$INCLUDE:'tree.def'
c
          integer unit1
          real xdc, ydc, xndc, yndc
c
          real xback(5),yback(5), tmat1(2,3),tmat2(2,3)
c
$INCLUDE:'gdefines.dat'
$INCLUDE:'devices.dat'
$INCLUDE:'hatch.dat'
$INCLUDE:'roe.dat'
$INCLUDE:'lake.dat'
$INCLUDE:'tree.dat'
c
          data unit1 /14/
c
          data xback /0, 10, 10, 0, 0/
          data yback /0, 0, 10, 10, 0/
c
          size = 12500
c
c
          open (unit1,file='errors.lst',status='new')
c
c*=================================================================
c
          call GOPKS (unit1, 1024)
          call GOPWK (crtdev, 0, crtdev)
          call GACWK (crtdev)
c
          call dsurf (crtdev, xdc, ydc, xndc, yndc)
c
          call GSWN (1,0.0,10.0,0.0,10.0)
          call GSVP (1,0.0,1.0,0.0,1.0)
c
          call GSWN (2,0.0,250.0,0.0,150.0)
          call GSVP (2,0.1,0.9,0.1,0.6)
c
          call GSWN (3,0.0,70.0,0.0,70.0)
          call GSVP (3,0.0,0.4,0.5,0.7)
```

```
c
            call GSWN (4,0.0,200.0,0.0,200.0)
            call GSVP (4,0.5,0.9,0.15,0.55)
c
            call GSCR (crtdev,8,0.6,0.6,0.0)
            call GSCR (crtdev,9,0.6,0.6,0.6)
c
            call GSLN (glsoli)
            call GSPLCI (0)
c
            call GSFAIS (gsolid)
c
c
c       *** Create Objects on current Workstation DISPLAY
c
c        ** Background
c
            call GSELNT (1)
            call GSFACI (9)
            call GFA (4,xback,yback)
c
c         ** Lake
c
            call GSELNT (2)
            call GSFACI (4)
            call GFA (15,xlake,ylake)
            call GPL (16,xlake,ylake)
c
c         ** Tree
c
            call GSELNT (3)
            call GSFACI (3)
            call GFA (59,xtree,ytree)
            call GPL (60,xtree,ytree)
c
c
c       *** Deactivate Workstation DISPLAY
c
            call GDAWK (crtdev)
c
c
c       *** OPEN AND ACTIVATE WISS
c
            call GOPWK (wssdev,0,wssdev)
            call GACWK (wssdev)
c
c
c       *** CREATE SEGMENT "ROE"
c
            call GCRSG (1)
              call GSELNT (4)
              call GSFAIS (ghatch)
              call GSFASI (nhatch)
              call GSFACI (8)
              call GFA (52,xroe,yroe)
              call GPL (53,xroe,yroe)
            call GCLSG
c
c
c       *** DEACTIVATE WISS
c
            call GDAWK (wssdev)
c
```

```
c
c          *** ACTIVATE WORKSTATION DISPLAY
c
           call GACWK (crtdev)
c
c
c          *** INSERT SEGMENT USING IDENTITY TRANSFORMATION
c
           call GCRSG (2)
             call GEVTM (0.0,0.0, 0.0,0.0, 0.0, 1.0,1.0, gwc, tmat1)
c
c            ** Insert Segment "Roe"
c
             call GINSG (1,tmat1)
c
           call GCLSG
c
c
c
c          *** INSERT SEGMENT USING NON-IDENTITY TRANSFORMATION
c
           call GCRSG (3)
             call GEVTM (0.61,0.22, -0.05,-0.025, 0.0, 0.5,0.5, 0, tmat2)
c
c            ** Insert Segment "Roe"
c
             call GINSG (1,tmat2)
c
           call GCLSG
c
c
c          *** CLOSE WISS
c
           call GCLWK (wssdev)
c
c*----------------------------------------------------------------
c
           call GDAWK (crtdev)
c
           read (5,*)
c
           call GCLWK (crtdev)
           call GCLKS
           close (unit1)
c
           end
```

See Plate 16(d).

```
C********************************************************************
c* E.30 SEGHLIT : Emphasizing Segments ("Roe","Tree") by          *
c*                Highlighting them                               *
C********************************************************************
c* Refers to chapter : 6.3                                        *
c* Used external subroutines : dsurf                              *
C********************************************************************
            program seghlit
c
            integer*4 size,intary(12500)
            integer*2 gerrnr, gfctid
c
            common /gracom/size,intary
            common /gercom/gerrnr, gfctid
c
$INCLUDE:'gdefines.def'
$INCLUDE:'devices.def'
$INCLUDE:'hatch.def'
$INCLUDE:'roe.def'
$INCLUDE:'lake.def'
$INCLUDE:'tree.def'
c
            integer unit1
            real xdc, ydc, xndc, yndc
c
            real xback(5),yback(5)
c
$INCLUDE:'gdefines.dat'
$INCLUDE:'devices.dat'
$INCLUDE:'hatch.dat'
$INCLUDE:'roe.dat'
$INCLUDE:'lake.dat'
$INCLUDE:'tree.dat'
c
            data unit1 /14/
c
            data xback /0, 10, 10, 0, 0/
            data yback /0, 0, 10, 10, 0/
c
            size = 12500
c
c
            open (unit1,file='errors.lst',status='new')
c
c*================================================================
c
            call GOPKS (unit1, 1024)
            call GOPWK (crtdev, 0, crtdev)
            call GACWK (crtdev)
c
            call dsurf (crtdev, xdc, ydc, xndc, yndc)
c
            call GSWN (1,0.0,10.0,0.0,10.0)
            call GSVP (1,0.0,1.0,0.0,1.0)
c
            call GSWN (2,0.0,250.0,0.0,150.0)
            call GSVP (2,0.1,0.9,0.1,0.6)
c
            call GSWN (3,0.0,70.0,0.0,70.0)
            call GSVP (3,0.1,0.4,0.5,0.65)
c
            call GSWN (4,0.0,200.0,0.0,200.0)
            call GSVP (4,0.5,0.9,0.15,0.55)
```

```
c
          call GSCR (crtdev,8,0.6,0.6,0.0)
          call GSCR (crtdev,9,0.6,0.6,0.6)
c
          call GSLN (glsoli)
          call GSPLCI (0)
c
          call GSFAIS (gsolid)
c
c
c      *** CREATE SEGMENTS INVISIBLE AND WITHOUT HIGHLIGHTING
c
c       ** Segment Background
c
          call GCRSG (1)
            call GSELNT (1)
            call GSFACI (9)
            call GFA (4,xback,yback)
            call GSVIS (1,ginvis)
          call GCLSG
c
c       ** Segment Lake
c
          call GCRSG (2)
            call GSELNT (2)
            call GSFACI (4)
            call GFA (15,xlake,ylake)
            call GPL (16,xlake,ylake)
            call GSVIS (2,ginvis)
          call GCLSG
c
c       ** Segment Tree
c
          call GCRSG (3)
            call GSELNT (3)
            call GSFACI (3)
            call GFA (59,xtree,ytree)
            call GPL (60,xtree,ytree)
            call GSVIS (3,ginvis)
          call GCLSG
c
c       ** Segment Roe
c
          call GCRSG (4)
            call GSELNT (4)
            call GSFAIS (ghatch)
            call GSFASI (nhatch)
            call GSFACI (8)
            call GFA (52,xroe,yroe)
            call GPL (53,xroe,yroe)
            call GSVIS (4,ginvis)
          call GCLSG
c
c
c      *** Make Segments visible
c
          do 50 i = 1,4
            call GSVIS (i,gvisi)
   50 continue
c
          call GSPLCI (4)
c
c
```

```
c               *** HIGHLIGHT SEGMENTS "ROE" AND "TREE"
c
          call GSHLIT (3,ghilit)
          call GSHLIT (4,ghilit)
c
c*---------------------------------------------------------------
c
          call GDAWK (crtdev)
c
          read (5,*)
c
          call GCLRWK (crtdev,galway)
          call GCLWK (crtdev)
          call GCLKS
          close (unit1)
c
          end
```

See Plate 17(a).

```
c********************************************************************
c* E.31 LOC : Locate the Positions of the vertices in Request    *
c*            Mode to create five-sided Polygons                 *
c*            (Compare with Loc.c)                               *
c********************************************************************
c* Refers to chapter : 8.1                                        *
c* Used external subroutines : dsurf                              *
c********************************************************************
            program loc
c
            integer*4 size,intary(12500)
            integer*2 gerrnr, gfctid
c
            common /gracom/size,intary
            common /gercom/gerrnr, gfctid
c
$INCLUDE:'gdefines.def'
$INCLUDE:'devices.def'
$INCLUDE:'echos.def'
c
            integer unit1
            real xdc, ydc, xndc, yndc, now
c
            real xini,yini, xact,yact ,xechmin,xechmax,yechmin,yechmax
            real xex(5), yex(5), xmult(6), ymult(6), realin(1)
            real xpos, ypos
            integer status, intin(7), ldr, c, col, i
            integer line(2), stat, seg, pk, nt
            character*80 datrec(1), charin(1), dr(1)
c
$INCLUDE:'gdefines.dat'
$INCLUDE:'devices.dat'
$INCLUDE:'echos.dat'
c
            data unit1 /14/
c
            data xex /0.0,100.0,100.0,0.0,0.0/
            data yex /0.0,0.0,100.0,100.0,0.0/
c
            size = 12500
c
c
            open (unit1,file='errors.lst',status='new')
c
c*================================================================
c
            call GOPKS (unit1, 1024)
            call GOPWK (crtdev, 0, crtdev)
            call GACWK (crtdev)
c
            call dsurf (crtdev, xdc, ydc, xndc, yndc)
c
            call GSWN (1,0.0,100.0,0.0,100.0)
            call GSVP (1,0.0,xndc,0.0,yndc)
c
            call GSWN (2,0.0,100.0,0.0,100.0)
            call GSVP (2,0.0,0.1,0.0,0.1)
c
c       *** SET VIEWPORT INPUT PRIORITY OF LOCATOR INPUT AREAS
c            HIGHER THAN DEFAULT NORMALIZATION TRANSFORMATION
c
            call GSVPIP (1, 0, ghighr)
            call GSVPIP (2, 1, ghighr)
```

```
c
c
c              *** CREATE SEGMENT "EXIT"
c
              call GCRSG (1)
c
c                ** Set Pick Identifier
                 call GSPKID (1)
c
                 call GSELNT (2)
                 call GSFACI (1)
                 call GSTXCI (3)
                 call GFA (4,xex,yex)
                 call GTX (10.0,10.0,' EXIT ')
c
c                *** SET DETECTABILITY TO "DETECTABLE"
c
                 call GSDTEC (1,gdetec)
                 call GSVIS  (1,ginvis)
              call GCLSG
c
c
 4000 call GSELNT (1)
c
c              ** Display Title
               call GSTXCI (4)
               call GTX (5.,95.,'ENTER THE POINTS OF A FIVE-SIDED POLYGON ')
               call GTX (5.,90.,'            USING THE MOUSE !          ')
               call GTX (5.,88.,'::::::::::::::::::::::::::::::::::::::::::::::')
c
c              ** Draw Frame
               call GSPLCI (1)
               call GPL (5,xex,yex)
c
c
               xpos = 50.0
               ypos = 50.0
c
c              ** define echo area for Locator
               xechmin = 0.0
               xechmax = xdc
               yechmin = 0.0
               yechmax = ydc


               nt = 1
c
c ******************** Loop over Number of Edges
c
c              *** INITIALIZE, REQUEST AND EVALUATE LOCATOR
c                ** initialize locator prompt and echo type -2
c                   -- inking
c                 * attribute control flag
                 intin(1) = gspec
c                 * linetype ASF
                 intin(2) = gindiv
c                 * linewidth scale factor ASF
                 intin(3) = gindiv
c                 * polyline colour index ASF
                 intin(4) = gindiv
c                 * polyline bundle index
                 intin(5) = 1
c                 * linetype index
                 intin(6) = glsoli
```

```
c               * polyline colour index
                intin(7) = 3
c
                realin(1) = 1.0
                charin(1) = ' '
c
c               ** Pack Data Record
                call GPRECS (7, intin, 1, realin, 0, 0, charin, 1,
       $                          errind, ldr, datrec)
c
                do 3000 c = 1,5
c
                    call GINLC (crtdev, msdev, nt, xpos, ypos, glrect,
       $                          xechmin, xechmax, yechmin, yechmax, 1, datrec)
c
c                   *** REQUEST LOCATOR
c
 100                call GRQLC (crtdev, msdev, status, nt, xmult(c), ymult(c) )
c
c
c                   *** EVALUATE LOCATOR
c
                    if (status .ne. gok) goto 100
c
c
                    call GSELNT (nt)
                    call GSPMCI (3)
                    call GSMK (1)
c
c                   ** Mark located Points with Polymarkers
c
                    call GPM (1,xmult(c),ymult(c))
c
c                   ** Calculate new Starting Position for Inking
c
                    xpos = xmult(c)
                    ypos = ymult(c)
c
 3000 continue
c
c ****************** End of Loop
c
c
c
c
c
c                   *** EVALUATE LOCATOR
c
                call GSELNT (1)
c
                xmult(6) = xmult(1)
                ymult(6) = ymult(1)
c
c               ** Create Polygon using Fill Area Output Primitive
c
                col = col + 1
                call GSFAIS (1)
                call GSFACI (col)
                call GFA (6,xmult,ymult)
```

```
c
c              *** EXIT OR CONTINUE ?
c
c              ** Set Segment "Exit" visible
               call GSVIS (1,gvisi)
               seg = 1
               pk  = 1
c
c              ** Initialize Pick
               call GINPK (crtdev,msdev,stat,gok,seg,pk,
      $                                  1, 0.0, 0.1, 0.0, 0.1, 0, dr)
c
 200           continue
c
c              ** Request Pick
               call GRQPK (crtdev, msdev, stat, seg, pk)
c
c              ** Evaluate Pick
               if (seg .eq. 1) goto 1000
c
               xpos = 50.0
               ypos = 50.0
c
c              ** Set Segment "Exit" invisible
               call GSVIS (1,ginvis)
c
c              *** UPDATE WORKSTATION
c
               call GUWK (crtdev, gperf)
c
               goto 4000
c
c
 1000 continue
c
c              ** Highlight Segment "Exit"
               call GSHLIT (seg, ghilit)
c
c
c              *** CLEAR WORKSTATION
c
               call GCLRWK (crtdev, galway)
c
c*----------------------------------------------------------------
c
               call GDAWK (crtdev)
               call GCLWK (crtdev)
               call GCLKS
c
               end
```

See Plates 17(b) and 17(c).

```
c*******************************************************************
c* E.32 PICK : Pick Segments in Request Mode for the purpose of   *
c*             Identification                                     *
c*******************************************************************
c* Refers to chapter : 8.6                                        *
c* Used external subroutines : dsurf                              *
c*******************************************************************
          program pick
c
          integer*4 size,intary(12500)
          integer*2 gerrnr, gfctid
c
          common /gracom/size,intary
          common /gercom/gerrnr, gfctid
c
$INCLUDE:'gdefines.def'
$INCLUDE:'devices.def'
$INCLUDE:'hatch.def'
$INCLUDE:'roe.def'
$INCLUDE:'lake.def'
$INCLUDE:'tree.def'
c
          integer unit1
          real xdc, ydc, xndc, yndc
c
          real xback(5),yback(5), xex(5),yex(5)
          real xechmin,xechmax, yechmin,yechmax, xout,yout
          integer sgid, pkid, segnam, pkident, echosw, status
          integer mode
          character*1 datrec(1)
c
$INCLUDE:'gdefines.dat'
$INCLUDE:'devices.dat'
$INCLUDE:'hatch.dat'
$INCLUDE:'roe.dat'
$INCLUDE:'lake.dat'
$INCLUDE:'tree.dat'
c
          data unit1 /14/
c
          data xback /0, 10, 10, 0, 0/
          data yback /0, 0, 10, 10, 0/
          data xex /0, 1, 1, 0, 0/
          data yex /0, 0, 1, 1, 0/
c
          size = 12500
c
c
          open (unit1,file='errors.lst',status='new')
c
c*===============================================================
c
          call GOPKS (unit1, 1024)
          call GOPWK (crtdev, 0, crtdev)
          call GACWK (crtdev)
c
          call dsurf (crtdev, xdc, ydc, xndc, yndc)
c
          call GSWN (1,0.0,10.0,0.0,10.0)
          call GSVP (1,0.0,1.0,0.0,1.0)
c
          call GSWN (2,0.0,250.0,0.0,150.0)
          call GSVP (2,0.1,0.9,0.1,0.6)
```

```
c
            call GSWN (3,0.0,70.0,0.0,70.0)
            call GSVP (3,0.0,0.4,0.5,0.7)
c
            call GSWN (4,0.0,200.0,0.0,200.0)
            call GSVP (4,0.5,0.9,0.15,0.55)
c
c
c       *** SET VIEWPORT INPUT PRIORITIES AS FOLLOWS :
c           Default NT - Background - Tree,Lake - Roe
c           lowest ------------------------> highest
c
            call GSVPIP (1, 0, ghighr)
            call GSVPIP (2, 1, ghighr)
            call GSVPIP (3, 1, ghighr)
            call GSVPIP (4, 2, ghighr)
c
            call GSCR (crtdev,8,0.6,0.6,0.0)
            call GSCR (crtdev,9,0.6,0.6,0.6)
c
            call GSLN (glsoli)
            call GSPLCI (0)
c
c       *** Create Background
c
            call GSELNT (1)
            call GSFAIS (gsolid)
            call GSFACI (9)
            call GFA (4,xback,yback)
c
c
c       *** CREATE SEGMENTS
c
c       ** Segment Lake
c
            call GCRSG (1)
              call GSELNT (2)
              call GSFAIS (gsolid)
              call GSFACI (4)
              call GFA (15,xlake,ylake)
              call GPL (16,xlake,ylake)
c
c             *** SET PICK IDENTIFIER
c
              call GSPKID (1)
c
c             *** SET DETECTABILITY
c
              call GSDTEC (1,gdetec)
c
            call GCLSG
c
c
c       ** Segment Tree
c
```

```
            call GCRSG (2)
              call GSELNT (3)
              call GSFAIS (gsolid)
              call GSFACI (3)
              call GFA (59,xtree,ytree)
              call GPL (60,xtree,ytree)
c
c           *** SET PICK IDENTIFIER
c
              call GSPKID (2)
c
c           *** SET DETECTABILITY
c
              call GSDTEC (2,gdetec)
c
            call GCLSG
c
c
c           ** Segment Roe
c
            call GCRSG (3)
              call GSLN (glsoli)
              call GSPLCI (0)
              call GSELNT (4)
              call GSFAIS (ghatch)
              call GSFASI (nhatch)
              call GSFACI (8)
              call GFA (52,xroe,yroe)
              call GPL (53,xroe,yroe)
c
c           *** SET PICK IDENTIFIER
c
              call GSPKID (3)
c
c           *** SET DETECTABILITY
c
              call GSDTEC (3,gdetec)
c
            call GCLSG
c
c
c
c           ** Segment Exit
c
            call GCRSG (4)
              call GSPLCI (1)
              call GSELNT (1)
              call GSFAIS (ghollo)
              call GSFACI (0)
              call GFA (4,xex,yex)
              call GSTXCI (3)
              call GTX (0.2,0.5,' EXIT ')
c
c           *** SET PICK IDENTIFIER
c
              call GSPKID (4)
c
c           *** SET DETECTABILITY
c
              call GSDTEC (4,gdetec)
c
            call GCLSG
c
```

```
c
c              ** define echo area
               xechmin = 0.0
               xechmax = xdc
               yechmin = 0.0
               yechmax = ydc
c
c              ** Initialize Segments and Pick Identifier
               sgid = 4
               pkid = 4
c
c              *** INITIALIZE PICK
c
               call GINPK (crtdev,msdev,gok,sgid,pkid,1,xechmin,xechmax,
      $              yechmin,yechmax,1,datrec)
c
c
c
               xout = 140.0
               yout = 140.0
c
c              ** Display Title
               call GSELNT (1)
               call GSTXCI (4)
               call GTX (5.0,7.0,' PICK SEGMENTS USING THE MOUSE ')
               call GTX (5.0,6.85,' **************************** ')
c
c
c              *** REQUEST PICK
c
  500 call GRQPK (crtdev, msdev, status, segnam, pkident)
c
c
               call GSTXCI (5)
               call GSELNT (2)
c
c
c              *** EVALUATE PICK
c
               if (status .eq. gnone) then
                    call GTX (xout,yout,'  NO SEGMENT   ')
                    goto 500
               endif
c
               if (segnam .eq. 1) goto 1000
c
               if (segnam .eq. 2) goto 2000
c
               if (segnam .eq. 3) goto 3000
c
               if (segnam .eq. 4) goto 4000
c
c
c              *** IDENTIFY SEGMENTS BY TEXT OUTPUT
c
 1000 call GTX (xout,yout,' SEGMENT LAKE ')
               goto 500
c
 2000 call GTX (xout,yout,' SEGMENT TREE ')
               goto 500
c
 3000 call GTX (xout,yout,' SEGMENT ROE   ')
               goto 500
```

```
c
4000 call GTX (xout,yout,' SEGMENT EXIT ')
          call GCLRWK (crtdev,1)
c
c*----------------------------------------------------------------
c
          call GDAWK (crtdev)
          call GCLWK (crtdev)
          call GCLKS
          close (unit1)
c
          end
```

See Plate 17(d).

```
C*********************************A A********************************************
c* E.33 CHOICE : Using the Choice Input Device (Function Keys)   *
c*               to select Segments to be made visible           *
C*****************************************************************************
c* Refers to chapter : 8.4                                       *
c* Used external subroutines : dsurf                             *
C*****************************************************************************
          program choice
c
          integer*4 size,intary(12500)
          integer gerrnr, gfctid
c
          common /gracom/size,intary
          common /gercom/gerrnr,gfctid
c
$INCLUDE:'gdefines.def'
$INCLUDE:'devices.def'
$INCLUDE:'hatch.def'
$INCLUDE:'roe.def'
$INCLUDE:'tree.def'
$INCLUDE:'lake.def'
c
          character datrec(1)
          real xback(5),yback(5)
          real xechmin, xechmax, yechmin, yechmax
          integer chnr, status, inich
          real xdc, ydc, xndc, yndc
          integer unit1
c
$INCLUDE:'gdefines.dat'
$INCLUDE:'devices.dat'
$INCLUDE:'hatch.dat'
$INCLUDE:'roe.dat'
$INCLUDE:'tree.dat'
$INCLUDE:'lake.dat'
c
          data unit1 /14/
          data xback /0, 10, 10, 0, 0/
          data yback /0, 0, 10, 10, 0/
c
          size = 12500
c
c
          open (unit1,file='errors.lst',status='new')
c
c*================================================================
c
          call GOPKS (unit1, 1024)
          call GOPWK (crtdev, 0, crtdev)
          call GACWK (crtdev)
c
          call dsurf (crtdev, xdc, ydc, xndc, yndc)
c
          call GSWN (1,0.0,10.0,0.0,10.0)
          call GSVP (1,0.0,1.0,0.0,1.0)
c
          call GSWN (2,0.0,250.0,0.0,150.0)
          call GSVP (2,0.1,0.9,0.1,0.6)
c
          call GSWN (3,0.0,70.0,0.0,70.0)
          call GSVP (3,0.0,0.4,0.5,0.7)
```

```
c
            call GSWN (4,0.0,200.0,0.0,200.0)
            call GSVP (4,0.5,0.9,0.15,0.55)
c
            call GSCR (crtdev,8,0.6,0.6,0.0)
            call GSCR (crtdev,9,0.6,0.6,0.6)
c
            call GSLN (glsoli)
            call GSPLCI (0)
c
c       *** Create Background
c
            call GSELNT (1)
            call GSFAIS (gsolid)
            call GSFACI (9)
            call GFA (4,xback,yback)
c
c       *** CREATE INVISIBLE SEGMENTS
c
c       ** Segment Lake
c
            call GCRSG (1)
              call GSELNT (2)
              call GSFACI (4)
              call GFA (15,xlake,ylake)
              call GPL (16,xlake,ylake)
              call GSVIS (1,ginvis)
            call GCLSG
c
c       ** Segment Tree
c
            call GCRSG (2)
              call GSELNT (3)
              call GSFACI (3)
              call GFA (59,xtree,ytree)
              call GPL (60,xtree,ytree)
              call GSVIS (2,ginvis)
            call GCLSG
c
c       ** Segment Roe
c
            call GCRSG (3)
              call GSELNT (4)
              call GSFAIS (ghatch)
              call GSFASI (nhatch)
              call GSFACI (8)
              call GFA (52,xroe,yroe)
              call GPL (53,xroe,yroe)
              call GSVIS (3,ginvis)
            call GCLSG
c
c
c       *** INITIALIZE CHOICE
c
c       ** Initial choice number
            inich = 4
c
c       ** Define echo area
            xechmin = 0.0
            xechmax = xdc/4.0
            yechmin = 0.0
            yechmax = ydc/4.0
c
```

```
c
          call GINCH (crtdev,crtdev,gok,inich,gecho,xechmin,xechmax,
     $        yechmin,yechmax,0,datrec)
c
c
c         *** Display Menu
          call GSELNT (2)
          call GSTXCI (2)
          call GTX (125.0,145.0,' MAKE SEGMENTS VISIBLE !')
          call GTX (125.0,140.0,' **********************')
          call GSTXCI (7)
          call GTX (0.5,20.0,'F1 = SEGMENT LAKE')
          call GTX (0.5,15.0,'F2 = SEGMENT TREE')
          call GTX (0.5,10.0,'F3 = SEGMENT ROE ')
          call GTX (0.5,5.0 ,'F4 = EXIT        ')
c
c         *** REQUEST CHOICE
c
 700      call GRQCH (crtdev, crtdev, status, chnr)
c
c         *** EVALUATE CHOICE
c
          if (status .ne. gok) goto 700
c
c
          if ((chnr .lt. 1).or.(chnr .gt. 4)) goto 700
          if (chnr .eq. 1) goto 1000
          if (chnr .eq. 2) goto 2000
          if (chnr .eq. 3) goto 3000
          if (chnr .eq. 4) goto 4000
c
c
c         *** MAKE SELECTED SEGMENT VISIBLE OR ELSE ABORT
c
c         ** Segment Lake
 1000 continue
          call GSVIS (1,gvisi)
          goto 700
c
c         ** Segment Tree
 2000 continue
          call GSVIS (2,gvisi)
          goto 700
c
c         ** Segment Roe
 3000 continue
          call GSVIS (3,gvisi)
          goto 700
c
c
 4000 continue
c
c*----------------------------------------------------------------
c
          call GDAWK (crtdev)
          call GCLRWK (crtdev,galway)
          call GCLWK (crtdev)
          call GCLKS
          close (unit1)
c
          end
```

See Plate 18(a).

```
c******************************************************************
c* E.34 STRING : Use the String Input Device to select Segments  *
c*               to be made visible                              *
c******************************************************************
c* Refers to chapter : 8.5                                       *
c* Used external subroutines : dsurf                             *
c******************************************************************
          program string
c
          integer*4 size,intary(12500)
          integer*2 gerrnr, gfctid
c
          common /gracom/size,intary
          common /gercom/gerrnr, gfctid
c
$INCLUDE:'gdefines.def'
$INCLUDE:'devices.def'
$INCLUDE:'hatch.def'
$INCLUDE:'roe.def'
$INCLUDE:'lake.def'
$INCLUDE:'tree.def'
c
          integer unit1
          real xdc, ydc, xndc, yndc
c
          real xback(5),yback(5)
          real xmin, xmax, ymin, ymax
          integer status, stlen, len, inipos, buflen
          character*80  datrec(1), datstr(1), inist(1)
          character*1   str(80)
          equivalence   (datstr,str)
c
$INCLUDE:'gdefines.dat'
$INCLUDE:'devices.dat'
$INCLUDE:'hatch.dat'
$INCLUDE:'roe.dat'
$INCLUDE:'lake.dat'
$INCLUDE:'tree.dat'
c
          data unit1 /14/
c
          data xback /0, 100, 100, 0, 0/
          data yback /0, 0, 100, 100, 0/
          data inist /'SELECTED SEGMENT =     '/
c
          size = 12500
c
c
          open (unit1,file='errors.lst',status='new')
c
c*================================================================
c
          call GOPKS (unit1, 1024)
          call GOPWK (crtdev, 0, crtdev)
          call GACWK (crtdev)
c
          call dsurf (crtdev, xdc, ydc, xndc, yndc)
c
          call GSWN (1,0.0,100.0,0.0,100.0)
          call GSVP (1,0.0,1.0,0.0,1.0)
c
          call GSWN (2,0.0,250.0,0.0,150.0)
          call GSVP (2,0.1,0.9,0.1,0.6)
```

```
c
            call GSWN (3,0.0,70.0,0.0,70.0)
            call GSVP (3,0.0,0.4,0.5,0.7)
c
            call GSWN (4,0.0,200.0,0.0,200.0)
            call GSVP (4,0.5,0.9,0.15,0.55)
c
            call GSCR (crtdev,8,0.6,0.6,0.0)
            call GSCR (crtdev,9,0.6,0.6,0.6)
c
            call GSLN (glsoli)
            call GSPLCI (0)
c
c       *** Create Background
c
            call GSELNT (1)
            call GSFAIS (gsolid)
            call GSFACI (9)
            call GFA (4,xback,yback)
c
c
c       *** CREATE INVISIBLE SEGMENTS
c
c       ** Segment Lake
c
            call GCRSG (1)
              call GSELNT (2)
              call GSFACI (4)
              call GFA (15,xlake,ylake)
              call GPL (16,xlake,ylake)
              call GSVIS (1,ginvis)
            call GCLSG
c
c       ** Segment Tree
c
            call GCRSG (2)
              call GSELNT (3)
              call GSFACI (3)
              call GFA (59,xtree,ytree)
              call GPL (60,xtree,ytree)
              call GSVIS (2,ginvis)
            call GCLSG
c
c       ** Segment Roe
c
            call GCRSG (3)
              call GSELNT (4)
              call GSFAIS (ghatch)
              call GSFASI (nhatch)
              call GSFACI (8)
              call GFA (52,xroe,yroe)
              call GPL (53,xroe,yroe)
              call GSVIS (3,ginvis)
            call GCLSG
c
c       *** INITIALIZE STRING
c
c       ** length
            stlen = 23
            buflen = 23
c
c       ** initial starting position
            inipos = 20
```

```
c
c           ** Define echo area
            xmin = 0.0
            xmax = 0.9*xdc
            ymin = 0.1*ydc
            ymax = 0.9*ydc
c
c
 500  call GINSTS (crtdev,crtdev,stlen,inist,1,
      $                xmin,xmax,ymin,ymax,buflen,inipos,1,datrec)
c
c
c           *** Display Instructions
            call GSELNT (1)
            call GSTXCI (3)
            call GTX (60.0,70.0,'  MAKE SEGMENTS VISIBLE !    ')
            call GSTXCI (7)
            call GTX (0.0,17.5,'"LAKE"')
            call GTX (0.0,15.0,'"TREE"')
            call GTX (0.0,12.5,'"ROE "')
            call GTX (0.0,10.0,'"NO  " to EXIT')
            call GSTXCI (3)
c
c           *** REQUEST STRING
c
            call GRQSTS (crtdev,crtdev,buflen,status,len,datstr)
c
c           *** EVALUATE STRING
c
            if ((status .eq. gnone) .or. (len .gt. buflen))
      $                goto  500
c
            if ((str(20).eq.'L') .and. (str(21).eq.'A') .and.
      $  (str(22).eq.'K') .and. (str(23).eq.'E'))
      $                goto 1000
c
c
            if ((str(20).eq.'T') .and. (str(21).eq.'R') .and.
      $  (str(22).eq.'E') .and. (str(23).eq.'E'))
      $                goto 2000
c
c
            if ((str(20).eq.'R') .and. (str(21).eq.'O') .and.
      $  (str(22).eq.'E') .and.
      $  ((str(23).eq.' ').or.(len.eq.22)))
      $                goto 3000
c
c
            if ((str(20).eq.'N') .and. (str(21).eq.'O') .and.
      $  (((str(22).eq.' ').and.(str(23).eq.' '))
      $   .or.(len .eq. 21)))
      $                goto 4000
c
c
            goto 500
c
c
c
c           *** MAKE SELECTED SEGMENT VISIBLE OR ABORT
c
c           ** Segment Lake
 1000 call GSELNT (2)
            call GSVIS (1,gvisi)
            goto 500
```

```
c
c            ** Segment Tree
 2000 call GSELNT (3)
           call GSVIS (2,gvisi)
           goto 500
c
c            ** Segment Roe
 3000 call GSELNT (4)
           call GSVIS (3,gvisi)
           goto 500
c
c
 4000 continue
c
c*-------------------------------------------------------------------
c
           call GDAWK (crtdev)
           call GCLRWK (crtdev,galway)
           call GCLWK (crtdev)
           call GCLKS
           close (unit1)
c
           end
```

See Plate 18(b).

```
c******************************************************************
c* E.35 ROBOT : Change the Position of a Robot Arm with three   *
c*              Joints using Segment Transformations, Pick Input *
c*              (Mouse), Choice Input (Function Keys) and String *
c*              Input                                            *
c******************************************************************
c* Refers to chapter :                                          *
c* Used external subroutines : dsurf                            *
c******************************************************************
          block data
c
          real  matrix(2,3,0:3)
          real  transl(3), angle(3), limit(3,2)
          real  x0,y0
          common /comrob/ matrix, transl, angle, x0, y0, limit
c
          data matrix(1,1,0), matrix(1,2,0),
     $             matrix(2,1,0), matrix(2,2,0)/
     $                 0.0, 1.0,
     $                 1.0, 0.0  /
          data x0, y0 /45.0, 5.0/
          data   transl /10.0, 5.0, 10.0/
          data angle  /0.0, -90.0, 0.0/
          data limit  /-75.0, 3.0, -135.0,
     $                  75.0, 10.0, 135.0/
c
          end
c
c
c*---------------------------------------------------------------
c
          program robot
c
          implicit logical (a-z)
          integer*4 size,intary(12500)
          integer*2 gerrnr, gfctid
c
          real  matrix(2,3,0:3)
          real  transl(3), angle(3), limit(3,2)
          real  x0,y0
c
          common /gracom/size,intary
          common /gercom/gerrnr, gfctid
          common /comrob/ matrix, transl, angle, x0, y0, limit
c
$INCLUDE:'gdefines.def'
$INCLUDE:'devices.def'
c
          integer unit1
          integer choice, i, err, sgnr, errid
          real x, y, val
          integer tl(5), pid
          integer    ldrec
          integer    asf(13), dl, stat, tnr, tus
          integer    inipos, buflen, stlen, len
          character*80    datrec(10), inist(1), datstr(1)
          real wn(4), vpl(4),vp2(4), rwn(4),cwn(4),cvp(4)
          real px(3), py(3), xndc, yndc, xmin, xmax, ymin, ymax
c
$INCLUDE:'gdefines.dat'
$INCLUDE:'devices.dat'
c
          data unit1 /14/
c
```

```
            data asf    /13 * 1/
            data wn     /0.0, 60.0, 0.0, 60.0/
            data vp1    /0.0, 1.0, 0.0, 1.0/
            data vp2    /0.0, 0.6, 0.0, 1.0/
c
            data stlen  /50/
            data buflen /50/
            data inist  /'ENTER THE VALUE FOR THE JOINT VARIABLE :    '/
            data inipos /42/
c
            size = 12500
c
c
c
c*------------------------------------------------------------------
c
            open (unit1,file='errors.lst',status='new')
            call GOPKS (unit1, 1024)
c
            call GOPWK (crtdev, 0, crtdev)
            call GACWK (crtdev)
c
c           *** Set All Aspect Source Flags to "Individual"
            call GSASF (asf)
c
            call dsurf (crtdev, cvp(2), cvp(4), xndc, yndc)
c
            cvp(1) = 0.0
            cvp(3) = 0.0
            xmin = 0.0
            xmax = cvp(2)
            ymin = 0.0
            ymax = cvp(4)
c
            call GSWN (1,wn(1),wn(2),wn(3),wn(4))
            call GSVP (1,vp1(1)*xndc,vp1(2)*xndc,vp1(3)*yndc,vp1(4)*yndc)
c
            call GSWN (2,wn(1),wn(2),wn(3),wn(4))
            call GSVP (2,vp2(1)*xndc,vp2(2)*xndc,vp2(3)*yndc,vp2(4)*yndc)
c
c           *** INITIALIZE PICK AND CHOICE
            call GINPK (crtdev, msdev, gok, 2,1, 1,cvp(2)*0.5,cvp(2),
          $                      cvp(3),cvp(4)*0.5, 1,datrec)
c
            call GINCH (crtdev,crtdev,gok,1,1,
          $                      cvp(1),cvp(2),cvp(3),cvp(4),1,datrec)
c
c           *** CALCULATE SEGMENT MATRICES STARTING WITH SEGMENT 0
            call segmat(0)
c
c           *** CREATE SEGMENTS
            call makeseg
c
c           *** TRANFORM SEGMENTS WITH IN "SEGMAT" CALCULATED SEGMENT
c                         MATRICES STARTING WITH SEGMENT 0
            call trseg(0,matrix,vp1,wn)
c
c
 111        continue
```

```
c
c          *** Display Choice Menu
           call GSELNT (2)
           call GTX (5.0,55.0,'CHOICE WANTED : ')
           call GTX (5.0,52.0,'^^^^^^^^^^^^^^    ')
           call GTX (5.0,48.0,'F1 = Exit        ')
           call GTX (5.0,45.0,'F2 = Pick & Move')
c
c          *** REQUEST AND EVALUATE CHOICE
           call GRQCH (crtdev,crtdev,stat,choice)
           if (choice.eq.2) then
                call GTX (5.0,55.0,'                    ')
                call GTX (5.0,52.0,'                    ')
                call GTX (5.0,48.0,'                    ')
                call GTX (5.0,45.0,'                    ')
                call GSELNT (1)
c               ** Redraw all Segments on Workstation
                call GRSGWK (crtdev)
           endif
           goto (999,200), choice
           goto 111
c
 200  continue
c
c          *** Display Instructions
           call GSELNT (2)
           call GTX (5.0,25.0,'PICK SEGMENT !')
           call GSELNT (1)
c
c          *** REQUEST AND EVALUATE PICK
           call GRQPK (crtdev,msdev,stat,sgnr,pid)
           call GSELNT (2)
           call GTX (5.0,25.0,'                    ')
           call GSELNT (1)
           if ((sgnr .lt. 1) .or. (sgnr .gt. 3)) goto 111
c
c          ** Highlight picked Segment
           call GSHLIT (sgnr, ghilit)
c
c          ** Initialize value for joint movements
           if (sgnr .eq. 2) val = transl(2)
           if (sgnr .ne. 2) val = angle(sgnr)
c
c          *** INITIALIZE STRING
           call GINSTS (crtdev,crtdev,stlen,inist(1),1,
     $             xmin,xmax,ymax*0.15,ymax,buflen,inipos,1,datrec)
c
c          ** Limit for joint movement values
           if (sgnr .eq. 1) call GTX (5.0,5.0,'[- 75, 75]')
           if (sgnr .eq. 2) call GTX (5.0,5.0,'[   3, 10]')
           if (sgnr .eq. 3) call GTX (5.0,5.0,'[-135,135]')
c
c          *** REQUEST STRING (angle between x-axes and segment or
c                               value for shift joint)
  10       call GRQSTS (crtdev,crtdev,buflen,stat,len,datstr)
           if ((stat .eq. gnone) .or. (len .eq. 0)) goto 10
           call GTX (5.0,5.0,'            ')
c
c          ** Convert string into real
           call convert (datstr,val)
c
           if ((limit(sgnr,1).gt.val) .or. (limit(sgnr,2).lt.val))
     $     goto 10
```

```
c
c               ** Stop Highlighting of selected segment
                call GSHLIT (sgnr, gnorml)
c
                if (sgnr .eq. 2) transl(2) = val
                if (sgnr .ne. 2) angle(sgnr) = val
c
c               *** CALCULATE SEGMENT MATRICES STARTING WITH PICKED SEGMENT
                call segmat(sgnr)

c               *** TRANSFORM SEGMENTS WITH SEGMENT MATRICES CALCULATED IN
c                     "SEGMAT"
c                     (START WITH SEGMENT 0)
                call trseg (sgnr, matrix,vpl,wn)
c
                goto 111
c
 999  continue
c
c
c
                call GDAWK (crtdev)
                call GCLWK (crtdev)
                call GCLKS
                close (unit1)
                stop
                end
```

See Plates 18(c) and (d) and 19(a).

```
c
c*======================================================================
c
c*---------------------------------------------------------------*
c* Makeseg : Defines geometry of robot segments and creates      *
c*           GKS segments                                        *
c*---------------------------------------------------------------*
                subroutine makeseg
c
                real  matrix(2,3,0:3)
                real  transl(3), angle(3), limit(3,2)
                real  x0,y0
c
                common /comrob/ matrix, transl, angle, x0, y0, limit
                integer    maxpn, maxln
                parameter (maxpn=13, maxln=13)
c
                integer    i, j, k, ntr, pli
                real  gpx(2), gpy(2)
                real  px(maxpn,0:3), py(maxpn,0:3)
                integer lines(2,maxln,0:3), nl(0:3)
                character*80    datrec(1)
c
$INCLUDE:'devices.def'
$INCLUDE:'gdefines.def'
$INCLUDE:'devices.dat'
$INCLUDE:'gdefines.dat'
c
c               ** Point list of each segment
                data px /-3.5, -0.5, -0.5, -3.5, 9*0,
      1              -9.5, -7, -1, -1, -7, -1, -1, 1, 1, 4*0,
      2              -10, -10, -2, -0.5, -2, 8*0,
      3              -9.5, -7.5, -2.5, -2.5, -7.5, -2.5, 0, 0, -2, -2,
      3              0, 0, -2.5/
```

```
                 data py /5, 5, -5, -5, 9*0,
     1                 0, -1, -1, 1, 1, -2, 2, -2, 2, 4*0,
     2                 -0.9, 0.9, 0.9, 0, -0.9, 8*0,
     3                 0, 0.9, 0.9, -0.9, -0.9, 1.25, 1.25, 0.9, 0.9, -0.9, -0.9,
     3                 -1.25, -1.25/
c
c                ** Number of edges in each segment
                 data nl /4, 7, 5, 13/
c
c                ** Edge list of each segment
                 data lines /1,2, 2,3, 3,4, 4,1, 18*0,
     1                 1,2, 2,3, 3,4, 4,5, 5,1, 6,7, 8,9, 12*0,
     2                 1,2, 2,3, 3,4, 4,5, 5,1, 16*0,
     3                 1,2, 2,3, 3,4, 4,5, 5,1, 6,7, 7,8, 8,9,
     3                 9,10, 10,11, 11,12, 12,13, 13,6/
c
                 ntr = 1
                 call GSELNT (ntr)
c
c                *** CREATE SEGMENTS
c
c                ==== for every segment
                 do 10 i=0,3
                   call GCRSG (i)
c
c                      ::: for every edge in current segment
                       do 20 j=1,nl(i)
c
c                          .. from starting to ending point of edge
                           do 30 k = 1,2
                                 gpx(k) = px(lines(k,j,i),i)
                                 gpy(k) = py(lines(k,j,i),i)
c                                     j is edge_id
c                                     i is segment_id
  30                         continue
c                          ....................................
c
                           call GSPLCI (2)
                           if (i .eq. 0) then
                                 call GSPLCI (1)
                           endif
                           if (i .eq. 2) then
                                 call GSPLCI (4)
                           endif
c
c                          ** Draw edge
                           call GPL(2,gpx,gpy)
  20                   continue
c                      :::::::::::::::::::::::::::::::::::::::::::::::
c
c                      ** Append ball-and-socket joints to segments 0 and 2
                       if ((i .eq. 0) .or. (i .eq. 2)) then
                             gpx(1) = 0.0
                             gpy(1) = 0.0
                             gpx(2) = 0.0
                             gpy(2) = 0.5
                             call GSFACI (3)
                             call GSFAIS (gsolid)
                             call GGDP (2,gpx,gpy,gcircl,1,datrec)
                             call GSFACI (1)
                             call GSFAIS (ghollo)
                       endif
                 call GCLSG
```

```
c
c
c              ** Make Segments detectable
               call GSDTEC (i,gdetec)
c
 10            continue
c              ========================================================
c
               call GSPLCI (1)
c
               return
               end
c
c*-----------------------------------------------------------------
c
c*-----------------------------------------------------------------*
c* Trseg : Transforms Segments using the current Transformation  *
c*         Matrix "matrix" starting with segment "nbegin"         *
c*         (picked segment)                                       *
c*-----------------------------------------------------------------*
               subroutine trseg(nbegin,matrix,vpl,wn)
c
               real  scalx, scaly
               real  matrix(2,3,0:3), mat(2,3), vpl(4),wn(4)
               integer nbegin, i, j, k
c
               scalx = (vpl(2) - vpl(1))/(wn(2) - wn(1))
               scaly = (vpl(4) - vpl(3))/(wn(4) - wn(3))
c
c              ** from picked segment to last segment
               do 10 i=nbegin,3
c
c                  ** over every element of 2x3-Transformation Matrix
                   do 20 j=1,2
                      do 20 k=1,3
                             mat(j,k) = matrix(j, k, i)
 20                continue
c
c                  ** Transformation from WC (matrix) to NDC (GSSGT)
                   mat(1,3) = mat(1,3) * scalx
                   mat(2,3) = mat(2,3) * scaly
c
c                  *** EXECUTE SEGMENT TRANSFORMATION
                   call GSSGT(i,mat)
 10            continue
               return
               end
c
c*-----------------------------------------------------------------
c
c*-----------------------------------------------------------------*
c* Calcmat : Calculates the Transformation Matrix "mat" relative *
c*            to translation "transl" and rotation angle "angle"  *
c*            (between x-axis of window coordinate system and      *
c*                       x-axis of segment coordinate system   )   *
c*-----------------------------------------------------------------*
               subroutine calcmat(mat,transl,angle)
c
               real mat(2,3), transl, angle
               real sine, cosine, a
c
               a = angle * 3.1415926 / 180.0
               sine = sin(a)
```

```
              cosine = cos(a)
c
              mat(1,1) = cosine
              mat(1,2) = - sine
              mat(1,3) = transl*cosine
              mat(2,1) = sine
              mat(2,2) = cosine
              mat(2,3) = transl*sine
c
              return
              end
c
c*------------------------------------------------------------------
c
c*----------------------------------------------------------------*
c* Segmat : Calculates the Transformation Matrices for the        *
c*          segments "seg_nr" to 3                                 *
c*----------------------------------------------------------------*
              subroutine segmat (seg_nr)
c
              real  matrix(2,3,0:3)
              real  transl(3), angle(3), limit(3,2)
              real  x0,y0
c
              common /comrob/ matrix, transl, angle, x0, y0, limit
c
              real amat(2,3)
              integer i, seg_nr, nbegin
c
              if ((seg_nr .lt. 0) .or. (seg_nr .gt. 3)) then
                   write (*,*) 'ERROR IN SEGMAT : ILLEGAL SEGMENT NR.'
                   return
              endif
c
              nbegin = seg_nr
c
              if (seg_nr .eq. 0) then
c
c                  ** Because segment 0 cannot be picked,here we
c                     perform the initial transformation
                   matrix(1,3,0) = x0
                   matrix(2,3,0) = y0
                   nbegin = 1
              endif
c
c             ** for the segments nbegin..3
              do 10 i=nbegin,3
c
c                  ** Calculate new transformation matrix
                   call calcmat(amat, transl(i), angle(i))
c
c                  ** Calculate matrix product of transformation matrix
c                     of current segment and transformation matrix of
c                     previous segment
                   call matprod(matrix(1,1,i),matrix(1,1,i-1),amat)
 10           continue
c
              return
              end
c
c*----------------------------------------------------------------
c
```

```
c*------------------------------------------------------------------*
c* Matprod : Calculates matrix product of "inmat1" and "inmat2"     *
c*            and stores the result in "outmat"                      *
c*------------------------------------------------------------------*
              subroutine matprod (outmat, inmat1, inmat2)
c
              real outmat(2,3), inmat1(2,3), inmat2(2,3)
              real help
              integer i, j, k
c
              do 10 i=1,2
                  do 20 j=1,3
                      outmat(i,j) = 0.0
c
                      do 30 k=1,2
                          outmat(i,j) = outmat(i,j)
     $                             + (inmat1(i,k)*inmat2(k,j))
c
 30                   continue
 20               continue
c
                  outmat(i,3) = outmat(i,3) + inmat1(i,3)
 10           continue
c
              return
              end
c
c*------------------------------------------------------------------
c
c*------------------------------------------------------------------*
c* Convert : Converts a string input into a real value              *
c*------------------------------------------------------------------*
              subroutine convert (str, ang)
c
              character*80 str
              character*80 strx
              character    stry(80)
              character    c
              integer      icount, sign
              real         ang, tens, mult, cmult
              equivalence (strx, stry)
c
              strx = str
              ang = 0.0
              tens = 10.0
              mult = 1.0
              cmult = 1.0
              sign = 1
              icount = 0
c
              c = ' '
 10           continue
c
c                 ** Recognize sign of value
                  if (c .EQ. '-') then
                      sign = -1
                  endif
c
                  icount = icount + 1
                  c = stry(icount)
c
```

```
c               ** look for first digit appearing in the string
                if ((c .GE. '0') .AND. (c .LE. '9') .OR. (c .EQ. '.')) then
                      goto 19
                else
                      goto 10
                endif
c
   19         continue
c
   20         continue
                if (c .EQ. '.') then
                      tens = 1.0
                      mult = 0.1
                      cmult = 0.1
                else
c                     ** Accumulate value
                      ang = ang * tens + float((ichar(c) - 48)) * mult
                      mult = mult * cmult
                endif
c
                icount = icount + 1
                c = stry(icount)
c
c               ** End of string reached ?
                if (icount .EQ. 80) then
                      goto 29
                endif
c
c               ** Abort accumulation of value
c                  if a character follows a digit
                if ((c .LT. '0') .OR. (c .GT. '9')) then
                      goto 29
                endif
c
                goto 20
   29         continue
c
c           ** Remember sign of value
            ang = ang * float(sign)
c
            return
            end
```

Shared FORTRAN
Subroutine
and
Include Files

```
c***********************************************************************
c* DSURF (Subroutine) : Set Workstation Transformation to adjust *
c*                      for differences in Display Space Size    *
c***********************************************************************
           subroutine dsurf (dev, xdc, ydc, xndc, yndc)
c
           integer dev, errind, dcunit
           real xdc,ydc, xndc,yndc, xras,yras, now
c
c          *** INQUIRE DISPLAY SPACE SIZE
c
           call GQDSP (dev, errind, dcunit, xdc,ydc, xras,yras)
c
c          *** CALCULATE WORKSTATION TRANSFORMATION
c
           now = xdc
           if (xdc .LT. ydc) now = ydc
           xndc = xdc / now
           yndc = ydc / now
c
c          *** SET WORKSTATION TRANSFORMATION
c
           call GSWKWN (dev,0.0,xndc,0.0,yndc)
           call GSWKVP (dev,0.0,xdc,0.0,ydc)
c
           return
           end
```

```
**************************************************************
**************************************************************
C
C *** LAKE.DEF
C
      real xlake(16), ylake(16)
C
**************************************************************
C
C *** LAKE.DAT
C
      data xlake / 15.0,   35.0,   55.0,   75.0, 105.0, 190.0,
     $           220.0, 225.0, 210.0, 185.0, 160.0, 110.0,
     $            80.0,  40.0,  15.0,  15.0/
      data ylake /100.0, 115.0, 115.0, 130.0, 135.0, 125.0,
     $           110.0,  80.0,  65.0,  55.0,  60.0,  60.0,
     $            55.0,  55.0,  70.0, 100.0/
C
**************************************************************
**************************************************************
C
C *** ROE.DEF
      real xroe(53), yroe(53)
C
**************************************************************
C
C *** ROE.DAT
C
      data xroe / 40,  47.5, 52.5, 57.5, 52.5, 47.5, 50, 60,
     $            65,  63  , 63  , 63  , 67  , 63  , 60, 75,
     $            70,  80  , 70  , 70  , 70  , 60  , 70, 65,
     $            80, 125  ,145  ,150  ,145  ,140  ,140,135,
     $           135, 130  ,130  ,125  ,125  ,120  , 85, 80,
     $            80,  75  , 75  , 70  , 70  , 65  , 65, 60,
     $            55,  50  , 50  , 50  , 40/
C
      data yroe / 80, 100, 102, 100,  98, 100, 110, 110,
     $           125, 120, 125, 120, 120, 120, 110, 125,
     $           120, 120, 120, 125, 120, 110, 110,  95,
     $            80,  85,  70,  65,  70,  50,  15,  15,
     $            35,  45,  25,  25,  40,  45,  50,  40,
     $            25,  25,  50,  35,  15,  15,  50,  70,
     $            85,  80,  85,  80,  80/
C
```

```
**************************************************************
**************************************************************
C
C *** TREE.DEF
C
      real xtree(60), ytree(60)
C
**************************************************************
C
c *** TREE.DAT
c
      data xtree /13.0, 16.0, 21.0, 22.0, 22.0, 25.0, 25.0, 22.0,
     $            17.0, 14.0, 11.0,  8.0,  7.0,  8.0, 10.0, 11.0,
     $            13.0, 16.0, 18.0, 20.0, 23.0, 25.0, 27.0, 30.0,
     $            35.0, 39.0, 39.0, 43.0, 47.0, 52.0, 56.0, 59.0,
     $            60.0, 61.0, 64.0, 65.0, 68.0, 69.0, 69.0, 67.0,
     $            64.0, 62.0, 59.0, 54.0, 52.0, 50.0, 47.0, 43.0,
     $            40.0, 38.0, 37.0, 36.0, 35.0, 37.0, 38.0, 39.0,
     $            40.0, 42.0, 22.0, 13.0/
C
      data ytree /11.0, 11.0, 13.0, 17.0, 20.0, 40.0, 44.0, 46.0,
     $            45.0, 48.0, 51.0, 51.0, 53.0, 54.0, 57.0, 59.0,
     $            63.0, 64.0, 65.0, 66.0, 65.0, 67.0, 66.0, 65.0,
     $            64.0, 66.0, 65.0, 63.0, 66.0, 65.0, 64.0, 63.0,
     $            62.0, 63.0, 60.0, 60.0, 59.0, 59.0, 57.0, 56.0,
     $            55.0, 54.0, 51.0, 49.0, 48.0, 47.0, 46.0, 45.0,
     $            44.0, 42.0, 49.0, 36.0, 32.0, 22.0, 16.0, 13.0,
     $            11.0,  9.0, 12.0, 11.0/
C
**************************************************************
**************************************************************
**************************************************************
**************************************************************
C
C *** DEVICES.DEF
C
      integer wssdev,crtdev, msdev,joydev,tabdev
      integer gmodev,gmidev,prtdev,pltdev,camdev
C
**************************************************************
C
C *** DEVICES.DAT
C
      data wssdev,crtdev, msdev,joydev,tabdev  /0,1,2,2,3/
      data gmodev,gmidev,prtdev,pltdev,camdev  /4,5,6,7,8/
C
**************************************************************
**************************************************************
C
C *** ECHOS.DEF
C
      integer glink, glrect, glstand, glrub
C
**************************************************************
C
C *** ECHOS.DAT
C
      data glink, glrect, glstand, glrub /-2, -1, 1, 4/
```

```
      C
      ************************************************************
      ************************************************************
      C
      C *** FONTS.DEF
      C
            integer hdware,gsimpx,gcompx,icompx
            integer gduplx,gtripx,itripx
      C
      ************************************************************
      C
      C *** FONTS.DAT
      C
            data hdware,gsimpx,gcompx,icompx /1,-101,-102,-103/
            data gduplx,gtripx,itripx /-104,-105,-106/
      C
      ************************************************************
      ************************************************************
      C
      C *** GDEFINES.DEF
      C
            integer gcurnt,gspec
            integer gbundl,gindiv
            integer gplbnd,gpmbnd,gtxbnd,gfabnd
            integer gdefd,gundef
            integer gnclip,gclip
            integer gpostp,gperf
            integer gcondi,galway
            integer gmonoc,gcolor
            integer gvalid,ginval
            integer gwc,gndc
            integer gmetre,gothu
            integer gasap,gbnig,gbnil,gasti
            integer gsuppd,gallow
            integer gnempt,gempty
            integer genone,geloc,gestrk,geval,gechc,gepick,gestr
            integer gnecho,gecho
            integer ghollo,gsolid,gpattr,ghatch
            integer gproff,gpron
            integer gnclas,glocat,gstrok,gvalua,gchoic,gpick,gstrin
            integer grequ,gsampl,gevent
            integer gset,greali
            integer girg,gimm
            integer gno,gyes
            integer ggkcl,ggkop,gwsop,gwsac,gsgop
            integer glma,glmb,glmc,gl0a,gl0b,gl0c
            integer gl1a,gl1b,gl1c,gl2a,gl2b,gl2c
            integer gld2d,glmdsh,glsoli,gldash,gldot,gldasd
            integer gdiam,gpoint,gplus,gast,gomark,gxmark
            integer gpline,gfilla
            integer gnone,gok,gnpck,gnchoi
            integer gabsnt,gprsnt
            integer gpostp,gperfo
            integer gundet,gdetec
            integer gnorml,ghilit
            integer ginvis,gvisi
            integer gnmore,gmore
            integer gahnor,galeft,gacent,garite
```

```
      integer gavnor,gatop,gacap,gahalf,gabase,gabott
      integer gright,gleft,gup,gdown
      integer gstrp,gcharp,gstrkp
      integer gnpend,gpend
      integer ghighr,glower
      integer goutpt,ginput,goutin,gwiss,gmo,gmi
      integer gvectr,grastr,gothwk
      integer ginact,gactiv
      integer gbar,garc,gpie,gcircl
C
***************************************************************
C
C *** GDEFINES.DAT
C
      data gcurnt,gspec /0,1/
      data gbundl,gindiv /0,1/
      data gplbnd,gpmbnd,gtxbnd,gfabnd /0,1,2,3/
      data gdefd,gundef /0,1/
      data gnclip,gclip /0,1/
      data gpostp, gperf /0,1/
      data gcondi,galway /0,1/
      data gmonoc,gcolor /0,1/
      data gvalid,ginval /1,0/
      data gwc,gndc /0,1/
      data gmetre,gothu /0,1/
      data gasap,gbnig,gbnil,gasti /0,1,2,3/
      data gsuppd, gallow /0, 1/
      data gnempt,gempty /0,1/
      data genone,geloc,gestrk,geval,gechc /0,1,2,3,4/
      data gepick,gestr /5,6/
      data gnecho,gecho /0,1/
      data ghollo,gsolid,gpattr,ghatch /0,1,2,3/
      data gproff,gpron /0,1/
      data gnclas,glocat,gstrok,gvalua,gchoic,gpick,gstrin
     *          /0,1,2,3,4,5,6/
      data grequ,gsampl,gevent /0,1,2/
      data gset,greali /0,1/
      data girg,gimm /0,1/
      data gno,gyes /0,1/
      data ggkcl,ggkop,gwsop,gwsac,gsgop /0,1,2,3,4/
      data glma,glmb,glmc,gl0a,gl0b,gl0c /-3,-2,-1,0,1,2/
      data glla,gllb,gllc,gl2a,gl2b,gl2c /3,4,5,6,7,8/
      data gld2d,glmdsh,glsoli,gldash,gldot,gldasd /-2,-1,1,2,3,4/
      data gdiam,gpoint,gplus,gast,gomark,gxmark /-1,1,2,3,4,5/
      data gpline,gfilla /0,1/
      data gnone,gok,gnpck,gnchoi /0,1,2,2/
      data gabsnt,gprsnt /0,1/
      data gundet,gdetec /0,1/
      data gnorml,ghilit /0,1/
      data ginvis,gvisi /0,1/
      data gnmore,gmore /0,1/
      data gahnor,galeft,gacent,garite /0,1,2,3/
      data gavnor,gatop,gacap,gahalf,gabase,gabott /0,1,2,3,4,5/
      data gright,gleft,gup,gdown /0,1,2,3/
      data gstrp,gcharp,gstrkp /0,1,2/
      data gnpend,gpend /0,1/
      data ghighr,glower /0,1/
      data goutpt,ginput,goutin,gwiss,gmo,gmi /0,1,2,3,4,5/
```

```
      data gvectr,grastr,gothwk /0,1,2/
      data ginact,gactiv /0,1/
      data gbar,garc,gpie,gcircl /-1,-2,-3,-4/
c
************************************************************
************************************************************
c
c *** HATCH.DEF
c
      integer nhatch,mhatch,whatch
      integer nxhtch,mxhtch,wxhtch
c
************************************************************
c
c *** HATCH.DAT
c
      data nhatch,mhatch,whatch /-1,-2,-3/
      data nxhtch,mxhtch,wxhtch /-4,-5,-6/
c
************************************************************
************************************************************
```

Appendix F
☐ ☐ ■ GKS C PROGRAMMING
■ EXAMPLES FOR THE IBM PC/AT

F.1 Device Environment

F.1.1 Recommended Hardware

The following hardware was used to check out the examples and produce the pictures. Other combinations of computer and display hardware may work as well. For example, the math co-processor is highly recommended because GKS uses a floating point world coordinate system. Furthermore, GSS does support many other graphics display devices. Contact them for the latest details regarding supported devices.

- IBM-compatible Personal Computer AT with 512 kbytes of RAM
- 1 floppy disk drive with at least 360 kbytes capacity
- 1 hard disk drive with at least 10 Mbytes capacity
- EGA-compatible graphics card
- Math co-processor
- Microsoft Mouse

F.1.2 Recommended Software

The following software was used to check out the examples and produce the pictures. Other combinations of IBM and GSS software may work as well. In addition, GSS does support other combinations of C compilers and linkers. Contact them for the latest details regarding supported environments.

- Graphic Software Systems Graphical Kernel System (GSS*GKS version 2.10 or later), which uses the GSS*CGI Virtual Device Interface software.
- GSS*CGI Device Driver for the IBM Extended Graphics Adaptor (IBMEGA.SYS).
- GSS*CGI Device Driver for the Microsoft Mouse (MSMOUSE.SYS).
- Microsoft Personal Computer Disk Operating System (MS-DOS) Version 2.1 or later.

- Microsoft Personal Computer Linker Version 3.55 or later.
- Microsoft C Version 5.0 or later.
- Microsoft Mouse Device Driver Version 6.0 or appropriate.

F.1.3   Comments

- Differences between what you see in this book and what you see on your display are to be expected if you use different hardware and software.
- In all the examples, it is assumed that the initial values of the aspect source flags are set to INDIVIDUAL.
- For a rigorous GKS program seeking maximum portability, each 'scanf("%s",str)' should be replaced by 'grq_str (...)'.
- For clarity and to keep the examples self-contained, the use of previously-defined subroutines has been avoided in the introductory programs (Chapters 3, 4 and 5).
- The non-interactive example programs are terminated by pressing any key and then the RETURN or ENTER key after you have finished viewing the picture on the display.
- The names of the program examples do not necessarily agree with the corresponding file names.
- The color descriptions used are specific to the EGA device.

Your AUTOEXEC.BAT file should contain at least:

- SET KERNEL=<path to a subdirectory where your KERNEL.SYS file will reside.>

Your CONFIG.SYS file should contain at least:

- device=[path]IBMEGA.SYS
- device=[path]GSSCGI.SYS
- files=20
- buffers=16

if possible, in that order.

F.2   Use of the Microsoft C Compiler

Compile your PROG.C program by typing

    [path]CL /c /AL /Gs /Zp prog.c

at the command line. Refer to your Microsoft C Compiler manual to find the appropriate options for your program.

F.3   Use of the Microsoft Linker

There are two possibilities:

1. type LINK;
   input the files requested;
   %%this procedure is awkward with frequent use%%
2. create a .BAT file with changeable parameters;
   start the .BAT file with the desired program name and parameters.

For example, the TEST.OBJ program compiled with CL should be connected to the procedure SUB.OBJ, the GKS Error Logging Routine GERR_LOG.OBJ, the GKS Error Handling Routine GERR_HND.OBJ and the required GKS and C libraries; the result should be filed under TEST.EXE, and a listing should be created under the name TEXT.MAP. (In the following, [path] stands for the respective path entries.)
Creating L.BAT:

[path]LINK %1 %2 [path]GERR_HND [path]GERR_LOG ,,,[path]MSCGKS /CO /SEG:1024 /ST:10000

(must be written on one line)

MSCGKS.LIB : GKS language binding for Microsoft C 5.0

To link, type:

L [path]TEST [path]SUB

If you want to link the example programs you have to type:

L [path]<prog>
or
L [path]<prog> [path]DSURF

where <prog> is the name of the C program taken from the table below. (See the comments in the header of the program listing to determine whether you need to link with the subroutine DSURF.)

Index of GKS C Programs on the IBM PC/AT

F.1	TREE	F.6	LOC
F.2	MULTNT	F.7	RECTROT
F.3	STATTEMP	F.8	CLOCK
F.4	SEGCRDEL	F.9	JULIA
F.5	CELL	F.10	MANDBROT

The headers of these files contain references to the chapters of the book where the functions illustrated by the programs are explained.

Include Files

The C programs share several include files and the procedure DSURF, which are listed following the listing of program F.10.

```
#include "stdio.h"
#include "devices.h"
#include "gdefines.h"
#include "tree.h"

/*******************************************************************
 *      F.1 TREE : Creating an object using different output       *
 *                 primitives                                      *
 *                 (Compare with Tree.for)                         *
 *******************************************************************
 *      Refers to chapter : 5.1                                    *
 *      Used external subroutines :                                *
 *******************************************************************/
main ()
{ int errfil;
  char str[50];
  extern short gerror_number, groutine;

  errfil = creat ("errors.lst", 0644);

/*===============================================================*/

  gopn_gks (errfil, 5000);
  if (gerror_number != 0)
    {gcls_gks ();
     exit (-999);
    }

  gopn_wk (DISPLAY, 0, DISPLAY);
  gact_wk (DISPLAY);

  gs_wind (1, 0.0, 70.0, 0.0, 70.0);
  gs_view (1, 0.0, 1.0, 0.0, 1.0);
  g_seltrn (1);

/* SET FILLAREA ATTRIBUTES */

  gsf_inter (GSOLID);
  gsf_color (3);

/* DISPLAY FILLAREA */

  g_fillarea (59, xtree, ytree);

/* SET POLYLINE ATTRIBUTES */

  gsl_type (GLSOLID);
  gsl_color (1);

/* DISPLAY POLYLINE */

  g_pline (60, xtree, ytree);

  scanf ("%s",str);

  gdct_wk (DISPLAY);
  gcls_wk (DISPLAY);
  gcls_gks ();

}
```

```
#include "stdio.h"
#include "devices.h"
#include "gdefines.h"
#include "hatch.h"
#include "tree.h"
#include "roe.h"
#include "lake.h"
#include "background.h"

/*******************************************************************
 *      F.2 MULTNT : Displaying Objects using different            *
 *                   Normalization Transformations                 *
 *                   (Compare with Multnt.for)                     *
 *******************************************************************
 *      Refers to chapter : 3.3                                    *
 *      Used external subroutines : dsurf                          *
 *******************************************************************/

main ()
{
  extern int dsurf ();
  int errfil, errind;
  float xdc, ydc, xndc, yndc;
  char str[50];
  extern short gerror_number, groutine;


  errfil = creat ("errors.lst", 0644);

/*===============================================================*/

  gopn_gks (errfil, 5000);
  if (gerror_number != 0)
    {gcls_gks();
     exit (-999);
    }

  gopn_wk (DISPLAY, 0, DISPLAY);
  gact_wk (DISPLAY);


/* SET WORKSTATION TRANSFORMATION */

  errind = dsurf (DISPLAY, &xdc, &ydc, &xndc, &yndc);


/* SET NORMALIZATION TRANSFORMATIONS */

                 /* Normalization Transformation for Background */
  gs_wind (1, 0.0, 10.0, 0.0, 10.0);
  gs_view (1, 0.0,  1.0, 0.0,  1.0);

                 /* Normalization Transformation for Lake */
  gs_wind (2, 0.0, 250.0, 0.0, 150.0);
  gs_view (2, 0.1,   0.9, 0.1,   0.6);

                 /* Normalization Transformation for Tree */
  gs_wind (3, 0.0, 70.0, 0.0, 70.0);
  gs_view (3, 0.0,  0.4, 0.5,  0.7);

                 /* Normalization Transformation for Roe */
  gs_wind (4, 0.0, 200.0, 0.0, 200.0);
  gs_view (4, 0.5,   0.9, 0.15,  0.55);
```

```
gscl_rep (DISPLAY, 8, 0.6, 0.6, 0.0);
gscl_rep (DISPLAY, 9, 0.6, 0.6, 0.6);

gsl_bindex (GLSOLID);
gsl_color (0);
gsf_inter (GSOLID);


/* CREATE OBJECTS USING DIFFERENT NORMALIZATION TRANSFORMATIONS */

g_seltrn (1);          /* Select Normalization Transformation */
gsf_color (9);
g_fillarea (4, xback, yback);    /* Display Object Background */

g_seltrn (2);          /* Select Normalization Transformation */
gsf_color (4);
g_fillarea (15, xlake, ylake);   /* Display Object Lake */
g_pline     (16, xlake, ylake);

g_seltrn (3);          /* Select Normalization Transformation */
gsf_color (3);
g_fillarea (59, xtree, ytree);   /* Display Object Tree */
g_pline     (60, xtree, ytree);

g_seltrn (4);          /* Select Normalization Transformation */
gsf_inter (GHATCH);
gsf_style (NHATCH);
gsf_color (8);
g_fillarea (52, xroe, yroe);      /* Display Object Roe  */
g_pline     (53, xroe, yroe);


scanf ("%s",str);


gdct_wk (DISPLAY);
gcls_wk (DISPLAY);
gcls_gks ();

}
```

See Plate 13(c).

```
#include "stdio.h"
#include "devices.h"
#include "gdefines.h"
#include "hatch.h"

/******************************************************************
*     F.3 STATTEMP : Displaying Statistics using the Generalized *
*                    Drawing Primitives "Circle", "Arc" and      *
*                                       "Pie slice"              *
*                    (Compare with Stattemp.for)                *
******************************************************************
*     Refers to chapter : 5.1                                    *
*     Used external subroutines : dsurf                          *
******************************************************************/

float xpsl[3] = { 90.0, 145.0,  55.5 }, /* Arc/Slice Starting */
      ypsl[3] = { 75.0,  75.0, 117.5 }, /* Coordinates        */

        xdiff[5] = { -19.0,   3.0,  3.0,107.0, 0.0 },
        ydiff[5] = { -52.0, -10.0, -7.5, 25.0, 0.0 },

                        /* Coordinates for Description */
                        /* of Statistics              */

        xtemp[5] = {150.0,  0.0, 12.5, 14.0, 90.0 },
        ytemp[5] = { 90.0, 85.0, 65.0, 55.0, 15.0 },

        xpct[5] = {110.0, 40.0, 14.0, 16.0, 90.0 },
        ypct[5] = {100.0, 85.0, 60.0, 50.0, 40.0 };

                        /* Description of Statistics */

char *temp[5] = {"0 -31 mph","32-37 mph","38-42 mph","43-48 mph",
                 "49-   mph"},

     *pct[5] = {"35.3 %","17.1 %","03.0 %","00.5 %","43.0 %"};

main ()
{
  extern int dsurf ();
  int errfil, errind, i;
  float xdc, ydc, xndc, yndc;
  float xcirc[2], ycirc[2], xnpsl, ynpsl;
  char str[50],datrec[1],*strbuf[6];
  extern short gerror_number, groutine;

  errfil = creat ("errors.lst", 0644);

/*===============================================================*/

  gopn_gks (errfil, 5000);
  if (gerror_number != 0)
    {gcls_gks();
     exit (-999);
    }

  gopn_wk (DISPLAY, 0, DISPLAY);
  gact_wk (DISPLAY);

  errind = dsurf (DISPLAY, &xdc, &ydc, &xndc, &yndc);

  gs_wind (1, 0.0, 280.0, 0.0, 280.0);
  gs_view (1, 0.0,   1.0, 0.0,   1.0);
```

```
g_seltrn (1);

g_text (60.0, 175.0, "  MEASURED DRIVING SPEED ");
g_text (60.0, 170.0, " ----------------------");
g_text (60.0, 165.0, "AT A SPEED LIMIT OF 50 MPH");
g_text (60.0, 160.0, "--------------------------");

gsf_color (1);
gsf_inter (GHATCH);

xnpsl = xpsl[1];
ynpsl = ypsl[1];

for (i=0;i<2;i++)                          /* Coordinates for Circles */
{ xcirc[i] = xpsl[i] + 3.0;
  ycirc[i] = ypsl[i] + 3.0;
}


/* DISPLAY CIRCLES */

for (i=0;i<2;i++)
{ g_gdp (2, xcirc, ycirc, GCIRCLE, 0, datrec);
  gsf_inter (GHOLLOW);
}


gsf_inter (GSOLID);
gst_align (GTNORMAL, GTV_HALF);
for (i=0;i<5;i++)
{ gst_color (i+1);
    gsf_color (i+1);

/* DISPLAY SLICES PARTIALLY SURROUNDED BY ARCS */

      g_gdp (3, xpsl, ypsl, GSLICE, 0, datrec);
      g_gdp (3, xpsl, ypsl, GARC  , 0, datrec);

                           /* Description for Statistics */
      g_text (xtemp[i],ytemp[i],temp[i]);
      gst_color (1);
      g_text (xpct[i],ypct[i],pct[i]);

      xpsl[1] = xpsl[2];      /* Final Point of an Arc/Slice is        */
      ypsl[1] = ypsl[2];      /* Starting Point of the next Arc/Slice */
      xpsl[2]+= xdiff[i];     /* New Final Point */
      ypsl[2]+= ydiff[i];
      if (i==3) {
        xpsl[2] = xnpsl;
        ypsl[2] = ynpsl;
      }
}
g_text (5.0, 5.0,    "PRESS <Y><RETURN> TO EXIT !");
do
  scanf ("%s",str);
while (str[0] != 'Y' && str[0] != 'y');

gdct_wk (DISPLAY);
gcls_wk (DISPLAY);
gcls_gks ();

}
```

```
#include "stdio.h"
#include "devices.h"
#include "gdefines.h"
#include "hatch.h"
#include "tree.h"
#include "roe.h"
#include "lake.h"
#include "background.h"

/*****************************************************************
*     F.4 SEGCRDEL : Creating and Deleting Segments             *
*                                                               *
*                    (Compare with Segcrdel.for)                *
*****************************************************************
*     Refers to chapter : 6.1                                   *
*     Used external subroutines : dsurf                         *
*****************************************************************/

main ()
{
  extern int dsurf ();
  int errfil, errind, i;
  float xdc, ydc, xndc, yndc;
  char str[50];
  extern short gerror_number, groutine;


  errfil = creat ("errors.lst", 0644);

/*==============================================================*/

  gopn_gks (errfil, 5000);
  if (gerror_number != 0)
    {gcls_gks();
     exit (-999);
    }

  gopn_wk (DISPLAY, 0, DISPLAY);
  gact_wk (DISPLAY);

  errind = dsurf (DISPLAY, &xdc, &ydc, &xndc, &yndc);

                        /* Normalization Transformation for Objects */

  gs_wind (1, 0.0, 10.0, 0.0, 10.0);          /* ... Background */
  gs_view (1, 0.0,  1.0, 0.0,  1.0);

  gs_wind (2, 0.0, 250.0, 0.0, 150.0);        /* ... Segment Lake */
  gs_view (2, 0.1,   0.9, 0.1,   0.6);

  gs_wind (3, 0.0, 70.0, 0.0, 70.0);          /* ... Segment Tree */
  gs_view (3, 0.0,  0.4, 0.5,  0.7);

  gs_wind (4, 0.0, 200.0, 0.0, 200.0);        /* ... Segment Roe */
  gs_view (4, 0.5,   0.9, 0.15,  0.55);

  gscl_rep (DISPLAY, 8, 0.6, 0.6, 0.0);
  gscl_rep (DISPLAY, 9, 0.6, 0.6, 0.6);

  gsl_bindex (GLSOLID);
  gsl_color (0);
  gsf_inter (GSOLID);
```

```
g_scltrn (1);
gsf_color (9);
g_fillarea (4, xback, yback);

g_seltrn (2);
do
{ g_text (10.0, 5.0, "PRESS <Y><RETURN> TO CREATE SEGMENTS !");
    scanf ("%s",str);
    if (str[0] == 'y') str[0] = 'Y';
}
while (str[0] != 'Y');
```

/* CREATE SEGMENTS */

```
gcreat_seg (1);                    /* Segment Lake */
    g_seltrn (2);
    gsf_color (4);
    g_fillarea (15, xlake, ylake);
    g_pline   (16, xlake, ylake);
gcls_seg ();

gcreat_seg (2);                    /* Segment Tree */
    g_seltrn (3);
    gsf_color (3);
    g_fillarea (59, xtree, ytree);
    g_pline   (60, xtree, ytree);
gcls_seg ();

gcreat_seg (3);                    /* Segment Roe */
    g_seltrn (4);
    gsf_inter (GHATCH);
    gsf_style (NHATCH);
    gsf_color (8);
    g_fillarea (52, xroe, yroe);
    g_pline   (53, xroe, yroe);
gcls_seg ();

g_seltrn (2);
do
{ g_text (10.0, 5.0, "PRESS <Y><RETURN> TO DELETE SEGMENTS !");
    scanf ("%s",str);
    if (str[0] == 'y') str[0] = 'Y';
}
while (str[0] != 'Y');
```

/* DELETE THE THREE SEGMENTS */

```
for (i=1;i<=3;i++)
  gdelet_seg (i);

do
{ g_text (10.0, 5.0, "    PRESS <Y><RETURN> TO TERMINATE !    ");
    scanf ("%s",str);
    if (str[0] == 'y') str[0] = 'Y';
}
while (str[0] != 'Y');

gdct_wk (DISPLAY);
gcls_wk (DISPLAY);
gcls_gks ();


}
```

```
#include "stdio.h"
#include "devices.h"
#include "gdefines.h"
#include "hatch.h"
#include "echos.h"
```

See Plate 13(d).

```
/*****************************************************************
*      F.5 CELL : Creating and zooming a trebleclef using the   *
*                 Cell Array Primitive ,                        *
*                 Normalization Transformations and the         *
*                 Locator Input Device                          *
*****************************************************************
*      Refers to chapter : 4.1                                  *
*      Used external subroutines : dsurf                        *
*****************************************************************/

#define col_rows      20      /* Dimensions of Color Index Array */
#define col_columns 20
#define cell_rows     20      /* Dimensions of Cell Array */
#define cell_columns 20

                              /* Trebleclef Coordinates in Cell Array */

int xdraw[44] = {11, 10,11,12, 10,12, 10,12, 10,12, 10,11, 10, 9,10,
                 8,10, 7,10, 7,9,10,11, 7,9,11,12, 7,8,10,11,
                 8,9,10,11, 10, 10, 8,9,10, 8,10, 9,10
                 },

    ydraw[44] = {19, 18,18,18, 17,17, 16,16, 15,15, 14,14, 13, 12,12,
                 11,11, 10,10, 9,9,9,9, 8,8,8,8, 7,7,7,7,
                 6,6,6,6, 5, 4, 3,3,3, 2,2, 1,1
                 };

main ()
{
  extern int dsurf ();
  void Frame ();

  int errfil, errind;
  extern short gerror_number, groutine;

  float xdc, ydc, xndc, yndc,
        x_min, y_min, x_max, y_max,
        x_win_min, x_win_max, y_win_min, y_win_max, xfact, yfact,
        x_up_left, y_up_left, x_low_right, y_low_right,
        xmin, xmax, ymin, ymax,
        xview_f, yview_f, xv_f, yv_f,
        xpos, ypos,
        rarray[2],
        red, green, blue;

  char str[50],
       datrec[80];

  int  i, k, l, m, n,
       nt2 = 2,
       nt3 = 3,
       ntc,
       max_len=80,
       rec_len,
       trans_nr,
```

```
        loc_status,
          iarray[7],
        echo_type,
          row_start, col_start,
          col_array[col_rows*col_columns];


  errfil = creat ("errors.lst", 0644);

/*==================================================================*/

  gopn_gks (errfil, 5000);
  if (gerror_number != 0)
    {gcls_gks();
     exit (-999);
    }

  gopn_wk (DISPLAY, 0, DISPLAY);
  gact_wk (DISPLAY);

  errind = dsurf (DISPLAY, &xdc, &ydc, &xndc, &yndc);

  x_win_min = 0.0;                            /* Initializing Window */
  x_win_max = (float)cell_columns;
  y_win_min = 0.0;
  y_win_max = (float)cell_rows;
  xfact = 20.0 / x_win_max;
  yfact = 20.0 / y_win_max;

  gs_wind (nt2,        0.0, 100.0, 0.0, 100.0);
  gs_view (nt2, 3*xndc/4,  xndc, 0.0,  yndc);
  gsview_pri (nt2,    0, 'GHIGHER);

  g_seltrn (nt2);
  Frame (0.0, 100.0, 0.0, 100.0);      /* Draw a Frame in Locator Area */
  g_text (20.0, 90.0, "Select here");
  g_text (20.0, 85.0, "to  display");
  g_text (20.0, 80.0, "      a      ");
  g_text (20.0, 75.0, "TREBLECLEF!");


/* initialize locator prompt and echo type -1 -- rubber rectangle */

    iarray[0] = GSPECIFIED;  /* attribute control flag */
    iarray[1] = GINDIVIDUAL; /* linetype ASF */
    iarray[2] = GINDIVIDUAL; /* linewidth scale factor ASF */
    iarray[3] = GINDIVIDUAL; /* polyline colour index ASF */
    iarray[4] = 1;           /* polyline bundle index */
    iarray[5] = GLSOLID;     /* linetype index */
    iarray[6] = 2;           /* polyline colour index */
    rarray[0] = 1.0;         /* linetype scale factor */
    str[0] = ' ';
    gpack_rec (7, iarray, 1, rarray, 0, str, 40, datrec);

  rec_len = 80;
  echo_type = LOC_RECTANGLE;
  xmin =  xdc*3/4;
  xmax =  xdc;
  ymin =  0.0;
  ymax =  ydc;
  xpos =  50.0;
```

```
ypos =  50.0;
g_loc_ini (DISPLAY, MOUSE, nt2, xpos,ypos, echo_type,
           xmin, xmax, ymin, ymax, rec_len, datrec);

do
 grq_loc (DISPLAY, MOUSE, &loc_status, &trans_nr, &xpos, &xpos);
while (loc_status != GOK || trans_nr != nt2);

g_seltrn (nt2);
g_text (20.0, 90.0, "Please wait!");
g_text (20.0, 85.0, "          ");
g_text (20.0, 80.0, "          ");
g_text (20.0, 75.0, "          ");


col_start = 0;
row_start = 0;


x_up_left    = x_win_min;        /* Define Color Index Array */
x_low_right = x_win_max;
y_up_left    = y_win_max;
y_low_right = y_win_min;


red    = 1.0;                            /* Initialize Colors for Color Index Array */
green = 0.25;
blue  = 0.75;

for (k=0;k<9;k+=4){

 for (i=0;i<col_rows;i++)        /* Reset Color Index Array */
  for (l=0;l<col_columns;l++)
   col_array[i*col_rows+l] = 0;

 if (k>0){
   g_seltrn (nt3);

/* DRAW CELL ARRAY */

   g_cell (x_up_left,y_up_left, x_low_right,y_low_right,
           col_columns,col_rows,col_start,row_start, cell_columns,
           cell_rows, col_array);
 }

/* PREPARE FOR ZOOMING */

 x_min = -(xfact*(k+1)-1.0)*x_win_max;
 y_min = -(yfact*(k+1)-1.0)*y_win_max;
 x_max = (xfact*(k+1))*x_win_max;
 y_max = (yfact*(k+1))*y_win_max;
 xview_f = (k<8) ? 0.0 : 1.0/(-2.25*x_min/x_win_max);
 yview_f = (k<8) ? 0.0 : 1.0/(-2.25*y_min/y_win_max);
 if (k<8){
                /* Window Zooming */

   gs_wind (nt3, x_min,    x_max, y_min, y_max);
   gs_view (nt3,   0.0, 3*xndc/4,   0.0,  yndc);
   gsview_pri (nt3, nt2, GLOWER);
 }
 else{
  ntc = 3;
```

```
for (n=2;n<6;n+=2)
  for (m=n;m<15;m+=6)
    for (l=n;l<17;l+=7){
      xv_f = xview_f*3*xndc/4;
      yv_f = yview_f*yndc;

              /* Viewport Zooming */

        gs_wind (ntc, 0.0, x_win_max, 0.0, y_win_max);
        gs_view (ntc, l*xv_f, (l+1)*xv_f, m*yv_f, (m+1)*yv_f);
        gsview_pri (ntc, ntc-1, GLOWER);
        ntc++;
        ntc = (ntc > 14) ? 1 : ntc;

    }
} /* if k<8 else */

for (i=0;i<44;i++){        /* Over Coordinates of Trebleclef */
  if (k==0){
                              /* Set Colors for Color Index Array */
    gscl_rep(DISPLAY, i+2, red, green, blue);
      red    -= 0.02272;
      green += 0.017;
    blue   -= 0.017;
  }
                            /* Set Color Index Array */
  col_array[((col_rows-ydraw[i])*col_rows)+(xdraw[i])]= i+2;
}  /* for i */

/* PERFORM ZOOMING */

if (k<8){
    g_seltrn (nt3);
    g_cell (x_up_left,y_up_left, x_low_right,y_low_right, col_columns,
            col_rows, col_start,row_start, cell_columns,cell_rows,
            col_array);
}
else
  for (ntc=3;ntc<16;ntc++){
          ntc = (ntc > 14) ? 1 : ntc;
          g_seltrn (ntc);
          g_cell (x_up_left,y_up_left, x_low_right,y_low_right, col_columns,
                  col_rows, col_start,row_start, cell_columns,cell_rows,
                  col_array);
          ntc = (ntc == 1) ? 16 : ntc;
    }


if (k<8){
  g_seltrn (nt2);
  g_text (20.0, 90.0, "Select here ");
  g_text (20.0, 85.0, "    to     ");
  g_text (20.0, 80.0, " continue  ");
  g_text (20.0, 75.0, "TREBLECLEF!");

  do
    grq_loc (DISPLAY, MOUSE, &loc_status, &trans_nr, &xpos, &xpos);
  while (loc_status != GOK || trans_nr != nt2);
```

```
     g_text (20.0, 90.0, "Please wait!");
     g_text (20.0, 85.0, "            ");
     g_text (20.0, 80.0, "            ");
     g_text (20.0, 75.0, "            ");
   }

 } /* for k */


 g_seltrn (nt2);
 g_text (20.0, 90.0, "Select here ");
 g_text (20.0, 85.0, " to abort !");
 g_text (20.0, 80.0, "            ");
 g_text (20.0, 75.0, "            ");
 do
  grq_loc (DISPLAY, MOUSE, &loc_status, &trans_nr, &xpos, &xpos);
 while (loc_status != GOK || trans_nr != nt2);


 gdct_wk (DISPLAY);
 gcls_wk (DISPLAY);
 gcls_gks ();

}

/*==================================================================*/

void Frame (xmin, xmax, ymin, ymax)
      float xmin, xmax, ymin, ymax;
{ float xframe[5], yframe[5];

 xframe[0] = xmin+5.0;
 xframe[1] = xmax-5.0;
 xframe[2] = xmax-5.0;
 xframe[3] = xmin+5.0;
 xframe[4] = xframe[0];

 yframe[0] = ymin+5.0;
 yframe[1] = ymin+5.0;
 yframe[2] = ymax-5.0;
 yframe[3] = ymax-5.0;
 yframe[4] = yframe[0];

 g_pline (5, xframe, yframe);
}
```

See Plates 19(b) and 19(c).

```c
#include "stdio.h"
#include "devices.h"
#include "gdefines.h"
#include "hatch.h"
#include "echos.h"

/*******************************************************************
 *      F.6 LOC : Interactive Creation of a five-sided Polygon     *
 *                using the Locator Input Device (Mouse)           *
 *                (Compare with Loc.for)                           *
 *******************************************************************
 *      Refers to chapter : 8.1                                    *
 *      Used external subroutines : dsurf                          *
 *******************************************************************/

main ()
{
  extern int dsurf ();

  int errfil, errind;
  extern short gerror_number, groutine;

  float xdc, ydc, xndc, yndc,
        xpos=50.0, ypos=50.0,
        xmult[5], ymult[5],
        xmin, xmax, ymin, ymax,
        rarray[2];

  char str[50],
       datrec[80];

  int  i, k,
       ntl = 1,
       max_len=80,
       rec_len,
         trans_nr,
       loc_status,
       echo_type;


  errfil = creat ("errors.lst", 0644);

/*===============================================================*/

  gopn_gks (errfil, 5000);
  if (gerror_number != 0)
    {gcls_gks();
     exit (-999);
     }

  gopn_wk (DISPLAY, 0, DISPLAY);
  gact_wk (DISPLAY);

  errind = dsurf (DISPLAY, &xdc, &ydc, &xndc, &yndc);

  gs_wind (ntl, 0.0, 100.0, 0.0, 100.0);
  gs_view (ntl, 0.0,  xndc, 0.0,  yndc);

  gsview_pri (ntl, 0, GHIGHER);

  g_seltrn (ntl);
  g_text (10.0,95.0,"CREATE A FIVE_SIDED POLYGON BY USING THE MOUSE !");
```

```
    rec_len = 80;          /* Initialize Locator Parameters*/
    echo_type = 1;
    xmin =  0.0;
    xmax =  xdc;
    ymin =  0.0;
    ymax =  ydc;

    xpos =  50.0;          /* Starting Position of Locator */
    ypos =  50.0;

    gsm_color (4);         /* Presentation of "Edge Points" of Polygon */
    gsm_type  (GXMARKER);
    gsm_scale (0.1);

    for (k=0;k<=4;)        /* For all Edges */
    {

/* INITIALIZE LOCATOR */

      g_loc_ini (DISPLAY, MOUSE, nt1, xpos, ypos, echo_type, xmin, xmax,
                          ymin, ymax, rec_len, datrec);
      do

    /* REQUEST LOCATOR */

          grq_loc (DISPLAY, MOUSE, &loc_status, &trans_nr, xmult+k,
                          ymult+k);
      while (loc_status != GOK || trans_nr != nt1);

      g_seltrn (nt1);
      g_pmarker (1, xmult+k, ymult+k);  /* Place Marker at current */
                                        /* Locator Position        */

      xpos = xmult[k];                   /* Initialize new Locator Position */
      ypos = ymult[k];
      k++;
    }

    gsf_color (3);                 /* Fill Area between located Edges */
    gsf_inter (GSOLID);
    g_fillarea (k,xmult,ymult);

    do
    { g_seltrn (nt1);
      g_text (30.0, 5.0, "PRESS <Y><RETURN> TO EXIT !");
        scanf ("%s",str);
        if (str[0] == 'y') str[0] = 'Y';
    }
    while (str[0] != 'Y');

    gdct_wk (DISPLAY);
    gcls_wk (DISPLAY);
    gcls_gks ();

}
```

```
#include "stdio.h"
#include "math.h"
#include "devices.h"
#include "gdefines.h"

/*********************************************************************
 *      F.7 RECTROT : Creating and Zooming a Rectangle using        *
 *                    Segment Transformations and Insertions        *
 *********************************************************************
 *      Refers to chapter : 6.2                                     *
 *      Used external subroutines : dsurf                           *
 *********************************************************************/

#define max(x,y) ((x>y) ? (x) : (y))

float xline[5] = { -100.0,  100.0, 100.0, -100.0, -100.0 },
      yline[5] = { -100.0, -100.0, 100.0,  100.0, -100.0 };


main ()
{
  extern short gerror_number, groutine;
  extern int dsurf ();
  int errfil, errind;

  float xdc, ydc, xndc, yndc;
  char str[50];

  float x_view_transl,
        PI = 3.141593,
        phi, scalx, scaly,
        tmout[2][3];

  double alpha;

  int     depth,
          i;

  for (i=0;i<25;i++)  printf ("\n");
  do {
    printf ("Enter number of rectangles ( > 0) : ");
      scanf ("%d",&depth);
      printf ("\n");
      if (depth <= 0)
          printf ("ILLEGAL INPUT !!\n");
  }
  while (depth <= 0);

  errfil = creat ("errors.lst", 0644);

/*================================================================*/

  gopn_gks (errfil, 5000);
  if (gerror_number |= 0)
    {gcls_gks ();
     exit (-999);
    }

  gopn_wk (DISPLAY, 0, DISPLAY);
  gopn_wk (WISS, 0, WISS);
  gact_wk (DISPLAY);
  gact_wk (WISS);
```

```
    errind = dsurf (DISPLAY, &xdc, &ydc, &xndc, &yndc);

                        /* Center Rectangles on Display */
    x_view_transl = fabs(xdc-ydc)/(2*max(xdc,ydc));
    gs_wind (1, -100.0, 100.0, -100.0, 100.0);
    gs_view (1, x_view_transl, xndc - x_view_transl, 0.0, yndc);
    g_seltrn (1);


/* CREATE SEGMENT RECTANGLE */

    gcreat_seg (1);
        g_pline (5,xline,yline);
    gcls_seg ();

    phi   = 2.0 * PI / (depth-1);    /* Calculate Rotation Angle */
    alpha = (double)phi;


/* CREATE SEGMENT FOR ZOOMED RECTANGLES */

    gcreat_seg (2);
        for (i=1;i<depth;i++){
                    /* Choose Scaling Factor so that the corners of
                       every rectangle touch the edges of the
                       previous rectangle                          */
            scalx = 1.0/pow((sin(alpha)+cos(alpha)),i);
            scaly = scalx;

            /* EVALUATE TRANSFORMATION MATRIX SEGMENT TO BE ZOOMED*/

            gev_stran (0.0,0.0, 0.0,0.0, phi, scalx,scaly, GWC,
                            tmout);

            /* INSERT SEGMENT UNDER TRANSFORMATION */

            ginsrt_seg (1, tmout);

            phi += (float)alpha;    /* Acculmulate Rotation Angle */
    }
    gcls_seg ();


    scanf ("%s",str);

    gdct_wk (WISS);
    gdct_wk (DISPLAY);
    gcls_wk (WISS);
    gcls_wk (DISPLAY);
    gcls_gks ();

}
```

See Plate 19(d).

```c
#include "stdio.h"
#include "math.h"
#include "devices.h"
#include "gdefines.h"
#include "fonts.h"


/*********************************************************************
 *      F.8 CLOCK : Realizing a Clock with Segments and            *
 *                  Segment Transformations                        *
 *********************************************************************
 *      Refers to chapter : 6.3                                    *
 *      Used external subroutines : dsurf                          *
 *********************************************************************/

#define max(x,y) ((x>y) ? (x) : (y))

char *digit[12] = {"3","2","1","12","11","10",
                             "9","8","7","6","5","4"};

                        /* Default Position of Hands */
float shx[5] = {-0.02, 0.0, 0.02, 0.0, -0.02},
      shy[5] = {0.0, -0.04, 0.0, 0.7, 0.0},
      mhx[6] = {-0.04, -0.02, 0.02, 0.04, 0.0, -0.04},
      mhy[6] = {0.0, -0.1, -0.1, 0.0, 0.65, 0.0},
      hhx[10]= {-0.015, -0.06, -0.02, 0.02, 0.06, 0.015,
                          0.1, 0.0, -0.1, -0.015},
      hhy[10]= {0.0, -0.1, -0.2, -0.2, -0.1, 0.0,
                          0.2, 0.4, 0.2, 0.0},
      PI = 3.141593;


main ()
{
  extern int dsurf();
  int errfil, errind;
  float xdc, ydc, xndc, yndc, x_view_transl;
  char ch[50],datrec[1],ch1,ch2;
  extern short gerror_number, groutine;
  float x[3], y[3],
             sec_mat[2][3], min_mat[2][3], hour_mat[2][3], buf_mat[2][3],
             run_time, rt1, rt2,
             phi;
  int i, k, l,
      hour_start,min_start,sec_start,again,
             ich,
             m,
             delay=1300; /* Adjust depending on the speed
                             of your CPU */


  errfil = creat ("errors.lst", 0644);


  for (i=0;i<25;i++)  printf ("\n");
  again = 0;
```

```
do{
    printf ("Enter current time [HH:MM:SS] : ");
    scanf ("%d%c%d%c%d",&hour_start,&ch1,&min_start,&ch2,&sec_start);
    printf ("\n");
  again = 0;
    if (  (hour_start<0) || (hour_start>24)
          || (min_start<0) || (min_start > 59)
          || (sec_start<0) || (sec_start > 59)
          || (ch1 !=':') || (ch2 !=':')){
          printf ("ILLEGAL TIME FORMAT !!\n");
          again = 1;
    }
} while (again == 1);

do{
    printf ("Enter running time in minutes : ");
    scanf ("%f",&run_time);
    printf ("\n");
  again = 0;
    if (run_time<0){
          printf ("ILLEGAL INPUT !!\n");
          again = 1;
    }
} while (again == 1);


/*================================================================*/

gopn_gks (errfil, 5000);
if (gerror_number != 0)
  {gcls_gks();
   exit (-999);
  }

gopn_wk (DISPLAY, 0, DISPLAY);
gopn_wk (WISS, 0, WISS);
gact_wk (DISPLAY);

errind = dsurf (DISPLAY, &xdc, &ydc, &xndc, &yndc);

                        /* Center Clock on Display */

x_view_transl = fabs(xdc-ydc)/(2*max(xdc,ydc));
gs_wind (1, -1.0,  1.0, -1.0,  1.0);
gs_view (1, x_view_transl, xndc-x_view_transl, 0.0, yndc);
g_seltrn (1);

x[0] = 0.0;
y[0] = 0.0;
x[1] = 1.0;
y[1] = 0.0;

gsf_inter (GSOLID);
gsf_color (1);

/* Draw Frame of Clock by two Circles */

g_gdp (2, x, y, GCIRCLE,1, datrec);
x[1] = 0.95;
gsf_color (0);
g_gdp (2, x, y, GCIRCLE,1, datrec);

x[1] = 0.01;
```

```
/* Draw Digits and Markers */

  gsc_height (0.1);
  for (i=0;i<48;i+=4){
      x[0] = cos(i*PI/24.0)*0.9;
      y[0] = sin(i*PI/24.0)*0.9;
      x[1] = x[0] * 0.95;
      y[1] = y[0] * 0.95;

      g_pline (2, x, y);

      x[2] = x[1] * 0.9 - 0.025;
      y[2] = y[1] * 0.9 - 0.025;
      if (((i+1) > 9) && ((i+1) < 22))  x[2]-=0.03;
      ich = (int)((i+3)/4);

      g_text (x[2],y[2],digit[ich]);
  }
  phi = -PI/30.0;

/* EVALUATE TRANSFORMATION MATRICES FOR THE THREE HANDS
   TRANSFORMING THEM FROM THEIR DEFAULT POSITION INTO THE DESIRED
   STARTING POSITION                                         */

  gev_stran (0.0,0.0, 0.0,0.0, sec_start*phi, 1.0,1.0, GWC, sec_mat);
  gev_stran (0.0,0.0, 0.0,0.0, min_start*phi, 1.0,1.0, GWC, min_mat);
  gev_stran (0.0,0.0, 0.0,0.0,hour_start*5*phi,1.0,1.0,GWC, hour_mat);

/* CREATE SEGMENTS IN WISS */

  gact_wk (WISS);

  gcreat_seg (4);            /* Create Segment "Center of Hands" */
    gs_svisi (4, GINVISIBLE);
     gs_sprior (4, 1.0);
    g_gdp (2, x, y, GCIRCLE,1, datrec);
  gcls_seg ();

  gsf_color (1);
  gsl_color (0);

  gcreat_seg (1);            /* Create Segment "Second Hand" */
    gs_svisi (1, GINVISIBLE);
     gs_sprior (1, 0.9);
     g_fillarea (4,shx,shy);
     g_pline (5,shx,shy);
  gcls_seg();

  gcreat_seg (2);            /* Create Segment "Minute Hand" */
    gs_svisi (2, GINVISIBLE);
     gs_sprior (2, 0.8);
     g_fillarea (5,mhx,mhy);
     g_pline (6,mhx,mhy);
  gcls_seg();

  gcreat_seg (3);            /* Create Segment "Hour Hand" */
    gs_svisi (3, GINVISIBLE);
     gs_sprior (3, 0.7);
     g_fillarea (9,hhx,hhy);
     g_pline (10,hhx,hhy);
  gcls_seg();
```

```
/* TRANSFORM HAND SEGMENTS INTO STARTING POSITION */

  gs_stran (1, sec_mat);
  gs_stran (2, min_mat);
  gs_stran (3, hour_mat);

/* Set Hand Segments and Center of Hands visible */

  for (i=1;i<=4;i++)
      gs_svisi (i, GVISIBLE);

/*-----------------------------------------------------------------*/

/* Clock running for entire Minutes of Running Time entered */

  for (l=0;l<floor((double)run_time);l++)  /* Minutes Loop    */
      for (i=0;i<12;i++){                    /* 5-Seconds Loop */
          for (k=0;k<5;k++){                  /* Seconds Loop   */

              /* ACCUMULATE TRANSFORMATION OF SECOND HAND SEGMENT */

              gac_stran (sec_mat, 0.0,0.0, 0.0,0.0, phi, 1.0,1.0, GWC,
                         buf_mat);
              gac_stran (buf_mat, 0.0,0.0, 0.0,0.0, 0.0, 1.0,1.0, GWC,
                         sec_mat);
              gs_stran (1,sec_mat);   /* Adjust Second Hand */

              if (k < 4){ /* Move Hour Hand and Minute Hand just
                             every 5 Seconds */

              /* COPY TRANSFORMED SEGMENTS FROM WISS TO DISPLAY */

                  gcopy_seg (DISPLAY, 3);
                  gcopy_seg (DISPLAY, 2);
                  gcopy_seg (DISPLAY, 1);
                  gcopy_seg (DISPLAY, 4);
              }
              for (m=0;m<delay;m++); /* Delay Loop to adjust Clock */
          }
                        /* Move all Hands every 5 Seconds*/

          /* ACCUMULATE TRANSFORMATION OF HOURS AND MINUTE HAND SEGMENT */

          gac_stran (hour_mat,0.0,0.0, 0.0,0.0,phi/144.0, 1.0,1.0, GWC,
                     buf_mat);
          gac_stran (buf_mat, 0.0,0.0, 0.0,0.0, 0.0, 1.0,1.0, GWC,
                     hour_mat);
          gac_stran (min_mat, 0.0,0.0, 0.0,0.0,phi/ 12.0, 1.0,1.0, GWC,
                     buf_mat);
          gac_stran (buf_mat, 0.0,0.0, 0.0,0.0, 0.0, 1.0,1.0, GWC,
                     min_mat);

                        /* Adjust all Hands and Center of Hands*/
          gs_stran (3, hour_mat);
          gs_stran (2, min_mat);
          gs_stran (1,sec_mat);
          gs_stran (4, hour_mat);
      }

      rt2 = (run_time - 1) * 60.0; /* Calculate number of 5 Second
      rt1 = rt2/5.0;                      Periods left */
```

```
/*------------------------------------------------------------------*/

/* Clock running for entire 5 Seconds of Running Time entered */

        if (rt1 > 0.0)
        for (i=0;i<floor((double)rt1);i++){ /* 5-Seconds Loop */
            for (k=0;k<5;k++){                    /* Seconds Loop    */

                /* ACCUMULATE TRANSFORMATION OF SECOND HAND SEGMENT */

                gac_stran (sec_mat, 0.0,0.0, 0.0,0.0, phi, 1.0,1.0, GWC,
                           buf_mat);
                gac_stran (buf_mat, 0.0,0.0, 0.0,0.0, 0.0, 1.0,1.0, GWC,
                           sec_mat);
                gs_stran (1,sec_mat);   /* Adjust Second Hand */

                if (k < 4){ /* Move Hour Hand and Minute Hand just
                               every 5 Seconds */

                /* COPY TRANSFORMED SEGMENTS FROM WISS TO DISPLAY */

                    gcopy_seg (DISPLAY, 3);
                    gcopy_seg (DISPLAY, 2);
                    gcopy_seg (DISPLAY, 1);
                    gcopy_seg (DISPLAY, 4);
                }
                for (m=0;m<delay;m++); /* Delay Loop to adjust Clock */
            }

            /* ACCUMULATE TRANSFORMATION OF HOURS AND MINUTE HAND SEGMENT */

            gac_stran (hour_mat,0.0,0.0, 0.0,0.0,phi/144.0, 1.0,1.0, GWC,
                       buf_mat);
            gac_stran (buf_mat, 0.0,0.0, 0.0,0.0, 0.0, 1.0,1.0, GWC,
                       hour_mat);
            gac_stran (min_mat, 0.0,0.0, 0.0,0.0,phi/ 12.0, 1.0,1.0, GWC,
                       buf_mat);
            gac_stran (buf_mat, 0.0,0.0, 0.0,0.0, 0.0, 1.0,1.0, GWC,
                       min_mat);

                             /* Adjust all Hands and Center of Hands */
            gs_stran (3, hour_mat);
            gs_stran (2, min_mat);
            gs_stran (1,sec_mat);
            gs_stran (4, hour_mat);
        }

    rt1 = (rt1 - i) * 5.0;          /* Calculate Seconds left */
    rt2 = (float)((int)rt1);
    rt2 = ((rt1 - rt2) < 0.5) ? rt2 : (rt2 + 1.0);

/*------------------------------------------------------------------*/

    if (rt2 > 0.0)
```

```
        for (k=0;k<rt2;k++){

                /* ACCUMULATE TRANSFORMATION OF SECOND HAND SEGMENT */

                gac_stran (sec_mat, 0.0,0.0, 0.0,0.0, phi, 1.0,1.0, GWC,
                                buf_mat);
                gac_stran (buf_mat, 0.0,0.0, 0.0,0.0, 0.0, 1.0,1.0, GWC,
                                sec_mat);
                gs_stran (1,sec_mat);   /* Adjust Second Hand */

                /* COPY TRANSFORMED SEGMENTS FROM WISS TO DISPLAY */

                gcopy_seg (DISPLAY, 3); /* Copy ALL Segments to prevent */
                gcopy_seg (DISPLAY, 2); /* incorrect overlapping        */
                gcopy_seg (DISPLAY, 1);
                gcopy_seg (DISPLAY, 4);
        }


        scanf ("%s",ch);

  gdct_wk (WISS);
  gdct_wk (DISPLAY);
  gcls_wk (DISPLAY);
  gcls_gks ();

}
```

See Plate 20(a).

```c
#include "stdio.h"
#include "devices.h"
#include "gdefines.h"
#include "math.h"
#include "stdlib.h"

/*********************************************************************
*      F.9 JULIA : Creating a Fractal (Julia Set for f(z)=z²+c ;  *
*                                   c=0.39054 + 0.586791      )*
*                using the Polymarker Output Primitive        *
*********************************************************************
*      Refers to chapter :                                    *
*      Used external subroutines : dsurf                      *
*********************************************************************/

#define sqr(x)    ((x) * (x))

#define    Firstpoint 50    /* number of iterations to approach
                                curve */
#define c0x 0.39054
#define c0y 0.58679
#define num_points    90000 /* number of iterations */

typedef struct   cplx { double x,y; } Complex;
float   x_win_min, x_win_max, y_win_min, y_win_max;

main ()
{
  extern int dsurf ();
  int errfil, errind;
  extern short gerror_number, groutine;
  float xdc, ydc, xndc, yndc;
  char      c;
  unsigned  long  int  i, k, l, m;
  Complex   z0;

  void           Julia_Set();

  errfil = creat ("errors.lst", 0644);

/*===============================================================*/

  gopn_gks (errfil, 5000);
  if (gerror_number != 0)
    {gcls_gks();
     exit (-999);
     }

  gopn_wk (DISPLAY, 0, DISPLAY);
  gact_wk (DISPLAY);

  errind = dsurf (DISPLAY, &xdc, &ydc, &xndc, &yndc);

  x_win_min = -xndc*1.2;
  x_win_max =  xndc*1.2;
  y_win_min = -xndc*1.1;
  y_win_max =  xndc*1.1;

  gs_wind (1, x_win_min,x_win_max, y_win_min, y_win_max) ;
  gs_view (1,  0.0,  xndc, 0.0,  yndc);

  g_seltrn (1);
```

```
    gst_align (GTH_CENTER, GTV_HALF);
    g_text (0.0,-0.5,"CALCULATING !");

    z0.x = 1.0;              /* Starting Value of Z */
    z0.y = 0.0;

    Julia_Set (z0);

    g_text (0.0,-0.5,"     READY !    ");
    scanf ("%s",c);
    gdct_wk (DISPLAY);
    gcls_wk (DISPLAY);
    gcls_gks ();
}

/*=================================================================*/

    void Julia_Set (z)
          Complex    z;
    {
          unsigned  long  int np,k;
          void  Iterate();
          void  Draw_Point();
          float random;
          Complex    buf;

          buf.x = z.x;
          buf.y = z.y;

                        /* Iterate to a Point which is on the Curve */
          for (k=1;k<=Firstpoint;k++){
                random =  (float)rand();
                Iterate(&buf.x,&buf.y,random);
          }

          /* SET POLYMARKER ATTRIBUTES */

          gsm_type (GPOINT);
          gsm_color (1);
          gsm_scale (0.01);

          for (k=1;k<=num_points;k++) {
                random =  (float)rand();
                Iterate(&buf.x,&buf.y,random);
                Draw_Point (buf.x, buf.y);
          }
    }

/*=================================================================*/

    void  Iterate (zx,zy,random)
          double     *zx,*zy;
          float random;
    {     Complex result;
          void  Sqrt_Cmplx ();

                  /* Calculate Zn-1=COMPLEX_SQRT(Zn - C) */

          result.x = *zx - c0x;
          result.y = *zy - c0y;
          Sqrt_Cmplx (&result.x,&result.y);
```

```
                                  /* Choose sign of sqrt by random */

            if (random < (RAND_MAX/2.0)){
                result.x = -(result.x);
                result.y = -(result.y);
            }
            *zx = result.x;
            *zy = result.y;

            return ;
        }
```

```
/*===================================================================*/

        void Sqrt_Cmplx (zx,zy)
            double      *zx,*zy;
        {   double  magnitude;
            Complex     result;

            magnitude = sqrt (sqr(*zx) + sqr(*zy));
            if ((magnitude + *zx) < 0.0)
                result.x = 0.0;
            else
                result.x = sqrt ((magnitude + *zx)/2.0);

            if ((magnitude - *zx) < 0.0)
                result.y = 0.0;
            else
                result.y = sqrt ((magnitude - *zx)/2.0);
            if (*zy < 0.0)   result.y = -(result.y);
            *zx = result.x;
            *zy = result.y;
            return;
        }
```

```
/*===================================================================*/

        void Draw_Point (x,y)
            double      x, y;
        {
            float x1[1],y1[1];

            if ((fabs(x) > x_win_max) || (fabs(y) > y_win_max))
                return;
            else {
                x1[0]=(float)x;
                y1[0]=(float)y;

                /* DRAW POLYMARKER ON SCREEN */

                g_pmarker (1,y1,x1);
            }
            return;
        }
```

See Plate 20(b).

```
#include "stdio.h"
#include "devices.h"
#include "gdefines.h"
#include "math.h"
#include "stdlib.h"

/****************************************************************
*      F.10 MANDBROT : Creating a Fractal (Mandelbrot Set for   *
*                                       f(z)=z²-c          )    *
*                       using the Polymarker Output Primitive   *
*                       (The Limits for C=a+ib are taken out of *
*                       the File MANDBROT.DAT :                 *
*                       Mand1bro.dat contains  -1.0 < a < 2.5   *
*                                              -1.2 < b < 1.2   *
*                                      num_points = 20          *
*                                      max_depth =200           *
*                    Mand2bro.dat contains                      *
*                                      0.915 < a <  0.9294      *
*                                     -0.315 < b < -0.305       *
*                                      num_points = 100         *
*                                      max_depth =  40          *
*                   So before starting MANDBROT copy one        *
*                   of these files to mandbrot.dat !    )       *
****************************************************************
*     Refers to chapter :                                       *
*     Used external subroutines : dsurf                         *
****************************************************************/

#define sqr(x)    ((x) * (x))
#define limit     100            /* Limit of Attractor */

typedef struct   cplx { double x,y; } Complex;

float  x_win_min, x_win_max, y_win_min, y_win_max;

main ()
{
  extern int dsurf ();
  extern short gerror_number, groutine;
  void           Draw_point ();
  int errfil, errind;
  float xdc, ydc, xndc, yndc,
        xfa[4], yfa[4],
        r_margin,l_margin,t_margin,b_margin;
  double x_res,y_res,
        absqu,
        sqrx, sqry;
  char      ch;
  FILE *fp, *fopen();

  unsigned  long  int  num_points,
                         i, k, n,
                         max_depth;

  int ready;

  Complex   c,z0,z;
```

```
fp = fopen ("mandbrot.dat","r");
fscanf (fp,"%f%f%f%f%d%d",&l_margin,              /* left margin    */
                                   &r_margin,     /* right margin   */
                                   &b_margin,     /* bottom margin  */
                                   &t_margin,     /* top margin     */
                                   &num_points,
                                   &max_depth);

errfil = creat ("errors.lst", 0644);

/*==================================================================*/

gopn_gks (errfil, 5000);
if (gerror_number != 0)
  {gcls_gks();
   exit (-999);
  }

gopn_wk (DISPLAY, 0, DISPLAY);
gact_wk (DISPLAY);

errind = dsurf (DISPLAY, &xdc, &ydc, &xndc, &yndc);

    /* Assure that the Window gets an Aspect Ratio of 5 : 3 */
x_win_min = 0.0;
x_win_max = 480.0;
y_win_min = 0.0;
y_win_max = (x_win_max-x_win_min) * 3.0 / 5.0;

xfa[0] = xfa[3] = x_win_min;      /* Background */
xfa[1] = xfa[2] = x_win_max;
yfa[0] = yfa[1] = y_win_min;
yfa[2] = yfa[3] = y_win_max;

gs_wind (1, x_win_min,x_win_max, y_win_min, y_win_max) ;
gs_view (1,  0.0,  xndc, 0.0,  yndc);

g_seltrn (1);

gsf_inter (GSOLID);
gsf_color (1);
g_fillarea (4, xfa, yfa);  /* Set Background to White and
                              Polymarker Color to Black
                              to draw Fractal in Reverse Mode */

/* SET POLYMARKER ATTRIBUTES */

gsm_type (GPOINT);
gsm_color (0);
gsm_scale (0.01);

                                  /* Resolution */
x_res = (r_margin-l_margin)/x_win_max;
y_res = (t_margin-b_margin)/y_win_max;

            /* Starting Value of Z */
z0.x = 0.0;
z0.y = 0.0;
```

```
                        /* For all Points on Screen
                           calculate Zn+1 = Zn² - C  */
    for (i=0;i<=y_win_max;i++)
        for (k=0;k<=x_win_max;k++){
            c.x = (l_margin+ (k*x_res));
            c.y = (b_margin+ (i*y_res));
            z.x = z0.x;
            z.y = z0.y;
            n   = 0;
            ready   = 0;
            sqrx = sqr(z.x);  /* Calculate Zn² */
            sqry = sqr(z.y);
            do{
                n++;
                z.y = (2.0 * z.x * z.y) - c.y;  /* Calculate Zn+1 */
                z.x = sqrx - sqry - c.x;
                sqrx = sqr(z.x);
                sqry = sqr(z.y);
                absqu = sqrx + sqry;
                ready = ((absqu > limit) || (n == num_points))
                        ? 1 : 0;
            } while (ready == 0);

            if (  (n == num_points)
               || (((int)(fmod((double)n,(double)3.0)) == 2)
                   && (n < max_depth)))

                Draw_point ((double)k,(double)i);
        }


    scanf ("%s",ch);
    gdct_wk (DISPLAY);
    gcls_wk (DISPLAY);
    gcls_gks ();
}

/*============================================================*/


    void Draw_point (x,y)
          double     x, y;
    {
          float x1[1],y1[1];

          if ((x > x_win_max) || (y > y_win_max))
               return;
          else {
                  x1[0]=(float)x;
                  y1[0]=(float)y;

                  /* DRAW POINT ON SCREEN */

                  g_pmarker (1,x1,y1);
          }
          return;
    }
```

See Plate 20(c) and (d).

Shared C
Subroutine
and
Include Files

```
/******************************************************************
 *     DSURF (Subroutine) : Inquires the Maximum Display Surface *
 *                          the Device and sets the Workstation  *
 *                          Transformation appropriately         *
 ******************************************************************
 *     Refers to chapter : 3.3.3                                 *
 *     Used external subroutines :                               *
 ******************************************************************/

int dsurf (dev, max_xdc, max_ydc, xndc, yndc)

     int   dev;
     float *max_xdc, *max_ydc, *xndc, *yndc;
{    int   dev_unit,
           errind,
           max_xras, max_yras;
     float now;


/* INQUIRE WORKSTATION DIMENSIONS */

     errind = gqmax_disp (dev, &dev_unit, max_xdc, max_ydc,
                     ·                   &max_xras, &max_yras);

/* ADAPTION OF WORKSTATION TRANSFORMATION TO WORKSTATION
   DIMENSIONS */

     now = (*max_xdc < *max_ydc) ? *max_ydc : *max_xdc;
     *xndc = *max_xdc/now;
     *yndc = *max_ydc/now;

   /* SET WORKSTATION WINDOW */

     gswk_wind (dev, 0.0,    *xndc, 0.0,    *yndc);

   /* SET WORKSTATION VIEWPORT */

     gswk_view (dev, 0.0, *max_xdc, 0.0, *max_ydc);

     return errind;

}
```

```
*****************************************************
include file:  backgrou.h
*****************************************************
float xback[5] = { 0, 10, 10,  0, 0 },
      yback[5] = { 0,  0, 10, 10, 0 };


*****************************************************
include file:  lake.h
*****************************************************
float xlake[16]={ 15.0,  35.0,  55.0,  75.0, 105.0, 190.0,
                 220.0, 225.0, 210.0, 185.0, 160.0, 110.0,
                  80.0,  40.0,  15.0,  15.0},

      ylake[16]={100.0, 115.0, 115.0, 130.0, 135.0, 125.0,
                 110.0,  80.0,  65.0,  55.0,  60.0,  60.0,
                  55.0,  55.0,  70.0, 100.0};


*****************************************************
include file:  roe.h
*****************************************************

float xroe[53]=
{ 40, 47.5, 52.5, 57.5, 52.5, 47.5,  50,  60,  65,  63,  63,
  63,   67,   63,   60,   75,   70,  80,  70,  70,  70,  60,
  70,   65,   80,  125,  145,  150, 145, 140, 140, 135, 135,
 130,  130,  125,  125,  120,   85,  80,  80,  75,  75,  70,
  70,   65,   65,   60,   55,   50,  50,  50,  40},

      yroe[53]=
{ 80,  100,  102,  100,   98,  100, 110, 110, 125, 120, 125,
 120,  120,  120,  110,  125,  120, 120, 120, 125, 120, 110,
 110,   95,   80,   85,   70,   65,  70,  50,  15,  15,  35,
  45,   25,   25,   40,   45,   50,  40,  25,  25,  50,  35,
  15,   15,   50,   70,   85,   80,  85,  80,  80};


*****************************************************
include file:  tree.h
*****************************************************

float xtree[60] =
{ 8.0, 11.0, 16.0, 17.0, 17.0, 20.0, 20.0, 17.0, 12.0,  9.0,
  6.0,  3.0,  2.0,  3.0,  5.0,  6.0,  8.0, 11.0, 13.0, 15.0,
 18.0, 20.0, 22.0, 25.0, 30.0, 34.0, 35.0, 38.0, 42.0, 47.0,
 51.0, 54.0, 55.0, 56.0, 59.0, 60.0, 63.0, 64.0, 64.0, 62.0,
 59.0, 57.0, 54.0, 49.0, 47.0, 45.0, 42.0, 38.0, 35.0, 33.0,
 32.0, 31.0, 30.0, 32.0, 33.0, 34.0, 35.0, 37.0, 27.0,  8.0},

      ytree[60] =
{11.0, 11.0, 13.0, 17.0, 20.0, 40.0, 44.0, 46.0, 45.0, 48.0,
 51.0, 51.0, 53.0, 54.0, 57.0, 59.0, 63.0, 64.0, 65.0, 66.0,
 65.0, 67.0, 66.0, 65.0, 64.0, 66.0, 65.0, 63.0, 66.0, 65.0,
 64.0, 63.0, 62.0, 63.0, 60.0, 60.0, 59.0, 59.0, 57.0, 56.0,
 55.0, 54.0, 51.0, 49.0, 48.0, 47.0, 46.0, 45.0, 44.0, 42.0,
 49.0, 36.0, 32.0, 22.0, 16.0, 13.0, 11.0,  9.0, 12.0, 11.0};
```

```
*******************************************************
include file:  devices.h
*******************************************************
/* Device defines */

#define WISS            0
#define DISPLAY         1
#define MOUSE           2
#define JOYSTIK         2
#define TABLET          3
#define PRINTER         6
#define PLOTTER         7
#define CAMERA          8

/* devices GMO and GMI are defined as 4 and 5, respectively
   in gdefines.h, hence the 'gap' between tablet and printer. */

*******************************************************
include file:  echos.h
*******************************************************
/* Prompt/echo types for the Locator device */

#define LOC_INK         -2
#define LOC_RECTANGLE   -1
#define LOC_CROSS        1
#define LOC_RUBBER       4

*******************************************************
include file:  fonts.h
*******************************************************
/* Text font defines */

#define HARDWARE     1
#define GSIMPLEX  -101
#define GCOMPLEX  -102
#define ICOMPLEX  -103
#define GDUPLEX   -104
#define GTRIPLEX  -105
#define ITRIPLEX  -106

*******************************************************
include file:  gdefines.h
*******************************************************
/* Attribute Control Flag */

#define GCURRENT               0
#define GSPECIFIED             1

/* Aspect Source Flag */
#define GBUNDLED               0
#define GINDIVIDUAL            1

/* Attributes Used */
#define GPOLYLINE              0
#define GPOLYMARKER            1
#define GTEXT                  2
#define GFILLAREA              3
```

```
/* Bundle Index Setting */
#define GDEFINED            1
#define GUNDEFINED          0

/* Clipping Indicator */
#define GNOCLIP             0
#define GCLIP               1

/* Clear Control Flag */
#define GCONDITIONALLY      0
#define GALWAYS             1

/* Color Availability */
#define GMONOCHROME         0
#define GCOLOUR             1

/* Color Values Valid */
#define GVALID              1
#define GINVALID            0

/* Coordinate Switch */
#define GWC                 0
#define GNDC                1

/* Device Coordinate Units */
#define GDC_METRES          0
#define GDC_OTHER           1

/* Deferral Mode */
#define GASAP               0
#define GBNIG               1
#define GBNIL               2
#define GASTI               3
#define GSUPPRESSED         0
#define GALLOWED            1

/* Display Surface */
#define GNOTEMPTY           0
#define GEMPTY              1

/* Event Class */
#define GE_NONE             0
#define GE_LOCATOR          1
#define GE_STROKE           2
#define GE_VALUATOR         3
#define GE_CHOICE           4
#define GE_PICK             5
#define GE_STRING           6

/* Echo Switch */
#define GNOECHO             0
#define     GECHO           1

/* Fill Area Interior Style */
#define GHOLLOW             0
#define GSOLID              1
#define GPATTERN            2
#define GHATCH              3
```

```
/* Initial Choice */
#define GOFF                    0
#define GON                     1

/* Input Class */
#define GIC_LOCATOR             0
#define GIC_STROKE              1
#define GIC_VALUATOR            2
#define GIC_CHOICE              3
#define GIC_PICK                4
#define GIC_STRING              5

/* Input Mode */
#define GREQUEST                0
#define GSAMPLE                 1
#define GEVENT                  2

/* Inquiry Type */
#define GSET                    0
#define GREALIZED               1

/* Dynamic Modification Type */
#define GIRG                    0
#define GIMM                    1

/* New Frame Action */
#define GNO                     0
#define GYES                    1

/* GKS Operating State */
#define GGKCL                   0
#define GGKOP                   1
#define GWSOP                   2
#define GWSAC                   3
#define GSGOP                   4

/* Level of GKS */
#define GLMA                   -3
#define GLMB                   -2
#define GLMC                   -1
#define GL0A                    0
#define GL0B                    1
#define GL0C                    2
#define GL1A                    3
#define GL1B                    4
#define GL1C                    5
#define GL2A                    6
#define GL2B                    7
#define GL2C                    8

/* Line Type */
#define GLDASH2DOT             -2
#define GLMDASH                -1
#define GLSOLID                 1
#define GLDASH                  2
#define GLDOT                   3
#define GLDASHDOT               4
```

```
/* Marker Type */
#define GDIAMOND                -1
#define GPOINT                   1
#define GPLUS                    2
#define GASTERISK                3
#define GOMARKER                 4
#define GXMARKER                 5

/* Polyline/Fill Area Control Flag */
#define GPF_POLYLINE             0
#define GPF_FILLAREA             1

/* Input Status */
#define GNONE                    0
#define GOK                      1
#define GNOPICK                  2
#define GNOCHOICE                2

/* Pixel Array */
#define GABSENT                  0
#define GPRESENT                 1

/* Regeneration Flag */
#define GPOSTPONE                0
#define GPERFORM                 1

/* Segment Detectability */
#define GUNDETECTABLE            0
#define GDETECTABLE              1

/* Segment Highlighting */
#define GNORMAL                  0
#define GHIGHLIGHTED             1

/* Segment Visibility */
#define GINVISIBLE               0
#define GVISIBLE                 1

/* Simultaneous Events */
#define GNOMORE                  0
#define GMORE                    1

/* Text Alignment Horizontal Component */
#define GTNORMAL                 0
#define GTH_LEFT                 1
#define GTH_CENTER               2
#define GTH_RIGHT                3

/* Text Alignment Vertical Component */
#define GTV_TOP                  1
#define GTV_CAP                  2
#define GTV_HALF                 3
#define GTV_BASE                 4
#define GTV_BOTTOM               5
```

```
/* Text Path */
#define GTP_RIGHT              0
#define GTP_LEFT               1
#define GTP_UP                 2
#define GTP_DOWN               3

/* Text Precision */
#define GSTRING                0
#define GCHAR                  1
#define GSTROKE                2

/* Generalized Drawing Primitive Identifier */
#define GBAR                  -1
#define GARC                  -2
#define GSLICE                -3
#define GCIRCLE               -4

/* Update States */
#define GNOTPENDING            0
#define GPENDING               1

/* Viewport Input Priority */
#define GHIGHER                0
#define GLOWER                 1

/* Workstation Category */
#define GOUTPUT                0
#define GINPUT                 1
#define GOUTIN                 2
#define GWISS                  3
#define GMO                    4
#define GMI                    5
#define GVDM                   6

/* Workstation Classification */
#define GVECTOR                0
#define GRASTER                1
#define GOTHER                 2

/* Workstation State */
#define GINACTIVE              0
#define GACTIVE                1


****************************************************
include file:  hatch.h
****************************************************

/* fill area hatch styles */
#define NHATCH  -1     /* narrow hatch */
#define MHATCH  -2     /* medium hatch */
#define WHATCH  -3     /* wide hatch */
#define NXHATCH -4     /* narrow cross hatch */
#define MXHATCH -5     /* medium cross hatch */
#define WXHATCH -6     /* wide cross hatch */
```

Appendix G
■ BIBLIOGRAPHY

Arnold, D.B. and Bono, P.R. (1988) *CGM and CGI: Metafile and Interface Standards for Computer Graphics*, Springer, Heidelberg.

Baker, P.M. and Hearn, D. (1986) *Computer Graphics*, Prentice Hall, Englewood Cliffs.

Berger, M. (1986) *Computer Graphics with Pascal*, Benjamin/Cummings, Menlo Park.

Bettels, J., Bono, P., McGinnis, E. and Rix, J. (1989) 'Guidelines for Determining When to Use GKS and When to Use PHIGS', *Computer & Graphics*, 13 (1).

Bono, P.R. (1983) 'Graphics Standards' in Tutorial 3.1, CAMP '83, Berlin.

Bono, P.R., ed. (1986) 'Special Issue on Graphics Standards', *IEEE Computer Graphics and Applications*, 6(8).

Brown, M.D. and Heck, M. (1985) *Understanding PHIGS*, Megatek Corp, San Diego, Calif.

Cuellar, G. (1984) *Graphics Made Easy for the IBM PC and XT*, Reston Publishing, Reston.

De Ruiter, M.M., ed. (1988) *Advances in Computer Graphics III*, Springer, Heidelberg.

Encarnação, J. and Schlechtendahl, E.G. (1983) *Computer Aided Design – Fundamentals and System Architectures*, Springer, Heidelberg.

Encarnação, J. and Schönhut, J. (1986) 'Interfaces and Data Transfer Formats' in *Advances in Computer Graphics I*, Springer, Heidelberg, pp. 237–54.

Encarnação, J., Schuster, R. and Vöge, E. (1983) *Product Data Interfaces in CAD/ CAM Applications – Design, Implementation, Experiences*, Springer, Heidelberg.

Encarnação, J. and Strasser, W. (1981) *Geräteunabhängige Graphische Systeme*, Oldenbourg, Munich.

Encarnação, J. and Strasser, W. (1988) *'Computer Graphics', Gerätetechnik, Programmierung und Anwendung Graphischer Systeme*, 3rd edn, Oldenbourg, Munich.

Enderle, G. (1986) 'Interfaces for Storage and Communication of Computer Graphics Information', in *Advances in Computer Graphics II*, Springer, Heidelberg, pp. 115–52.

Enderle, G., Grave, M. and Lillhagen, F., eds. (1986) *Advances in Computer Graphics I*, Springer, Heidelberg.

Enderle, G., Kansy, K. and Pfaff, G. (1987) *Computer Graphics Programming: GKS – The Graphics Standard*, 2nd edn, Springer, Heidelberg.

Fuchs, H. (1985) 'VLSI and Computer Graphics', Tutorial Notes No. 7. EUROGRAPHICS '85 (Nice, France), EUROGRAPHICS Association, Geneva.

Guedj, R. *et al.*, eds. (1980) *Methodology of Interaction*, North-Holland, Amsterdam.

Guibas, L., Ingalls, D. and Pike, R. (1984) 'Bitmap Graphics', AT&T Bell Laboratories, SIGGRAPH 84 Course Notes.

Hopgood, F.R.A., Duce, D.A., Fielding, E.V.C., Robinson, K. and Williams, A.S., eds. (1986a) *Methodology of Window Management*, Springer, Heidelberg.

Hopgood, F.R.A., Hubbold, R.J. and Duce, D.A., eds. (1986b) *Advances in Computer Graphics II*, Springer, Heidelberg.

Hopgood, F.R.A., Gallop, J.R., Duce, D.A. and Sutcliffe, D.C. (1988) *Introduction to the Graphical Kernel System (GKS)*, 2nd edn, Academic Press, New York.

Hübner, W., Lux-Mülders, G. and Muth, M. (1987) 'Designing a System to Provide Graphical User Interfaces: The THESEUS Approach', *Proc: EUROGRAPHICS '87*, North-Holland, Amsterdam.

International Standardization Organization (1980) *The Programming Language Fortran77*, ISO 1539.

International Standardization Organization (1985) *Graphical Kernel System (GKS) – Functional Description*, ISO 7942.

International Standardization Organization (1987) *Computer Graphics – Metafile for the Transfer and Storage of Picture Description Information (CGM)*, ISO 8632.

International Standardization Organization (1988a) *Computer Graphics – Interfacing Techniques for Dialogues with Graphical Devices (CGI)*, ISO DP 9636.

International Standardization Organization (1988b) *Computer Graphics – Programmer's Hierarchical Interactive Graphics System (PHIGS)*, ISO 9592.

International Standardization Organization (1988c) *GKS Language Bindings, Part 1: FORTRAN*, ISO 8651–1.

International Standardization Organization (1988d) *GKS Language Bindings, Part 2: Pascal*, ISO/IEC 8651–2.

International Standardization Organization (1988e) *GKS Language Bindings, Part 3: Ada*, ISO/IEC 8651–3.

International Standardization Organization (1988f) *GKS-3D Language Bindings, Part 1: FORTRAN*, ISO/DIS 8806–1.

International Standardization Organization (1988g) *Information Processing Systems – Computer Graphics – Graphical Kernel System for Three Dimensions (GKS-3D), Functional Description*, ISO 8805.

International Standardization Organization (1988h) *PHIGS Language Bindings, Part 2: Pascal*, ISO/IEC DP 9593–2.

International Standardization Organization (1989a) *CGI Language Bindings, Part 1: FORTRAN*, ISO DP 9637–1.

International Standardization Organization (1989b) *CGI Language Bindings, Part 4: C*, ISO DP 9637–4.

International Standardization Organization (1989c) *GKS Language Bindings, Part 4: C*, ISO/IEC DIS 8651–4.

International Standardization Organization (1989d) *GKS-3D Language Bindings, Part 2: Pascal*, ISO DP 8806–2.

International Standardization Organization (1989e) *GKS-3D Language Bindings, Part 3: Ada*, ISO DIS 8806–3.

International Standardization Organization (1989f) *GKS-3D Language Bindings, Part 4: C*, ISO DIS 8806–4.

International Standardization Organization (1989g) *PHIGS Language Bindings, Part 1: FORTRAN*, ISO/IEC 9593–1.

International Standardization Organization (1989h) *PHIGS Language Bindings, Part 3: Ada*, ISO/IEC 9593–3.

International Standardization Organization (1989i) *PHIGS Language Bindings, Part 4: C*, ISO/IEC DIS 9593–4.

Magnenat-Thalmann, N. and Thalmann, D. (1985) *Computer Animation – Theory and Practice*, Springer, Tokyo.

Mumford, A.M. and Skall, M.W., eds. (1989) *CGM in the Real World*, Springer, Heidelberg.

Noll, S., Poller, J. and Rix, J. (1986) 'An Approach to Solve the Compatibility Problem Between GKS and PHIGS', *Proceedings of Workshop on Standardization in Computer Graphics*, Genoa, Italy.

Poller, J., Noll, S. and Rix, J. (1989) 'Migration of GKS/GKS-3D and PHIGS Discussed under the View of the Computer Graphics Reference Model', *Computer Graphics Forum*, 8(3), North-Holland, Amsterdam.

Reeves, W.T. (1983) 'Particle Systems – A Technique for Modelling a Class of Fuzzy Objects', *ACM Transactions on Graphics*, 2 (2).

Requicha, A. (1980) 'Representation of Rigid Solids Theory, Methods & Systems', *Computing Surveys*, 12.

Rogers, D.F. and Earnshaw, R.A., eds. (1987) *Techniques for Computer Graphics*, Springer, New York.

Schlechtendahl, E.G. (1986) 'CAD Interfaces (CAD I)', *Reports of the ESPRIT CIM Research and Development Project*, no. 322.

Schönhut, J. (1986) 'Are PHIGS and GKS Necessarily Incompatible?' *IEEE Computer Graphics and Applications*, 6(7).

Straayer, D.H. (1986) 'Setting Standards', *Computer Graphics World*, November, pp. 73–8.

Strasser, W. (1986) 'VLSI-oriented Graphics System Design' in *Advances in Computer Graphics II*, Springer, Heidelberg.

Willis, P.S. and Watters, G.W. (1988) 'Colour Raster Operations', *Computer Graphics Forum*, 7(3), September.

Van Dam, A. *et al.* (1988) 'PHIGS PLUS, ACM-SIGGRAPH', *Computer Graphics*, 22(3), pp. 125ff.

 INDEX

Numbers in **bold** type denote principal entries

Accumulate (transformation matrix), **86**, 224
Ada, 12
Annex E (of GKS), 94
Application (program, system), **2**, 91, 154
  independent, 8
  interface, **2**, 8
Archives (in PHIGS), 152
ASCII, 94, 142
Aspect source flags (ASF), 64
Associate (segment with workstation), 81, 230
Attributes
  default values for, 65
  of output primitives, 14, 29, **53**
  of segments, 85
  workstation dependent, 62, 90
  workstation independent, 63, 65
Audit trail, 90

Binary encoding, 144
Bitblt, 6
Bitmap, 6
Bundle (table), 70

C (language), 12, 276
CAD, CAE, CAI, CAM, 2
CalComp (on GKS), 38–40
Character encoding, 141
Choice (input), 15, 99, 106, **108**, 254
Cell array, **44**, 129, 276, 287
Cell array 3, 143
Circles, 141
Clear text encoding, 145
Clipping, **114**, 182
Color, **54**, 208
Computer graphics, 1
  interface (CGI), 13, **146**
  metafile (CGM), 13, 97, **139**
Coordinate systems, 15, **30**, 122, 180

Deferral control, 49
Description tables, 18
Descriptor, 140
Detectability (of segments), 88
Device
  coordinates (DC), 15, **36**
  independent, 15
  interface, 2, 3
Disjoint polyline, 141

Echo, 101
EDIF, 4
Edge, 131–3
Ellipses, 141
Emergency (close GKS), 115
Encodings, 94, 97
Error handling, 16, **114**, 126, 152
Escape, 51
Evaluate (transformation matrix), 86, 224
Even/odd-rule, 42
Event (input mode), 15, **101**

Fill area, 41
  attributes, 56, 67
Fillarea set, 122
Fill area set 3, 130
Fill area 3, 128
FORTRAN, 12, 21, 172
Fractals, 120, 302, 305
Functions, viii

Generalized drawing primitive (GDP), **46**, 202,
    205, 283
Generative computer graphics, 1
GKS
  control, 20
  functions, 12

L.-Brault   DATE DUE

1 OCT. 1991

8 DEC. 199

2 8 NOV. 1992

2 1 JAN. 1994

2 1 MARS 1994

RÉSERVE

2 8 NOV. 199

1 7 JAN. 1996